Nutshell Series

of

WEST PUBLISHING COMPANY

P.O. Box 64526

St. Paul, Minnesota 55164–0526

Accounting—Law and, 1984, 377 pages, by E. McGruder Faris, Late Professor of Law, Stetson University.

Administrative Law and Process, 2nd Ed., 1981, 445 pages, by Ernest Gellhorn, Former Dean and Professor of Law, Case Western Reserve University, and Barry B. Boyer, Professor of Law, SUNY, Buffalo.

Admiralty, 2nd Ed., 1988, 379 pages, by Frank L. Maraist, Professor of Law, Louisiana State University.

Agency-Partnership, 1977, 364 pages, by Roscoe T. Steffen, Late Professor of Law, University of Chicago.

American Indian Law, 2nd Ed., 1988, about 319 pages, by William C. Canby, Jr., Adjunct Professor of Law, Arizona State University.

Antitrust Law and Economics, 3rd Ed., 1986, 472 pages, by Ernest Gellhorn, Former Dean and Professor of Law, Case Western Reserve University.

Appellate Advocacy, 1984, 325 pages, by Alan D. Hornstein, Professor of Law, University of Maryland.

Art Law, 1984, 335 pages, by Leonard D. DuBoff, Professor of Law, Lewis and Clark College, Northwestern School of Law.

Banking and Financial Institutions, 2nd Ed., 1988, about 455 pages, by William A. Lovett, Professor of Law, Tulane University.

Church-State Relations—Law of, 1981, 305 pages, by Leonard F. Manning, Late Professor of Law, Fordham University.

NUTSHELL SERIES

Civil Procedure, 2nd Ed., 1986, 306 pages, by Mary Kay Kane, Professor of Law, University of California, Hastings College of the Law.

Civil Rights, 1978, 279 pages, by Norman Vieira, Professor of Law, Southern Illinois University.

Commercial Paper, 3rd Ed., 1982, 404 pages, by Charles M. Weber, Former Professor of Business Law, The Wharton School of Finance and Commerce, University of Pennsylvania and Richard E. Speidel, Professor of Law, Northwestern University.

Community Property, 2nd Ed., 1988, 432 pages, by Robert L. Mennell, Former Professor of Law, Hamline University, and Thomas M. Boykoff.

Comparative Legal Traditions, 1982, 402 pages, by Mary Ann Glendon, Professor of Law, Harvard University, Michael Wallace Gordon, Professor of Law, University of Florida, and Christopher Osakwe, Professor of Law, Tulane University.

Conflicts, 1982, 470 pages, by David D. Siegel, Professor of Law, St. John's University.

Constitutional Analysis, 1979, 388 pages, by Jerre S. Williams, Professor of Law Emeritus, University of Texas.

Constitutional Federalism, 2nd Ed., 1987, 411 pages, by David E. Engdahl, Professor of Law, University of Puget Sound.

Constitutional Law, 1986, 389 pages, by Jerome A. Barron, Professor of Law, George Washington University, and C. Thomas Dienes, Professor of Law, George Washington University.

Consumer Law, 2nd Ed., 1981, 418 pages, by David G. Epstein, Dean and Professor of Law, Emory University, and Steve H. Nickles, Professor of Law, University of Minnesota.

Contract Remedies, 1981, 323 pages, by Jane M. Friedman, Professor of Law, Wayne State University.

Contracts, 2nd Ed., 1984, 425 pages, by Gordon D. Schaber, Dean and Professor of Law, McGeorge School of Law, and Claude D. Rohwer, Professor of Law, McGeorge School of Law.

Corporations—Law of, 2nd Ed., 1987, 515 pages, by Robert W. Hamilton, Professor of Law, University of Texas.

Corrections and Prisoners' Rights—Law of, 2nd Ed., 1983, 386 pages, by Sheldon Krantz, Professor of Law, University of San Diego.

Criminal Law, 2nd Ed., 1987, 321 pages, by Arnold H. Loewy, Professor of Law, University of North Carolina.

Criminal Procedure—Constitutional Limitations, 4th Ed., 1988, 461 pages, by Jerold H. Israel, Professor of Law, University of Michigan, and Wayne R. LaFave, Professor of Law, University of Illinois.

Debtor-Creditor Law, 3rd Ed., 1986, 383 pages, by David G. Epstein, Dean and Professor of Law, Emory University.

Employment Discrimination—Federal Law of, 2nd Ed., 1981, 402 pages, by Mack A. Player, Professor of Law, Florida State University.

Energy Law, 1981, 338 pages, by Joseph P. Tomain, Professor of Law, University of Cincinnatti.

Environmental Law, 2nd Ed., 1988, about 348 pages by Roger W. Findley, Professor of Law, University of Illinois, and Daniel A. Farber, Professor of Law, University of Minnesota.

Estate and Gift Taxation, Federal, 3rd Ed., 1983, 509 pages, by John K. McNulty, Professor of Law, University of California, Berkeley.

Estate Planning—Introduction to, 3rd Ed., 1983, 370 pages, by Robert J. Lynn, Professor of Law, Ohio State University.

Evidence, Federal Rules of, 2nd Ed., 1987, 473 pages, by Michael H. Graham, Professor of Law, University of Miami.

Evidence, State and Federal Rules, 2nd Ed., 1981, 514 pages, by Paul F. Rothstein, Professor of Law, Georgetown University.

Family Law, 2nd Ed., 1986, 444 pages, by Harry D. Krause, Professor of Law, University of Illinois.

Federal Jurisdiction, 2nd Ed., 1981, 258 pages, by David P. Currie, Professor of Law, University of Chicago.

Future Interests, 1981, 361 pages, by Lawrence W. Waggoner, Professor of Law, University of Michigan.

Government Contracts, 1979, 423 pages, by W. Noel Keyes, Professor of Law Emeritus, Pepperdine University.

Historical Introduction to Anglo-American Law, 2nd Ed., 1973, 280 pages, by Frederick G. Kempin, Jr., Professor of Business Law, Wharton School of Finance and Commerce, University of Pennsylvania.

Immigration Law and Procedure, 1984, 345 pages, by David Weissbrodt, Professor of Law, University of Minnesota.

Injunctions, 1974, 264 pages, by John F. Dobbyn, Professor of Law, Villanova University.

Insurance Law, 1981, 281 pages, by John F. Dobbyn, Professor of Law, Villanova University.

Intellectual Property—Patents, Trademarks and Copyright, 1983, 428 pages, by Arthur R. Miller, Professor of Law, Harvard University, and Michael H. Davis, Professor of Law, Cleveland State University, Cleveland-Marshall College of Law.

International Business Transactions, 3rd Ed., 1988, about 484 pages, by Ralph H. Folsom, Professor of Law, University of San Diego, Michael Wallace Gordon, Professor of Law, University of Florida, and John A. Spanogle, Jr., Professor of Law, State University of New York, Buffalo.

International Human Rights, 1988, about 275 pages, by Thomas Buergenthal, Professor of Law, Emory University.

International Law (Public), 1985, 262 pages, by Thomas Buergenthal, Professor of Law, Emory University, and Harold G. Maier, Professor of Law, Vanderbilt University.

Introduction to the Study and Practice of Law, 1983, 418 pages, by Kenney F. Hegland, Professor of Law, University of Arizona.

Judicial Process, 1980, 292 pages, by William L. Reynolds, Professor of Law, University of Maryland.

Jurisdiction, 4th Ed., 1980, 232 pages, by Albert A. Ehrenzweig, Late Professor of Law, University of California, Berkeley, David W. Louisell, Late Professor of Law, University of

California, Berkeley, and Geoffrey C. Hazard, Jr., Professor of Law, Yale Law School.

Juvenile Courts, 3rd Ed., 1984, 291 pages, by Sanford J. Fox, Professor of Law, Boston College.

Labor Arbitration Law and Practice, 1979, 358 pages, by Dennis R. Nolan, Professor of Law, University of South Carolina.

Labor Law, 2nd Ed., 1986, 397 pages, by Douglas L. Leslie, Professor of Law, University of Virginia.

Land Use, 2nd Ed., 1985, 356 pages, by Robert R. Wright, Professor of Law, University of Arkansas, Little Rock, and Susan Webber Wright, Professor of Law, University of Arkansas, Little Rock.

Landlord and Tenant Law, 2nd Ed., 1986, 311 pages, by David S. Hill, Professor of Law, University of Colorado.

Law Study and Law Examinations—Introduction to, 1971, 389 pages, by Stanley V. Kinyon, Late Professor of Law, University of Minnesota.

Legal Interviewing and Counseling, 2nd Ed., 1987, 487 pages, by Thomas L. Shaffer, Professor of Law, University of Notre Dame, and James R. Elkins, Professor of Law, West Virginia University.

Legal Research, 4th Ed., 1985, 452 pages, by Morris L. Cohen, Professor of Law and Law Librarian, Yale University.

Legal Writing, 1982, 294 pages, by Lynn B. Squires and Marjorie Dick Rombauer, Professor of Law, University of Washington.

Legislative Law and Process, 2nd Ed., 1986, 346 pages, by Jack Davies, Professor of Law, William Mitchell College of Law.

Local Government Law, 2nd Ed., 1983, 404 pages, by David J. McCarthy, Jr., Professor of Law, Georgetown University.

Mass Communications Law, 3rd Ed., 1988, 538 pages, by Harvey L. Zuckman, Professor of Law, Catholic University, Martin J. Gaynes, Lecturer in Law, Temple University, T. Barton Carter, Professor of Public Communications, Boston University, and Juliet Lushbough Dee, Professor of Communications, University of Delaware.

Medical Malpractice—The Law of, 2nd Ed., 1986, 342 pages, by Joseph H. King, Professor of Law, University of Tennessee.

Military Law, 1980, 378 pages, by Charles A. Shanor, Professor of Law, Emory University, and Timothy P. Terrell, Professor of Law, Emory University.

Oil and Gas Law, 2nd Ed., 1988, about 402 pages, by John S. Lowe, Professor of Law, Southern Methodist University.

Personal Property, 1983, 322 pages, by Barlow Burke, Jr., Professor of Law, American University.

Post-Conviction Remedies, 1978, 360 pages, by Robert Popper, Dean and Professor of Law, University of Missouri, Kansas City.

Presidential Power, 1977, 328 pages, by Arthur Selwyn Miller, Professor of Law Emeritus, George Washington University.

Products Liability, 3rd Ed., 1988, 307 pages, by Jerry J. Phillips, Professor of Law, University of Tennessee.

Professional Responsibility, 1980, 399 pages, by Robert H. Aronson, Professor of Law, University of Washington, and Donald T. Weckstein, Professor of Law, University of San Diego.

Real Estate Finance, 2nd Ed., 1985, 262 pages, by Jon W. Bruce, Professor of Law, Vanderbilt University.

Real Property, 2nd Ed., 1981, 448 pages, by Roger H. Bernhardt, Professor of Law, Golden Gate University.

Regulated Industries, 2nd Ed., 1987, 389 pages, by Ernest Gellhorn, Former Dean and Professor of Law, Case Western Reserve University, and Richard J. Pierce, Professor of Law, Southern Methodist University.

Remedies, 2nd Ed., 1985, 320 pages, by John F. O'Connell, Dean and Professor of Law, Southern California College of Law.

Res Judicata, 1976, 310 pages, by Robert C. Casad, Professor of Law, University of Kansas.

Sales, 2nd Ed., 1981, 370 pages, by John M. Stockton, Professor of Business Law, Wharton School of Finance and Commerce, University of Pennsylvania.

Schools, Students and Teachers—Law of, 1984, 409 pages, by Kern Alexander, President, Western Kentucky University and M. David Alexander, Professor, Virginia Tech University.

Sea—Law of, 1984, 264 pages, by Louis B. Sohn, Professor of Law, University of Georgia, and Kristen Gustafson.

Secured Transactions, 3rd Ed., 1988, about 390 pages, by Henry J. Bailey, Professor of Law Emeritus, Willamette University, and Richard B. Hagedorn, Professor of Law, Willamette University.

Securities Regulation, 3rd Ed., 1988, 316 pages, by David L. Ratner, Dean and Professor of Law, University of San Francisco.

Sex Discrimination, 1982, 399 pages, by Claire Sherman Thomas, Lecturer, University of Washington, Women's Studies Department.

State Constitutional Law, 1988, about 300 pages, by Thomas C. Marks, Jr., Professor of Law, Stetson University, and John F. Cooper, Professor of Law, Stetson University.

Taxation and Finance, State and Local, 1986, 309 pages, by M. David Gelfand, Professor of Law, Tulane University, and Peter W. Salsich, Professor of Law, St. Louis University.

Taxation of Individuals, Federal Income, 4th Ed., 1988, about 500 pages, by John K. McNulty, Professor of Law, University of California, Berkeley.

Torts—Injuries to Persons and Property, 1977, 434 pages, by Edward J. Kionka, Professor of Law, Southern Illinois University.

Torts—Injuries to Family, Social and Trade Relations, 1979, 358 pages, by Wex S. Malone, Professor of Law Emeritus, Louisiana State University.

Trial Advocacy, 1979, 402 pages, by Paul B. Bergman, Adjunct Professor of Law, University of California, Los Angeles.

Trial and Practice Skills, 1978, 346 pages, by Kenney F. Hegland, Professor of Law, University of Arizona.

Trial, The First—Where Do I Sit? What Do I Say?, 1982, 396 pages, by Steven H. Goldberg, Professor of Law, University of Minnesota.

Unfair Trade Practices, 2nd Ed., 1988, about 430 pages, by Charles R. McManis, Professor of Law, Washington University.

Uniform Commercial Code, 2nd Ed., 1984, 516 pages, by Bradford Stone, Professor of Law, Stetson University.

Uniform Probate Code, 2nd Ed., 1987, 454 pages, by Lawrence H. Averill, Jr., Dean and Professor of Law, University of Arkansas, Little Rock.

Water Law, 1984, 439 pages, by David H. Getches, Professor of Law, University of Colorado.

Welfare Law—Structure and Entitlement, 1979, 455 pages, by Arthur B. LaFrance, Professor of Law, Lewis and Clark College, Northwestern School of Law.

Wills and Trusts, 1979, 392 pages, by Robert L. Mennell, Former Professor of Law, Hamline University.

Workers' Compensation and Employee Protection Laws, 1984, 274 pages, by Jack B. Hood, Former Professor of Law, Cumberland School of Law, Samford University and Benjamin A. Hardy, Former Professor of Law, Cumberland School of Law, Samford University.

Hornbook Series

and

Basic Legal Texts

of

WEST PUBLISHING COMPANY

P.O. Box 64526

St. Paul, Minnesota 55164–0526

Admiralty and Maritime Law, Schoenbaum's Hornbook on, 1987, 692 pages, by Thomas J. Schoenbaum, Professor of Law, University of Georgia.

Agency and Partnership, Reuschlein & Gregory's Hornbook on the Law of, 1979 with 1981 Pocket Part, 625 pages, by Harold Gill Reuschlein, Professor of Law Emeritus, Villanova University, and William A. Gregory, Professor of Law, Georgia State University.

Antitrust, Sullivan's Hornbook on the Law of, 1977, 886 pages, by Lawrence A. Sullivan, Professor of Law, University of California, Berkeley.

Civil Procedure, Friedenthal, Kane and Miller's Hornbook on, 1985, 876 pages, by Jack H. Friedental, Dean and Professor of Law, George Washington University, Mary Kay Kane, Professor of Law, University of California, Hastings College of the Law, and Arthur R. Miller, Professor of Law, Harvard University.

Common Law Pleading, Koffler and Reppy's Hornbook on, 1969, 663 pages, by Joseph H. Koffler, Professor of Law, New York Law School, and Alison Reppy, Late Dean and Professor of Law, New York Law School.

Conflict of Laws, Scoles and Hay's Hornbook on, 1982, with 1986 Pocket Part, 1085 pages, by Eugene F. Scoles, Professor of Law, University of Illinois, and Peter Hay, Dean and Professor of Law, University of Illinois.

Constitutional Law, Nowak, Rotunda and Young's Hornbook on, 3rd Ed., 1986, with 1988 Pocket Part, 1191 pages, by John E. Nowak, Professor of Law, University of Illinois, Ronald D. Rotunda, Professor of Law, University of Illinois, and J. Nelson Young, Late Professor of Law, University of North Carolina.

Contracts, Calamari and Perillo's Hornbook on, 3rd Ed., 1987, 1049 pages, by John D. Calamari, Professor of Law, Fordham University, and Joseph M. Perillo, Professor of Law, Fordham University.

Contracts, Corbin's One Volume Student Ed., 1952, 1224 pages, by Arthur L. Corbin, Late Professor of Law, Yale University.

Corporations, Henn and Alexander's Hornbook on, 3rd Ed., 1983, with 1986 Pocket Part, 1371 pages, by Harry G. Henn, Professor of Law Emeritus, Cornell University, and John R. Alexander.

Criminal Law, LaFave and Scott's Hornbook on, 2nd Ed., 1986, 918 pages, by Wayne R. LaFave, Professor of Law, University of Illinois, and Austin Scott, Jr., Late Professor of Law, University of Colorado.

Criminal Procedure, LaFave and Israel's Hornbook on, 1985 with 1986 pocket part, 1142 pages, by Wayne R. LaFave, Professor of Law, University of Illinois, and Jerold H. Israel, Professor of Law University of Michigan.

Damages, McCormick's Hornbook on, 1935, 811 pages, by Charles T. McCormick, Late Dean and Professor of Law, University of Texas.

Domestic Relations, Clark's Hornbook on, 2nd Ed., 1988, 1050 pages, by Homer H. Clark, Jr., Professor of Law, University of Colorado.

Economics and Federal Antitrust Law, Hovenkamp's Hornbook on, 1985, 414 pages, by Herbert Hovenkamp, Professor of Law, University of Iowa.

Employment Discrimination Law, Player's Hornbook on, 708 pages, 1988, by Mack A. Player, Professor of Law, Florida State University.

HORNBOOKS & BASIC TEXTS

Environmental Law, Rodgers' Hornbook on, 1977 with 1984 Pocket Part, 956 pages, by William H. Rodgers, Jr., Professor of Law, University of Washington.

Evidence, Lilly's Introduction to, 2nd Ed., 1987, 585 pages, by Graham C. Lilly, Professor of Law, University of Virginia.

Evidence, McCormick's Hornbook on, 3rd Ed., 1984 with 1987 Pocket Part, 1156 pages, General Editor, Edward W. Cleary, Professor of Law Emeritus, Arizona State University.

Federal Courts, Wright's Hornbook on, 4th Ed., 1983, 870 pages, by Charles Alan Wright, Professor of Law, University of Texas.

Federal Income Taxation, Rose and Chommie's Hornbook on, 3rd Ed., 1988, 923 pages, by Michael D. Rose, Professor of Law, Ohio State University, and John C. Chommie, Late Professor of Law, University of Miami.

Federal Income Taxation of Individuals, Posin's Hornbook on, 1983 with 1987 Pocket Part, 491 pages, by Daniel Q. Posin, Jr., Professor of Law, Catholic University.

Future Interest, Simes' Hornbook on, 2nd Ed., 1966, 355 pages, by Lewis M. Simes, Late Professor of Law, University of Michigan.

Insurance, Keeton and Widiss on, 1988, about 1050 pages, by Robert E. Keeton, Professor of Law Emeritus, Harvard University, and Alan I. Widiss, Professor of Law, University of Iowa.

Labor Law, Gorman's Basic Text on, 1976, 914 pages, by Robert A. Gorman, Professor of Law, University of Pennsylvania.

Law Problems, Ballentine's, 5th Ed., 1975, 767 pages, General Editor, William E. Burby, Late Professor of Law, University of Southern California.

Legal Ethics, Wolfram's Hornbook on, 1986, 1120 pages, by Charles W. Wolfram, Professor of Law, Cornell University.

Legal Writing Style, Weihofen's, 2nd Ed., 1980, 332 pages, by Henry Weihofen, Professor of Law Emeritus, University of New Mexico.

Local Government Law, Reynolds' Hornbook on, 1982 with 1987 Pocket Part, 860 pages, by Osborne M. Reynolds, Professor of Law, University of Oklahoma.

New York Estate Administration, Turano and Radigan's Hornbook on, 1986, 676 pages, by Margaret V. Turano, Professor of Law, St. John's University, and Raymond Radigan.

New York Practice, Siegel's Hornbook on, 1978 with 1987 Pocket Part, 1011 pages, by David D. Siegel, Professor of Law, St. John's University.

Oil and Gas Law, Hemingway's Hornbook on, 2nd Ed., 1983, with 1986 Pocket Part, 543 pages, by Richard W. Hemingway, Professor of Law, University of Oklahoma.

Property, Boyer's Survey of, 3rd Ed., 1981, 766 pages, by Ralph E. Boyer, Professor of Law Emeritus, University of Miami.

Property, Law of, Cunningham, Whitman and Stoebuck's Hornbook on, 1984 with 1987 Pocket Part, 916 pages, by Roger A. Cunningham, Professor of Law, University of Michigan, Dale A. Whitman, Professor of Law, University of Missouri, Columbia, and William B. Stoebuck, Professor of Law, University of Washington.

Real Estate Finance Law, Nelson and Whitman's Hornbook on, 2nd Ed., 1985, 941 pages, by Grant S. Nelson, Professor of Law, University of Missouri, Columbia, and Dale A. Whitman, Professor of Law, University of Missouri, Columbia.

Real Property, Moynihan's Introduction to, 2nd Ed., 1988, 239 pages, by Cornelius J. Moynihan, Late Professor of Law, Suffolk University.

Remedies, Dobbs' Hornbook on, 1973, 1067 pages, by Dan B. Dobbs, Professor of Law, University of Arizona.

Secured Transactions under the U.C.C., Henson's Hornbook on, 2nd Ed., 1979 with 1979 Pocket Part, 504 pages, by Ray D. Henson, Professor of Law, University of California, Hastings College of the Law.

Securities Regulation, Hazen's Hornbook on the Law of, 1985 with 1988 Pocket Part, 739 pages, by Thomas Lee Hazen, Professor of Law, University of North Carolina.

HORNBOOKS & BASIC TEXTS

Sports Law, Schubert, Smith and Trentadue's, 1986, 395 pages, by George W. Schubert, Dean of University College, University of North Dakota, Rodney K. Smith, Professor of Law, Delaware Law School, Widener University, and Jesse C. Trentadue, Former Professor of Law, University of North Dakota.

Torts, Prosser and Keeton's Hornbook on, 5th Ed., 1984 with 1988 Pocket Part, 1286 pages, by William L. Prosser, Late Dean and Professor of Law, University of California, Berkeley, Page Keeton, Professor of Law Emeritus, University of Texas, Dan B. Dobbs, Professor of Law, University of Arizona, Robert E. Keeton, Professor of Law Emeritus, Harvard University, and David G. Owen, Professor of Law, University of South Carolina.

Trial Advocacy, Jeans' Handbook on, Soft cover, 1975, 473 pages, by James W. Jeans, Professor of Law, University of Missouri, Kansas City.

Trusts, Bogert's Hornbook on, 6th Ed., 1987, 794 pages, by George T. Bogert.

Uniform Commercial Code, White and Summers' Hornbook on, 3rd Ed., 1988, about 1200 pages, by James J. White, Professor of Law, University of Michigan, and Robert S. Summers, Professor of Law, Cornell University.

Urban Planning and Land Development Control Law, Hagman and Juergensmeyer's Hornbook on, 2nd Ed., 1986, 680 pages, by Donald G. Hagman, Late Professor of Law, University of California, Los Angeles, and Julian C. Juergensmeyer, Professor of Law, University of Florida.

Wills, Atkinson's Hornbook on, 2nd Ed., 1953, 975 pages, by Thomas E. Atkinson, Late Professor of Law, New York University.

Wills, Trusts and Estates Including Taxation and Future Interests, McGovern, Rein and Kurtz' Hornbook on, 1988, about 924 pages by William M. McGovern, Professor of Law, University of California, Los Angeles, Jan Ellen Rein, Professor of Law, Gonzaga University, and Sheldon F. Kurtz, Professor of Law, University of Iowa.

Advisory Board

FEDERAL INCOME TAXATION OF CORPORATIONS AND STOCKHOLDERS

IN A NUTSHELL

Third Edition

By

PETER P. WEIDENBRUCH, JR.

Dwan Professor of Taxation
Georgetown University Law Center

and

KAREN C. BURKE

Associate Professor of Law
University of Minnesota Law School

ST. PAUL, MINN.
WEST PUBLISHING CO.
1989

Library of Congress Cataloging-in-Publication Data

Weidenbruch, Peter P., 1929–
     Federal income taxation of corporations and stockholders in a
  nutshell / by Peter P. Weidenbruch, Jr. and Karen C. Burke.—3rd
  ed.
     p.   cm. — (Nutshell series) Second ed. by Jonathan Sobeloff
  and Peter P. Weidenbruch, Jr. Includes index.
     ISBN 0–314–49944–X
     1. Corporations—Taxation—Law and legislation—United States. I.
  Burke, Karen C., 1951–   . II. Sobeloff, Jonathan. Federal
  income taxation of corporations and stockholders in a nutshell. III.
  Title.
  KF6465.S58 1989
  343.7305'267—dc 19
  [347.3035267]
                                                        88–38321
                                                        CIP

ISBN 0–314–49944–X

(W. & B.) Fed.Inc.Tax. 3rd Ed. NS

PREFACE TO THE THIRD EDITION

Since the second edition of this work appeared in 1981, federal income taxation of corporations and shareholders has undergone numerous changes. The third edition has been completely revised to reflect developments in the statute, regulations and case law through November 1988, including the Technical and Miscellaneous Revenue Act of 1988.

Despite significant changes in emphasis and direction, many of the basic principles of corporate taxation prove remarkably durable. This edition retains the essential organizational structure of its predecessors. Chapter 1 introduces several fundamental issues in the taxation of corporations and shareholders, followed by a discussion of the corporation as a taxable entity in Chapter 2. Chapters 3 through 6 track the corporate life cycle from incorporations through nonliquidating distributions and redemptions to complete liquidations. Chapters 7 through 10 address more advanced problems in corporate taxation, including stock dividends, reorganizations, corporate divisions and carryover of corporate attributes. Chapter 11 provides an overview of the tax treatment of S corporations.

PREFACE TO THE THIRD EDITION

This work is intended to introduce students to the basic structure of corporate taxation.

KAREN C. BURKE

Minneapolis, MN
November, 1988

OUTLINE

Chapter 1. Introduction

Chapter 2. Corporation as Taxable Entity

Chapter 3.   Incorporations

Chapter 4.　Nonliquidating Distributions

Chapter 5. Redemptions

Chapter 7. Stock Dividends

Chapter 8. Reorganizations

Chapter 9. Corporate Divisions

OUTLINE

TABLE OF CASES

References are to Pages

TABLE OF CASES

L

M

N

TABLE OF CASES

P

R

S

T

TABLE OF CASES

U

United States v. ____(see opposing party)

W

Y

Z

TABLE OF INTERNAL REVENUE CODE SECTIONS, REGULATIONS AND RULINGS

UNITED STATES

UNITED STATES CODE ANNOTATED

26 U.S.C.A.--Internal Revenue Code

INTERNAL REVENUE CODE SECTIONS

26 U.S.C.A.--Internal Revenue Code

INTERNAL REVENUE CODE SECTIONS

26 U.S.C.A.--Internal Revenue Code

26 U.S.C.A.--Internal Revenue Code

INTERNAL REVENUE CODE SECTIONS

26 U.S.C.A.--Internal Revenue Code

XLIX

26 U.S.C.A.--Internal Revenue Code

L

INTERNAL REVENUE CODE SECTIONS

26 U.S.C.A.--Internal Revenue Code

26 U.S.C.A.--Internal Revenue Code

INTERNAL REVENUE CODE SECTIONS

26 U.S.C.A.--Internal Revenue Code

26 U.S.C.A.--Internal Revenue Code

INTERNAL REVENUE CODE SECTIONS

26 U.S.C.A.--Internal Revenue Code

26 U.S.C.A.--Internal Revenue Code

INTERNAL REVENUE CODE SECTIONS

26 U.S.C.A.--Internal Revenue Code

26 U.S.C.A.--Internal Revenue Code

INTERNAL REVENUE CODE SECTIONS

26 U.S.C.A.--Internal Revenue Code

INTERNAL REVENUE CODE SECTIONS

26 U.S.C.A.--Internal Revenue Code

26 U.S.C.A.--Internal Revenue Code

LXVII

TREASURY REGULATIONS

INTERNAL REVENUE CODE SECTIONS

TREASURY REGULATIONS

PROPOSED TREASURY REGULATIONS

TEMPORARY TREASURY REGULATIONS

TEMPORARY TREASURY REGULATIONS

REVENUE PROCEDURE

REVENUE RULINGS

INTERNAL REVENUE CODE SECTIONS

REVENUE RULINGS

INTERNAL REVENUE CODE SECTIONS

REVENUE RULINGS

LETTER RULINGS

*

CHAPTER 1

INTRODUCTION

§ 1. The Corporate Double Tax and the Tax Reform Act of 1986

One of the underlying premises of Subchapter C is the double tax on distributed corporate earnings. A corporation is taxed as a separate entity on its taxable income, and shareholders are taxed on the distribution of the corporation's after-tax earnings. In effect, the same income is taxed once at the corporate level and again at the shareholder level. Double taxation of distributed earnings is a significant disadvantage of the corporate form of business. The Tax Reform Act of 1986 (the "1986 Act") introduced several changes that generally strengthen the double tax system and lessen the attractiveness of the corporate form of business.

(a) *Distributions of Appreciated Property.* The 1986 Act eliminated the *General Utilities* doctrine that permitted a corporation to distribute appreciated property to its shareholders without recognizing gain on the appreciation. *See* General Utilities & Operating Co. (1935). Congress believed that the *General Utilities* doctrine was subject to abuse and tended to undermine the corporate income tax. Prior to the 1986 Act, the *General Utilities* doctrine had been substantially eroded by several tax acts.

1

Under Subchapter C, a corporation recognizes gain on both liquidating and nonliquidating distributions of appreciated property, as discussed in Chapters 4 and 6. Losses are recognized, however, only on liquidating distributions of property. These changes affect not only distributions of property, but also sales of assets prior to liquidation and stock purchases treated as asset purchases, as discussed in Chapter 6.

(b) *Capital Gains.* The 1986 Act also eliminated preferential treatment for capital gains. Prior to the 1986 Act, an issue of primary importance with respect to corporate distributions was whether the distribution would be taxed at the shareholder level as ordinary income (to the extent the distribution constituted a dividend) or as capital gain from a sale or exchange of stock. In the case of a redemption of stock treated as a sale or exchange, the shareholder is generally permitted to recover his basis in the redeemed stock tax free; only the excess is taxed as capital gain, as discussed in Chapter 5. Because ordinary income and capital gains are taxed at the same rate under the 1986 Act, the focal point at the shareholder level will be whether the shareholder is entitled to tax-free basis recovery.

Although the 1986 Act has generally reduced the tax stakes, there have been no substantial changes in the complex provisions of Subchapter C that are designed to prevent shareholders from availing themselves of capital gains rates in connection with a bailout of corporate assets (including § 306 discussed in Chapter 7). Indeed, the legislative history of the 1986 Act makes clear that the Code retains the separate treatment of capital gains from prior law in order to facilitate reinstatement of a capital gains rate differential in the event of a future tax rate increase. Even in the absence of a preferential capital gains rate, shareholders may still prefer capital gains to ordinary income in order to offset capital losses. If the elimination of the capital gains preference proves permanent, however, many of the traditional corporate tax planning strategies will become obsolete because they will have little effect on the amount of tax payable at the shareholder level.

(c) *Corporate Tax Rates.* The 1986 Act inverted the relationship between the income tax rates for corporations and other taxpayers. Under prior law, corporate tax rates had consistently been lower than individual tax rates. Effective in 1988, however, the maximum corporate tax rate is 34% while the maximum individual rate is 28%. *See* Chapter 2. This inversion of the rates, combined with the elimination of the preferential capital gains rates, removes the advantage to shareholders of accumulating corporate earnings within the corporation and converting the corporation's undistributed earnings into cash at capital gains rates by selling their stock.

(d) *Revenue Effects.* The 1986 Act attempts to shift some of the federal income tax burden from individuals to businesses. Although the maximum corporate tax rate is significantly lower than the 50% maximum rate in effect under prior law, the effective corporate tax rate is actually projected to increase, resulting in an estimated $120 billion revenue increase from corporate taxes in 1987–1991. The estimated revenue increase is attributable to provisions of the 1986 Act limiting deductions and credits for businesses and expanding the alternative minimum tax applicable to corporations.

§ 2. Future Reform

The 1986 Act has thus had a profound impact on the federal income taxation of corporations and shareholders, and further changes may be forthcoming. The 1986 Act directs the Treasury "to conduct a study of proposals to reform the provisions of subchapter C" and to report to Congress "[n]ot later than January 1, 1988". Publication of the Treasury's proposals has been delayed and is not expected until 1989.

(a) *Nonrecognition.* The Code provides nonrecognition treatment for certain transactions which are viewed as mere changes in the form of a continuing investment. Nonrecognition transactions include incorporation transfers (Chapter 3) and certain corporate rearrangements broadly described as reorganizations (Chapter 8). Typically, the nonrecognition provisions ensure that any realized gain or loss is merely deferred rather than permanently eliminated. Technically, deferral is accomplished by requiring that a taxpayer's basis in property received in a nonrecognition transaction be determined (in whole or in part) either by reference to the basis of other property formerly held by the same taxpayer ("exchanged basis") or by reference to the basis of the same property in the hands of a previous owner ("transferred basis"). For convenience, the general term "substituted basis" is used to refer to exchanged basis as well as transferred basis. *See* §§ 7701(a)(42)-(44). The 1986 Act has enhanced the importance of tax-free reorganizations in contrast to taxable acquisitions which trigger tax at both the corporate and shareholder levels. Although the 1986 Act left the nonrecognition provisions virtually intact, reorganizations may be a principal focus of future reform.

(b) *Integration Proposals.* Several proposals for integrating federal income taxation of corporations and individuals have also been advanced in recent years. These proposals reflect concern that the present system of double taxation of corporate earnings may inhibit capital formation and impose an excessive tax burden on corporations as compared to proprietorships and partnerships. In part because of the potential revenue loss, it seems unlikely that a formal integration system will be adopted in the near future.

§ 3. Choice of Business Form

In the case of small businesses which are essentially similar to partnerships, Congress has expressed the policy goal that federal income tax considerations should not unduly influence the choice of the form of business. Accordingly, Subchapter S of the Code offers small business entities an alternative to the double tax system without sacrificing the non-tax advantages of doing business in corporate form, as discussed in Chapter 11. In the case of electing corporations, both distributed and undistributed corporate earnings are generally taxed only at the shareholder level. The choice of business form is increasingly important after the 1986 Act. A detailed comparison of the tax consequences of corporate as compared to noncorporate (proprietorship or partnership) form of business, however, is beyond the scope of this work.

CHAPTER 2

CORPORATION AS TAXABLE ENTITY

§ 1. Definition and Classification Issues

Under § 7701(a)(3), the term "corporation" is defined to include associations. The § 7701 Regulations list the following corporate characteristics to be taken into account in determining whether an unincorporated organization will be classified as an association for income tax purposes: (i) associates, (ii) an objective to carry on business and divide the gains therefrom, (iii) continuity of life, (iv) centralized management, (v) limited liability, and (vi) free transferability of interests. The first two characteristics are essential for classification as an association. In distinguishing an association from a partnership or other type of organization sharing any of these corporate characteristics, however, the shared characteristics are disregarded, and an unincorporated organization is classified as an association only if it has a majority of the remaining corporate characteristics. Reg. § 301.7701–2(a)(3).

For example, a trust will be classified as a corporation for federal tax purposes only if it has both of the first two corporate characteristics. *See* Morrissey (1935) (trust taxed as corporation); Bedell

(1986) (testamentary trust lacked "associates" and therefore could not be classified as a corporation). An organization which is a partnership under state law will be treated as an association for federal income tax purposes only if, in addition to the first two corporate characteristics listed above, it also exhibits more than two of the remaining corporate characteristics. In the Omnibus Budget Reform Act of 1987 (the "1987 Act"), Congress required certain publicly-traded partnerships, as defined in § 7704(b), to be taxed as associations. § 7704(a).

In some cases, taxpayers have argued that a corporation's income should be taxed directly to its shareholders, rather than to the corporation, on the theory that (i) the corporation's separate existence should be ignored or (ii) the corporation acts merely as the shareholders' agent. In *Moline Properties* (1943), the Supreme Court held that a corporation may be treated as a separate taxable entity even if it is wholly dominated by a single shareholder. The Court noted that the corporation was not merely the shareholder's alter ego, and its independent corporate existence was not fictitious. In *Bollinger* (1988), the Supreme Court addressed the argument that a corporation might act merely as the agent of its shareholders. The Court held that an agency relationship is sufficiently established if (i) the agency relationship is set forth in writing at the time the corporation acquires the relevant assets, (ii) the corporation functions as an agent with respect to those assets for all purposes, and (iii) the corporation's status as an agent is disclosed in all dealings with third parties relating to those assets.   Thus, *Bollinger* indicates that agency status is essentially a factual matter to be determined by reference to criteria other than the control of the corporation inherent in the corporate-shareholder relationship.

§ 2. Corporate Tax Rate Structure

(a) *General.* For taxable years beginning on or after July 1, 1987, a corporation's taxable income is taxed at the following graduated marginal rates under § 11(b):

Taxable Income	Marginal Rate
First $50,000 ($0–50,000)	15%
Next $25,000 ($50,001—$75,000)	25
Over $75,000	34

The benefit of graduated rates, however, is phased out by a 5% surtax on taxable income between $100,000 and $335,000. The maximum surtax liability is equal to 5% of the amount of taxable income in the phase-out range ($335,000 less $100,000, or $235,000), which exactly offsets the difference between the 34% rate and the lower rates applicable to the first $75,000 of taxable income ((34% − 15%) x $50,000 plus (34% − 25%) x $25,000). As a result, a corporation with taxable income of $335,000 or more pays tax at an effective (as well as a marginal) rate of 34%.

(b) *Capital Gains and Losses.* Before the 1986 Act, corporations were taxed on "net capital gain" at a rate equal to the lesser of the regular tax rates or a flat 28% tax. (Net capital gain is defined as the excess of net long-term capital gain over net short-term capital loss, under § 1222(11).) For taxable years beginning on or after July 1, 1987, the rate of tax under § 1201(a) applicable to net capital gain is increased to 34%. Although the differential between ordinary income and net capital gain tax rates is currently in abeyance, a subsequent increase in ordinary income tax rates, without a corresponding change under § 1201(a), could renew the importance of capital gain treatment.

A corporation may deduct capital losses only to the extent of capital gains during the year. § 1211(a). Any excess capital losses may be carried back for 3 years and carried forward for 5 years. § 1212(a)(1).

§ 3. Corporate Taxable Income

The gross income of a corporation is defined under § 61 in much the same manner as that of an individual, and corporate taxable income is determined under § 63(a) by subtracting allowable deductions from gross income. Corporations may deduct their ordinary and necessary business expenses under § 162 and interest expense under § 163. Corporations are also allowed deductions for certain security and debt losses under §§ 165 and 166. Corporate net operating losses are deductible subject to the 3–year carryback and 15–

year carryforward provisions of § 172. Section 291
imposes special percentage limitations on allowable deductions for certain corporate preference
items, such as the ordinary income portion on the
sale of certain § 1250 property (real property subject to accelerated depreciation) and certain preference items of financial institutions. The passive
loss limitations of § 469, enacted by the 1986 Act
to curb tax shelters, do not apply to corporations
(other than certain closely-held corporations and
personal service corporations). §§ 469(a)(2) and
469(j)(1)-(2). In the case of S corporations, the
passive loss limitations are determined separately
on the individual shareholders' tax returns.

§ 4. Special Rules Relating to Corporate-Shareholder Transactions

(a) *Related-Party Transactions.* Section 267(a)
(1) disallows deductions for losses on sales or exchanges of property between certain related parties. Under § 267(b), an individual and a corporation are treated as related parties if the individual
owns directly or indirectly more than 50% in value
of the corporation's outstanding stock. For this
purpose, stock ownership is determined under the
constructive ownership rules of § 267(c).

The "matching" rules of § 267(a)(2) also defer
deductions for an item of expense or interest owed
by a taxpayer who uses the accrual method to a
related party who uses the cash method, until the
item is actually included in the payee's gross income (generally when paid). This provision is in-

tended, for example, to prevent a corporation from deducting currently an amount for accrued but unpaid salary owed to a controlling shareholder-employee. The 1986 Act amended § 267(a)(2) to cover any shareholder-employee of a personal service corporation (as defined in § 441(i)(2)) as a related party, regardless of the amount of stock ownership.

(b) *Corporate Takeover Expenses.* Section 162(*l*), added by the 1986 Act, denies a deduction for any amount paid or incurred by a corporation "in connection with the redemption of its stock." Although the deductibility of such expenses was doubtful even under prior law, the new provision is aimed expressly at "greenmail" payments by a corporation purchasing its stock from corporate raiders. In addition, new § 5881 imposes an excise tax of 50% on any gain realized (whether or not recognized) by a person who receives greenmail. "Greenmail" is defined as any consideration paid by a corporation in redemption of its stock if the shareholder has held such stock for less than 2 years before agreeing to transfer the stock to the corporation, provided that the shareholder (or any person acting in concert with the shareholder or a related person) "made or threatened to make a public tender offer for stock" of the corporation during the 2-year period. § 5881(b). The excise tax does not apply, however, if the redemption is pursuant to an offer which is available to all other shareholders on the same terms.

Section 280G, enacted in 1984, disallows deductions for certain "golden parachute" payments designed to cushion the departure of management from corporations subject to hostile takeovers. This provision disallows a deduction for payments to a "disqualified individual" (officer, shareholder or other highly compensated individual), if the payment is contingent on a change in ownership or control of a company and the present value of the payments exceeds 3 times a defined base amount. The base amount is determined by reference to the individual's annual average compensation for the 5–year period preceding the change of ownership or control, with certain adjustments. In addition, § 280G disallows any amounts paid under an agreement in violation of generally enforced securities laws or regulations. A companion provision, § 4999, imposes an excise tax of 20% on the recipient of a golden parachute payment.

Section 279, enacted in 1969, disallows a deduction for corporate interest in excess of $5 million per year on certain "corporate acquisition indebtedness", which is defined to include certain convertible subordinated debt. The limitations of § 279 were circumvented relatively easily during the acquisition activities of the early 1980s; and, in 1987, further limitations on acquisition indebtedness were proposed but not enacted. These proposals included disallowance of deductions for interest on indebtedness incurred to purchase 20% or more of another corporation's stock pursuant to a hostile tender offer.

§ 5. Dividends-Received Deduction

(a) *Section 243.* Dividends received by a corporate taxpayer normally qualify for the dividends-received deduction under § 243. Prior to the 1987 Act, the amount of the § 243 deduction was generally 80% of the dividends received from domestic corporations (100% in the case of certain dividends received from at least 80% subsidiaries). Section 243 reduces the effective maximum tax rate on dividends eligible for the 80% deduction to 6.8%; that is, a 34% tax is imposed on only 20% of the dividends received. The 1987 Act reduced the dividends-received deduction from 80% to 70% for corporations which own less than 20% (by voting power and value) of the distributing corporation's stock, on the theory that such corporations lack a sufficient ownership interest in the distributing corporation to justify an 80% deduction. §§ 243(a) and 243(c).

(b) *Sales of Stock Ex-dividend.* Section 246(c) denies any dividends-received deduction unless the corporation has held the stock on which the dividend is paid for more than 45 days (90 days in the case of certain preferred stock). This provision was intended to close the loophole permitted when a corporation bought stock just before a dividend became payable (at a price reflecting the full value of the dividend) and then immediately sold the stock after payment of the dividend, thereby claiming a deductible loss in addition to the dividends-received deduction.

(c) *Basis Reduction for Extraordinary Dividends.* Section 1059 requires a corporate shareholder to reduce its basis to the extent of the deductible portion of any "extraordinary dividend." Generally, an extraordinary dividend is defined by § 1059(c) as a dividend equalling or exceeding 10% (5% for preferred stock) of the shareholder's adjusted basis in the underlying stock. The basis of the stock cannot be reduced below zero by the § 1059 basis adjustment. If this special limitation applies, § 1059(a)(2) treats the remainder as gain at the time of sale. No basis reduction is required generally, however, if the underlying stock has been held for more than 2 years before the dividend announcement date or certain other conditions are met. The Technical and Miscellaneous Revenue Act of 1988 (the "1988 Act") clarified that the 2–year safe harbor does not apply if the payment constitutes a non-pro-rata distribution or a partial liquidation. *See* § 1059(e)(1).

Example: P Corp. purchases T Corp.'s preferred stock for $100 and T immediately distributes to P a $10 dividend. If P is entitled to an 80% dividends-received deduction under § 243, the deductible portion of the dividend is $8. Under § 1059, P would be required to reduce its basis in the T stock to $92. Assuming that P immediately thereafter sells the T stock for $90 (the value of the T stock once the dividend has been paid), P would be entitled to a loss of $2 on its investment, which equals the $2 portion of the earlier distribution taxed to P. This result is economically correct because the transaction produces a "wash" for P, *i.e.,* P has just recovered its initial $100 investment through the $10 distribution and $90 sales proceeds. If P were not required to reduce its basis for the untaxed portion of the dividend, P would have an additional artificial loss of $8 on the sale (the difference between the cost basis of $100 and the reduced basis of $92).

(d) *Debt-Financed Portfolio Stock Dividends.* Section 246A, enacted in 1984, is aimed at "tax arbitrage" when a corporation receives an interest deduction for "debt-financed portfolio stock" and the associated dividend is eligible for the § 243 deduction. In this situation, the § 243 deduction is reduced by a percentage equal to the portion of the stock which is debt financed. For example, if half of the stock basis is debt financed, only half of the § 243 deduction is allowed. The reduction, however, cannot exceed the amount of deductible interest on the debt financing attributable to the stock. Section 246A applies only if the indebtedness is "directly attributable" to the investment in the stock, *i.e.,* where the indebtedness is clearly incurred for the purpose of acquiring or carrying the stock. *See* § 246A(d)(3); Rev. Rul. 88–66. A recipient corporation is not subject to the § 246A reduction if it owns at least 50% of the stock of the paying corporation (or owns at least 20% of the

stock and 5 or fewer corporations own at least 50%
of the stock).

§ 6. Taxable Year and Method of Accounting

A corporation, like other taxpayers, must choose
a taxable year and method of accounting for tax
purposes. §§ 441 and 446. Generally, corporations
may adopt either a calendar or a fiscal year. Section 441(i), added by the 1986 Act, requires certain
personal service corporations (defined in § 269A as
a corporation of which the principal activity is
performance of personal services by its shareholders) to use a calendar year, unless allowed to select
a fiscal year by the Service. Similarly, an S corporation is generally required to use a calendar year.
§ 1378. These rules are intended to eliminate the
advantages of tax deferral arising from a difference between the taxable year of the entity and
that of its shareholders.

The 1987 Act added three new provisions that
significantly modify these rules. New § 444 allows
S corporations and personal service corporations to
elect to retain their previous fiscal years, or, if
newly formed, to adopt fiscal years ending no earlier than September 30. New § 7519 requires that S
corporations that elect fiscal years must make certain payments on behalf of their owners to offset
the advantage of tax deferral. Finally, new
§ 280H provides that personal service corporations
which "disproportionately postpone" payments to
employee-owners until after December 31 must

postpone some or all of their deductions until the following fiscal year. *See* Temp. Reg. § 1.280H–1T.

The 1986 Act also added § 448, which requires most Subchapter C corporations to use the accrual method of accounting, except for certain farming corporations, "qualified personal service corporations" (as defined in § 448(d)(2)) and entities having average annual gross receipts of $5 million or less for the 3–year period preceding the taxable year. Qualified personal service corporations are defined as corporations substantially all of whose activities involve the performance of services in certain specified fields (including health, law and accounting), provided that substantially all of the stock in such corporations is owned by employees, retired employees or their estates. Temporary Regulations § 1.448–1T(e) provide guidance concerning when a corporation will be considered a qualified personal service corporation based on the type of services provided. Under the 1987 Act, qualified personal service corporations are taxed at a flat rate of 34%, without the benefit of the graduated rates. § 11(b)(2).

§ 7. Allocation of Income and Deductions Among Related Taxpayers

Section 482 authorizes the Service to reallocate income, deductions, and certain other items among two or more "organizations, trades, or businesses" under common control in order clearly to reflect the income of such organizations. The major purpose of § 482 is to prevent shifting or distortion of income or deductions reported by related parties. The term "organizations, trades or businesses" has been broadly construed to cover virtually any type of taxable entity having independent tax significance. *See* Keller (1981). For example, § 482 clearly applies to transactions between a corporation and a sole proprietorship owned by a controlling shareholder. In *Foglesong* (1982), the Seventh Circuit considered whether § 482 applies to a taxpayer whose only trade or business is the performance of services for a controlled corporation. Because the taxpayer and the controlled corporation were engaged in the identical business, the court held that the two-trades-or-businesses requirement of § 482 was not satisfied. *But see* Dolese (1987) (two separate trades or businesses found). The Service has announced that it will not follow the holding in *Foglesong* that § 482 does not apply to a shareholder-employee who works exclusively for a controlled corporation. Rev. Rul. 88–38.

Under § 269A, the Service may reallocate income or deductions between a personal service corporation and its employee-owners. Thus, § 269A sidesteps the issue of whether the rendering of services by an employee is a separate trade or business. This provision, however, applies only to a narrow category of personal service corporations performing services primarily for one other entity. In addition, the principal purpose for forming or using the corporation must be avoidance or evasion of federal income tax by reducing the in-

come of, or securing tax benefits that would otherwise not be available to, an employee-owner.

§ 8. Alternative Minimum Tax

(a) *Purpose of the AMT.*   In addition to the regular corporate tax, the corporation may also be
subject to an alternative minimum tax (AMT) under § 55. The primary objective of Congress in
enacting the AMT was to ensure that taxpayers
with substantial economic income could not reduce
their tax liability to nominal levels by using exclusions, deductions and credits allowable under the
regular tax. Thus, the income tax base used in
determining the AMT ("alternative minimum taxable income," or AMTI) is broader than the regular
taxable income base and is intended to provide a
better measure of the corporation's economic income.

(b) *Mechanics.*   Section 55 imposes a tentative
minimum tax of 20% on the corporation's AMTI,
computed after allowance of an exemption amount
of $40,000 which is phased out between $150,000
and $310,000. *See* §§ 55(b) and 55(d). AMTI is
defined in § 55(b)(2) as regular taxable income,
adjusted as provided by §§ 56 and 58 and increased
by the tax preference items listed in § 57. If the
corporation's tentative minimum tax exceeds the
regular tax for the taxable year, the excess amount
is the AMT.

Example: X Corp. has a tentative minimum tax
of $1.5 million and a regular tax of $1 million. X

must pay total taxes (AMT and regular tax) of $1.5 million, comprising $1 million of regular tax and $.5 million of AMT. In this sense, the AMT is an "add-on" tax rather than an alternative tax. This distinction is important when the taxpayer computes its AMT credits under § 53 against the regular tax, discussed below. The § 53 credit is limited to the excess of the tentative minimum tax over the regular tax, or $.5 million in this example.

(c) *Tax Preference Items: § 57.* The tax preference adjustments are relatively straightforward and are simply added back to regular taxable income in arriving at AMTI. The tax preferences listed in § 57 include excess percentage depletion, certain intangible drilling costs, certain tax-exempt interest, excess deductions by financial institutions for bad debt reserves, the appreciated portion of property claimed as a charitable deduction, and accelerated depreciation for property placed in service before 1987.

(d) *Adjustments Other Than Book Income Adjustment: §§ 56 and 58.* In computing AMTI, § 56 requires certain adjustments that generally increase taxable income. For example, these adjustments lengthen the recovery period for real and personal property placed in service after 1986, accelerate the timing of income from long-term contracts, and disallow installment sale treatment of property described in § 1221(1) (inventory and property held primarily for sale to customers). *See* §§ 56(a)(1), 56(a)(3) and 56(a)(6). Section 56(d) also requires recomputation of net operating losses to reflect AMTI and limits the deductible portion to 90% of AMTI.

In addition, § 58 imposes special rules in computing AMTI for certain farming and passive activity losses, but these adjustments generally do not apply to corporations (except for personal service corporations).

(e) *Timing Differences.* Many of the adjustments required in arriving at AMTI affect merely the timing rather than the amount of a corporation's deductions. In effect, these adjustments represent a downpayment on the corporation's regular tax liability, since the AMT denies certain income tax deferrals and accelerated deductions that are allowable for regular tax purposes. The corporation may receive no tax benefit from a corresponding reduction in AMTI in later years, however, if its regular tax reflects some items which generated AMT in earlier years. In these situations, § 53 provides relief by allowing a credit against the corporation's regular tax for the AMT paid in earlier years.

Example: X Corp. owns depreciated real property which is used in its trade or business. For regular tax purposes, the depreciation will be taken ratably over 27.5 years under § 168. For AMT purposes, however, the recovery period for the property will be 40 years, resulting in smaller AMT deductions (and higher AMTI) in the early years. The basis of the property will be fully recovered for regular tax purposes at the end of 27.5 years, but the corporation will still be entitled to AMT depreciation deductions for another 12.5 years, resulting in lower AMTI. In this situation, § 53 would allow a credit against X's regular tax liability in later years for the AMT generated in the earlier years attributable to the timing differences in the depreciation deductions.

The amount of the § 53 credit is the corporation's alternative minimum tax liability attributable to adjustments reflecting timing differences. Section 53 calculates this amount by reference to the AMT payable in prior years reduced by the § 53 credits allowable for prior years; the amount of the credit in any year may not reduce the regular tax below the AMT for the current year. No credit is allowed, however, for AMT allocable to so-called exclusion preferences, *i.e.,* those items involving permanent exclusions rather than timing differences. Since these items (such as charitable contributions of appreciated property or tax-exempt interest) can never generate any regular tax liability, no credit is appropriate. For purposes of the § 53 credit, the taxpayer's AMT can be carried forward indefinitely (until applied against the regular tax), but may not be carried back. Since no credit carryback is permitted, § 53 does not provide relief if an item generates regular tax liability in an earlier year and also generates AMT liability in a later year.

(f) *Parallel Tax System.* In effect, the AMT is a separate tax system, and taxpayers must keep records of ongoing AMT adjustments even for years in which no AMT is payable. The AMT adjustments will affect the AMT basis of the corporation's property, which can have surprising results upon sale of the property in subsequent years.

Example: Assume that X Corp. in the above example has depreciated the basis of its real property to zero for regular tax purposes, but that the property still has a basis of $1,000 for AMT purposes. If the property is sold for $500, the corporation will have a $500 gain for regular tax purposes and a $500 loss for AMT purposes.

(g) *Book Income Adjustment.* Despite the comprehensive AMT base, Congress was concerned that companies with substantial income for financial accounting purposes might still pay insufficient tax. To address these concerns, in 1986 Congress provided for a "book income" adjustment in determining AMTI. For taxable years beginning in 1987–1989, § 56(f) increases AMTI by one-half of the excess of a corporation's "book income" over its "pre-adjustment" AMTI (AMTI computed before the book income adjustment). *See* Temp. Reg. § 1.56–1T(a). Book income is determined by reference to a corporation's "applicable financial statement" (as defined in § 53(f)(3)(A)), which generally means a financial statement filed with the SEC or, if there is no such statement, an audited statement used for obtaining credit, reporting to shareholders or other substantial non-tax purposes.

Example: X Corp. has regular taxable income of $500, § 57 tax preferences of $200, and book income of $1,200. X's AMTI base is $950, calculated as $500 of regular taxable income, plus $200 of tax preferences, plus $250 of book income adjustment under § 56(f) (one-half of the $500 excess of $1,200 (book income) over $700 (pre-adjustment AMTI)). Suppose that the tax preference of $200 consists entirely of tax-exempt interest on "specified private activity bonds" under § 57(a)(5). Because the $200 both enters into the AMTI base as a tax preference item of $200 and gives rise to a further book income adjustment of $100, there is arguably a double-counting problem.

For taxable years beginning after 1989, the book income adjustment is to be replaced by an adjustment based on "adjusted current earnings" (ACE) under § 56(g), a similar but even more complex provision. If the ACE adjustment becomes fully effective, AMTI will be increased by 75% of the excess, if any, of ACE over AMTI (computed before this adjustment).

§ 9. Capital Structure

(a) *Debt vs. Equity.* A corporation's capital structure often includes substantial amounts of debt in addition to the shareholders' equity. From the corporation's standpoint, interest payments on corporate debt give rise to a deduction while distributions with respect to stock do not. From the investor's standpoint, corporate debt is often preferable to stock because the repayment of principal at maturity or on redemption is generally tax free, while a redemption of stock may trigger recognition of ordinary or capital gain to the shareholder. A corporate shareholder, however, may prefer to hold stock rather than debt, since a portion of the dividends received may be excludable under § 243 of the Code.

In general, the parties are free to choose debt or equity financing or a combination of each. If the ratio of debt to equity in the corporation's capital structure is unreasonably high, however, the Service may treat purported debt instruments as stock for tax purposes, with the result that no deduction is allowed for payments reported as interest by the corporation. In 1969, Congress added § 385 to the Code which authorized the Treasury to issue regulations determining the classification of instruments as debt or stock. The Regulations issued under § 385 proved unworkable, however, and never became effective in final form. The debt-equity classification, therefore, depends on a judicially-developed facts-and-circumstances test. The courts tend to take an all-or-nothing approach to debt-equity classification, rather than fragmenting particular interests into debt and equity components.

(b) *Gain or Loss on Investments.* Stock and debt instruments in the hands of a shareholder are generally capital assets, so that any gain or loss on disposition is capital gain or loss. Under § 1271, retirement of a debt instrument is treated as an exchange. Section 1276 may require a portion of the gain on so-called market discount bonds, however, to be reported as ordinary income rather than capital gain to the extent allocable to accrued market discount.

Worthless stock or debt is subject to the rules of § 165(g) or § 166. Generally, § 165(g) provides for capital loss treatment if a loss results from worthlessness of stock or debt evidenced by a "security" which is a capital asset. If a loss is sustained on a debt not evidenced by a security, the bad debt deduction rules of § 166 are applicable. Business bad debts are treated as ordinary losses, while nonbusiness bad debts are treated as short-term capital losses. §§ 166(a) and 166(d). If a shareholder-employee sustains a loss in his capacity as a creditor, nonbusiness bad debt treatment is virtually unavoidable. *See* Generes (1972) (shareholder-employee lacked "dominant" business motivation for loan to corporation). The nonbusiness bad debt rule of § 166(d) does not apply to corporations. Thus, a corporate creditor generally receives ordinary loss treatment under § 166(a), unless the debt is a "security" under § 165(g). A special rule, however, permits ordinary loss treatment for securities in an "affiliated" corporation. § 165(g)(3).

If a corporation purchases stock in another corporation, it may seek ordinary loss treatment on a sale of the stock on the ground that it purchased the stock predominantly for business rather than investment purposes. In *Arkansas Best Corp.* (1988), the Supreme Court denied ordinary loss treatment on a corporation's sale of stock in another corporation which it acquired and held for purposes of protecting its business reputation. The Court adopted a narrow reading of its earlier decision in *Corn Products Refining Co.* (1955), which allowed an ordinary loss on certain futures contracts acquired as an integral part of the taxpayer's business. Since the stock held by the taxpayer in *Arkansas Best* fell within the definition of a capital asset in § 1221, the Court held that capital loss treatment was appropriate regardless of the taxpayer's motive in acquiring the stock.

(c) *Section 1244 Stock.* An individual investor in a corporation which meets the requirements of § 1244 is entitled to treat up to $50,000 ($100,000 in the case of a joint return) of loss on "§ 1244 stock" as an ordinary (rather than a capital) loss for the taxable year; losses in excess of the § 1244 ceiling amount are generally allowable as capital losses. Section 1244 formerly applied only to common stock, but in 1984 this restriction was eliminated.

§ 10. Special Corporate Taxes

In addition to the regular corporate tax and the AMT, the Code also imposes special penalty taxes (the accumulated earnings tax and the personal holding company tax) on the undistributed income of certain corporations. The practical significance of these penalty taxes is greatly reduced as a result of the 1986 Act because corporations no longer offer significant income-sheltering opportunities. In view of the reduced importance and possible repeal of the penalty taxes, only their main outlines are summarized here.

(a) *Accumulated Earnings Tax.* The accumulated earnings tax imposed by § 531 is intended to penalize corporations with excessive accumulated earnings. When applicable, this penalty tax is imposed on "accumulated taxable income" at a flat 28% tax rate (for taxable years beginning after 1987), corresponding to the maximum tax rate for individuals under the 1986 Act. Accumulated taxable income is defined in § 535 as taxable income, with specified adjustments, less a dividends-paid deduction and an accumulated earnings credit. Since the penalty tax is aimed only at undistributed corporate earnings, the dividends-paid deduction is allowed both for dividends actually paid and for so-called "consent dividends," that is, amounts treated as dividends with shareholder consent even though not actually distributed by the corporation. §§ 561–565. The accumulated earnings credit permits most corporations to accumulate at least $250,000 without incurring accumulated earnings tax liability. § 535(c). Prior to 1984, it was often assumed that the accumulated earnings tax did not apply to publicly-held corporations, but the 1984 Act amended § 532(c) to make the tax applicable without regard to the number of shareholders.

The accumulated earnings tax is imposed only on a corporation "formed or availed of for the purpose of avoiding the income tax with respect to its shareholders. . . . " § 532(a). The proscribed purpose is presumed in any case where earnings and profits are allowed to accumulate "beyond the reasonable needs of the business" (including "reasonably anticipated needs"), unless the corporation proves the contrary by a preponderance of the evidence. §§ 533(a) and 537(a)(1). This presumption may be determinative where tax avoidance is not the primary or dominant purpose for an accumulation, but only a contributing purpose. Donruss Co. (1969). The Regulations provide a nonexclusive list of factors for determining whether accumulations are reasonable. Reg. §§ 1.537–2(b) and 1.537–2(c). Although the reasonable needs of the business might ordinarily be financed either with equity capital or with borrowed funds, the courts tend to permit financing of operations and expansion entirely from retained earnings.

(b) *Personal Holding Company Tax.* The personal holding company tax is imposed by § 541 on certain closely-held corporations that might otherwise serve as a vehicle to shelter passive income. Section 542 defines a personal holding company generally as a corporation of which more than half of the stock is owned (actually or constructively) by not more than 5 individuals, if at least 60% of the corporation's "adjusted ordinary gross income" (as defined in § 543(b)(2)) for the taxable year is "personal holding company income." Section 543 defines personal holding company income primarily as passive investment income (dividends, interest, rents, royalties and annuities). In addition, § 543(a)(7) includes certain personal service income in personal holding company income, in order to reach so-called "incorporated talents," *i.e.*, a corporation designed simply to market the personal services of a movie actor or other highly-compensated individual.

If the personal holding company provisions apply, § 541 imposes a tax of 28% (for taxable years beginning after 1987), in addition to the regular corporate tax, on "undistributed personal holding company income," defined in § 545 as taxable income for the year with certain adjustments minus the dividends-paid deduction described in § 561. The adjustments to taxable income under § 545 include allowances for regular federal taxes and net capital gains (less taxes allocable thereto), as well as a disallowance of the § 243 dividends-received deduction. § 545(b). Thus, if a closely-held corporation's sole annual income consists of $30,000 of fully deductible dividends, it will generally be a personal holding company subject to the § 541 tax unless it distributes all of its income to its shareholders each year.

The § 541 tax (but not interest or penalties) is subject to refund if the corporation follows certain dividend-deficiency procedures contained in § 547. Thus, the effect of this tax is primarily to force distributions to shareholders rather than to raise revenue. To the extent that corporations no longer serve as effective tax shelters, the § 541 tax may constitute a mere trap for unwary corporations.

§ 11. Multiple Corporations and Consolidated Returns

The Code contains numerous provisions designed to prevent taxpayers from exploiting statutory allowances or graduated rates by conducting businesses through several corporations with similar ownership. *See, e.g.,* §§ 1551, 1561 and 1563. The narrowing of the corporate tax brackets under the 1986 Act has reduced the importance of some of these provisions.

A group of corporations related through one 80% "parent" corporation (an "affiliated group" under § 1504) may elect to file a consolidated return treating the group as a single unit for tax purposes. Thus, current losses of one corporation may, for example, be offset against current income of another corporation. The detailed rules for consolidated returns, contained in lengthy Regulations under § 1502, are beyond the scope of this work.

CHAPTER 3

INCORPORATIONS

§ 1. General

Section 351 reflects a longstanding policy that the incorporation of a business should generally be tax free both to the shareholders and to the corporation. This nonrecognition policy rests on the assumption that a contribution of property to a corporation represents a continuation in modified form, rather than a liquidation, of the shareholder's investment. At the shareholder level, § 351 provides that no gain or loss is recognized when "property is transferred to a corporation by one or more persons solely in exchange for stock or securities in such corporation," if the transferor or transferors are in "control" of the corporation "immediately after the exchange." Section 357 generally preserves nonrecognition treatment at the shareholder level if the corporation assumes liabilities or takes property subject to liabilities in a § 351 transaction. Gain will be recognized at the shareholder level, however, under § 351(b), to the extent that the taxpayer receives "boot" in addition to stock and securities. At the corporate level, § 1032 provides that a corporation does not recognize gain or loss "on the receipt of money or other property in exchange for [its] stock (including treasury stock)." These nonrecognition provisions are

33

accompanied by the basis provisions of §§ 358 and 362 which prescribe the basis of the stock or securities (in the shareholder's hands) and the basis of the transferred assets (in the corporation's hands) generally by reference to the basis of the transferred assets in the shareholder's hands before the § 351 transfer, thus preserving any unrecognized gain or loss.

§ 2. Requirements to Qualify for Tax-Free Exchange

Section 351 provides nonrecognition treatment only if (i) one or more persons (the "transferors") transfer "property" to a corporation (the "transferee") in exchange for "stock or securities" in the corporation and (ii) the transferors viewed as a group are in "control" of the corporation "immediately after" the transfer.

(a) *Property.* Although the term "property" is not specifically defined, it has been construed broadly to include cash, tangible property, accounts receivable, nonexclusive licenses and industrial know-how. The inclusion of cash does not specifically affect a person who transfers only cash, since he would recognize no gain or loss in any case. The treatment of cash as property may be important to the other transferors, however, because it means that a person transferring cash will be counted in the group of property transferors for purposes of determining whether the control requirement is met.

The major exclusion from the definition of property is "services." § 351(d)(1). The purpose of this exclusion is to ensure that a person who provides services will be taxed under § 61 or § 83 on the fair market value of any stock (or other property) received from the corporation in exchange for the services. This rule also prevents a person who contributes only services from being counted in the group of property transferors for purposes of the control requirement. In some cases, it may be possible to characterize a previously untaxed claim for services as property, although the Service is likely to challenge such a characterization. *See, e.g.,* Stafford (1984) (real estate developer's "letter of intent" treated as property for analogous provisions of § 721).

If the services were performed for a third party and the service provider received stock from a corporation controlled by the third party, the stock may be viewed as having been constructively issued to the third party and then transferred to the service provider (as compensation) in a taxable transaction. If a transferor contributes a combination of property and services to a corporation in exchange for stock as part of a mixed transaction, the receipt of stock for property may qualify for nonrecognition treatment if the other requirements of § 351(a) are met. The receipt of stock attributable to services, however, will generally be treated as a separate transaction outside the scope of § 351, except for the limited purpose of determining whether the control requirement (discussed below) is met.

(b) *Stock or Securities.* Section 351(a) provides for nonrecognition treatment only if the transferors receive "stock or securities." The term "securities" has been construed to exclude short-term notes because of their similarity to cash. *See, e.g.,* Pinellas Ice & Cold Storage Co. (1933). Although the cases indicate that classification as a security is based on the "overall nature of the note," the time factor is nevertheless likely to be the most crucial element. Camp Wolters Enterprises, Inc. (1954). Generally, a note maturing in less than 5 years does not qualify as a security, while a note with a maturity of 10 years or more is treated as a security. *See, e.g.,* Bradshaw (1982) (notes with serial maturities of 6.5 years or less not treated as securities).

The "stock or securities" requirement of § 351(a) is clearly met if a transferor receives stock, or a combination of stock and securities. The underlying premise is that a shareholder who transfers property to a controlled corporation is merely continuing his investment in a different form, *i.e.,* his equity interest in the corporation. The rule is different in the case of a transferor who is not a shareholder: if a transferor who has no equity interest in a corporation transfers property to the corporation solely in exchange for securities, the nonrecognition provisions of § 351(a) do not apply and the transferor must recognize any gain on the exchange. Rev. Rul. 73–472. If the transferor already holds stock in the corporation and transfers additional property solely in exchange for securities, however, the Service has ruled that § 351(a) applies to the receipt of securities. Rev. Rul. 73–473.

Although § 351(a) provides for nonrecognition treatment if property is transferred "solely" in exchange for stock and securities, this does not mean that the entire exchange will be taxable if the transferors receive cash or other property ("boot") in addition to stock and securities. If some boot is received, § 351 nonrecognition treatment still applies to the receipt of stock and securities, but the boot may trigger partial gain recognition under § 351(b). *See* § 3 below.

(c) *Control.* The transferor group must be in control of the corporation immediately after the transfer. For this purpose, "control" means direct ownership of stock possessing at least 80% of the total combined voting power of all classes of voting stock and at least 80% of the total number of shares of each class of nonvoting stock. § 368(c). *See* Rev. Rul. 59–259. The requisite percentage of stock must actually be owned by the transferors; the constructive ownership rules of § 318 do not apply to § 351.

There is no specific limit on the number of transferors or the timing of the transfers. For purposes of control, transfers need not be simultaneous, but may generally be aggregated as long as they are part of a prearranged plan and are carried out reasonably expeditiously. *See* Reg. § 1.351–1(a)(1). In a typical incorporation of a business in which the transferors receive 100% of the stock in exchange for property, the control test is easily satisfied. Moreover, § 351 also covers transfers to an existing corporation, if the transferors own the requisite amount of stock (including any stock previously owned and retained after the transfer) and the other requirements of § 351 are satisfied.

As noted above, if a transferor contributes a combination of property and services to a corporation in exchange for stock, the portion of the stock attributable to services is counted (along with the rest of the transferor's stock) in determining whether the control requirement is met. On the other hand, if the transferor contributes no property but only services, none of his stock is counted because the transaction falls entirely outside § 351.

Example: A transfers appreciated property worth $50,000, and B transfers appreciated property worth $15,000 and contributes services worth $35,000 to X Corp. in exchange for all of the stock of X. A and B are each treated as transferors of property, and together they are in control of X. Neither A nor B will recognize any gain on the transferred property. B, however, will recognize $35,000 of ordinary income as compensation for his services. *See* Reg. § 1.351–1(a)(2), Example (3).

(d) *Nominal Transfers.* If a transferor contributes a nominal amount of property in exchange for stock or securities, with the primary purpose of obtaining § 351(a) nonrecognition treatment for an exchange by another transferor, the Regulations provide that the nominal transferor will not be counted as part of the transferor group. Reg. § 1.351–1(a)(1). The transferred property will be considered to be of nominal value only if its fair market is less than 10% of the fair market value of the stock already owned (or to be received in exchange for services) by the transferor. Rev. Proc. 77–37.

Example: X, a newly-formed corporation, issues 67% of its stock to A in exchange for appreciated property worth $67,000 and 33% of its stock to B in exchange for services worth $33,000. The transaction fails to qualify under § 351 since A, the only property transferor, lacks 80% control. As a result, A recognizes gain equal to the excess of the fair market value of the stock over A's basis in the transferred property; and B recognizes $33,000 of ordinary income. If B instead transferred $3,000 of cash in addition to $30,000 worth of services, the 10% safe-harbor rule would apply, and all of B's stock (including the 30% received for services) would count toward the control requirement. Because A and B together would receive 100% of the stock, A's transfer of appreciated property and B's transfer of cash would be tax free under § 351(a); B would still have $30,000 of ordinary income as compensation for services. If B transferred less than $3,000 cash, B's transfer would be considered nominal, and the entire transaction would fail to qualify under § 351(a).

A majority shareholder who makes a nominal transfer to enable a minority shareholder to qualify for § 351(a) treatment may have difficulty meeting the 10% safe-harbor test. *See, e.g.,* Estate of Kamborian (1972) (disregarding accommodation transfer because of lack of economic nexus).

Example: A owns 78% of the stock of X Corp., and B owns the remaining 22%; the fair market value of a share of X stock is $1,000. If B wishes to make an additional tax-free transfer to X of property worth $22,000, under § 351(a) A must transfer an additional $7,800 in order to be included with B in the group of transferors.

(e) *Disposition of Stock.* Section 351(a) requires that the transferors be in control of the corporation immediately after the transfer. If some of the transferors promptly sell or dispose of their stock pursuant to a prearranged plan and fail to retain sufficient stock to meet the 80% control requirement, the entire transaction may become ineligible for nonrecognition treatment. In *American Bantam Car Co.* (1948), the transferors contributed cash and other property to a new corporation in exchange for 100% of its common stock; five days later, the transferor-shareholders entered into an agreement to transfer a portion of the common stock to underwriters as compensation for their

services if the underwriters succeeded in selling
the corporation's preferred stock to the public.
Upon successful completion of the public offering
approximately 15 months later, more than 20% of
the common stock was transferred to the underwriters. The court held that the control requirement of § 351(a) was satisfied, despite the subsequent transfer, because the § 351 exchange and
the subsequent transfer to the underwriters were
not "mutually interdependent" and therefore could
not be viewed as a single transaction.

Revenue Ruling 79–294 clarifies the effect of a
post-incorporation public offering in two situations,
one involving a "best efforts" underwriting agreement and the other a "firm commitment" underwriting agreement. In the first situation, the Service held that the public investors who purchased
50% of the corporation's stock from the "best efforts" underwriter should be treated, together with
the incorporator, as transferors for control purposes. In the second situation, the Service treated
the "firm commitment" underwriter and the incorporator as transferors, since the underwriter assumed the risk of reselling the stock to the public.
If a third party purchases previously issued stock
from a member of the original control group, however, control may be broken. *See, e.g.,* Intermoun-
tain Lumber Co. (1976) (binding commitment by
primary incorporator to sell 50% of the stock broke
control). *See also* Rev. Rul. 79–70 (stock sold by
transferor of property broke control, even though

purchaser also contributed cash to the corporation in exchange for securities).

(f) *Disproportionate Receipt of Stock or Securities.* When two or more transferors contribute property in exchange for stock or securities, § 351 does not require as a condition for nonrecognition treatment that each transferor receive stock or securities in proportion to the value of his respective property contribution. The Regulations, however, provide that the transaction may be recast "in accordance with its true nature." Reg. § 1.351–1(b)(1). Thus, the transaction may be treated as an initial proportionate issuance of stock or securities, followed by a transfer between the shareholders in the nature of a gift or compensation.

Example: A and B transfer property of equal value to X, a newly-formed corporation, and in exchange A receives 60 shares of X stock and B receives 40 shares. The transaction may be treated as if A and B each initially received 50 shares of X stock and B then transferred 10 shares to A. If A and B are related family members, then B's transfer may be treated as a gift to A. Alternatively, if B is indebted to A for services, B's constructive transfer may be treated as compensation to A and relief of indebtedness to B. *See* Reg. § 1.351–1(b)(2), Example (1).

(g) *Investment Companies.* Section 351(e) denies § 351(a) nonrecognition treatment for transfers to an "investment company." This provision is aimed at so-called "swap funds" in which unrelated investors seek to achieve a tax-free diversification of their investment by transferring appreciated, readily marketable stock or securities in exchange for stock or securities of a newly-formed corporation. The Regulations provide that § 351(e) applies if (i) the transfer results, directly or indirectly, in diversification of the transferors' interests and (ii) the transferee is a regulated investment company, a real estate investment trust, or a corporation more than 80% of whose assets (other than cash and nonconvertible debt) consists of readily marketable stock, securities or similar assets held for investment. Reg. § 1.351–1(c)(1). If two or more persons transfer identical assets to a newly-formed corporation, the transfer will generally not be treated as resulting in diversification, unless it is part of a plan to achieve diversification without recognition of gain. Reg. § 1.351–1(c)(5); Rev. Rul. 88–32. If § 351(e) applies, losses as well as gains will be recognized. *See* Rev. Rul. 87–9.

§ 3. Boot

(a) *General.* Section 351(b) applies when a transferor receives cash or other property ("boot") in addition to stock or securities qualifying for § 351(a) nonrecognition treatment. Under § 351(b), the transferor recognizes gain to the extent of cash and the fair market value of any other boot received. Both the shareholder's basis in the stock or securities received and the corporation's basis in the transferred property is increased to reflect any gain recognized by the transferor under § 351(b). *See* §§ 5 and 6 below. The transferor recognizes no loss in a § 351 transaction regardless of whether any boot is received. § 351(b)(2). Any unrecognized loss is preserved in the shareholder's adjusted basis in the stock or securities received and in the corporation's basis in the transferred property. *See* §§ 5 and 6 below.

Example: In a § 351 transaction, A transfers land with an adjusted basis of $10,000 and a fair market value of $50,000 to a corporation in exchange for consideration consisting of $20,000 stock, $10,000 securities, $5,000 cash and $15,000 of other property. A's realized gain is $40,000 ($50,000 aggregate fair market value of consideration received less $10,000 basis in the transferred property), but A recognizes only $20,000 gain (fair market value of boot, consisting of $5,000 cash and $15,000 of other property). If A's basis in the transferred property were $40,000 instead of $10,000, the entire $10,000 of gain would be recognized since it does not exceed the amount of boot received. If A's basis in the transferred property were instead $60,000, A would realize a loss of $10,000, but none of the loss would be recognized.

(b) *Character of Gain.* The character of any recognized gain is determined by reference to the nature of the transferred assets. Recognized gain is treated as ordinary income to the extent that it represents depreciation recapture under § 1245 or § 1250. In addition, § 1239 may require ordinary income treatment if the transferor owns, actually or constructively, more than 50% of the corporation's stock and the property is depreciable in the corporation's hands.

(c) *Allocation.* If a transferor transfers several different assets and receives some boot (in addition to stock or securities), it is necessary to allocate the consideration received separately to each asset for purposes of determining the amount and character of gain recognized. *See* Rev. Rul. 68–55, amplified by Rev. Rul. 85–164. Any loss realized on an asset is not recognized and cannot be offset against gain realized on any other asset.

Example: A transfers two assets in exchange for $50,000 stock and $50,000 of cash in a § 351 transaction. Each of the assets has a basis of $20,000, but Asset # 1 has a fair market value of $10,000 and Asset # 2 has a fair market value of $90,000. The stock and cash must be allocated between the two assets in proportion to their respective fair market values. Accordingly, A is treated as receiving 1/10 of the stock and cash for Asset # 1 and 9/10 for Asset # 2. Thus, A receives $5,000 of cash and $5,000 stock for Asset # 1, and $45,000 of cash and $45,000 stock for Asset # 2. A's realized loss of $10,000 on Asset # 1 ($20,000 adjusted basis less $10,000 consideration received) is not recognized. A's realized gain of $70,000 on Asset # 2 is recognized only to the extent of the boot received ($45,000). An alternative approach might be to allocate the boot to the appreciated property (Asset

2) to the extent of the gain realized on that asset. Under this approach, A would recognize $50,000 gain on Asset # 2.

(d) *Installment Treatment of Notes.* A short-term note that does not qualify as a security will be treated as boot. If the note qualifies for § 453 installment sale treatment, the shareholder may be able to defer recognition of gain. § 453(f)(6). *See* Prop. Reg. § 1.453–1(f)(3)(ii). Under § 453(i), the shareholder must report gain immediately, however, to the extent of any depreciation recapture. Any deferred gain may be treated as ordinary or capital gain as payments are received, depending on the nature of the assets transferred. If the transferor reports gain under § 453, the transferee corporation's basis in the transferred property is not stepped up until the transferor recognizes gain. Prop. Reg. § 1.453–1(f)(3)(ii).

§ 4. Relief of Liabilities

(a) *General.* If a corporation assumes a liability or acquires property subject to a liability in a § 351 transfer, the transferor must include the liabilities relieved in the amount realized. § 1001. Section 357(a), however, provides that the assumption of liabilities or acquisition of property subject to liabilities is not treated as the receipt of boot, and does not disqualify the transaction from non-recognition treatment under § 351. The principal effect of § 357(a) is to prevent the transferor from recognizing gain immediately on relief of liabilities. Instead, recognition of gain attributable to relief of liabilities is deferred under § 358, which requires a downward adjustment in the shareholder's basis in the stock or securities received to reflect the relief of liabilities. *See* § 5 below.

Example: A transfers property with a basis of $50,000 and a fair market value of $100,000, subject to a liability of $20,000, to X Corp. in exchange for stock worth $80,000 (the net value of the transferred property). A will realize gain of $50,000 (total consideration of $100,000, consisting of $80,000 of stock and $20,000 of liabilities relieved, less $50,000 adjusted basis). A will recognize no gain, however, since § 357(a) does not treat the relief of liabilities as boot. A's basis in the stock received will be $30,000 under § 358 ($50,000 adjusted basis of the transferred property, less $20,000 of liabilities relieved).

(b) *Tax-Avoidance Transactions.* An important exception to the general rule of § 357(a) is provided in § 357(b) for certain tax-avoidance transactions. Section 357(b) treats as taxable boot the entire amount of liabilities assumed (or taken subject to) by the corporation, if the transferor's principal purpose was tax avoidance or was not a bona fide business purpose. Section 357(b) is intended to prevent the transferor from bailing cash out of a corporation by borrowing against the property immediately before the transfer with the intention of keeping the borrowed funds and arranging for the corporation to pay the liability. Section 357(b) might apply, for example, if a taxpayer borrowed against business assets shortly before a § 351 transfer and used the borrowed proceeds to purchase a personal residence. If the borrowing is incurred in the course of the taxpayer's business or is used to acquire or improve the contributed property, however, § 357(b) should not apply because the borrowed funds are not retained by the transferor for a prohibited purpose. If § 357(b) applies, then all of the liabilities (not merely the liabilities with respect to which a prohibited purpose exists) are treated as cash boot. Reg. § 1.357–1(c).

Example: The facts are the same as in the previous example, except that A incurs the $20,000 of liabilities shortly before the § 351 transfer to purchase an automobile for personal use. Under § 357(b), the $20,000 relief of liabilities will be treated as cash boot. Accordingly, A's realized gain of $50,000 will be recognized to the extent of the $20,000 boot.

(c) *Liabilities in Excess of Basis.* Section 357(c) (1) provides another important exception to the general rule of § 357(a). Under § 357(c)(1), any liabilities relieved (or taken subject to) in excess of the transferor's basis are treated as gain from the sale or exchange of the transferred property. This provision is necessary to prevent the transferor's substituted basis in stock or securities from being reduced below zero under § 358. Section 357(c)(1) applies even if the transferor remains personally liable (usually as a guarantor) on a liability assumed by the corporation. *See* Smith (1985). Section 357(c)(1) applies to each transferor separately, not to the transferors as a group. Each transferor may aggregate the basis of all assets transferred by him, however, for purposes of § 357(c)(1). Reg. § 1.357–2(a). Thus, gain attributable to excess liabilities may normally be avoided by transferring additional cash or other property. The amount and character of any recognized gain must be allocated among the assets in proportion to their respective fair market values if more than one asset is transferred. Reg. § 1.357–2(b).

Example: A transfers two assets to a corporation in a § 351 transaction in exchange for $30,000 of stock. Asset # 1 has a basis of $15,000 and a fair market value of $30,000, and is subject to a liability of $20,000; Asset # 2 has a basis of $15,000 and a fair market value of $50,000, and is subject to a liability of $30,000. Under § 357(c)(1), A will recognize $20,000 of gain ($50,000 total liabilities relieved, less $30,000 total basis). If Asset # 1 is a capital asset and Asset # 2 is an ordinary income asset in A's hands, $7,500 of the gain will be capital gain allocable to Asset # 1 ($20,000 x $30,000/$80,000) and the remaining $12,500 will be ordinary income allocable to Asset # 2 ($20,000 x $50,000/$80,000). A could avoid recognizing any gain by transferring an additional $20,000 of cash (or unencumbered property with a basis of $20,000) to the corporation.

If the purpose for assumption of the liability is tax avoidance or is not a bona fide business pur-

pose, however, § 357(b) applies instead of § 357(c)
(1), and the entire liability (not merely the excess
over total adjusted basis) is treated as taxable boot.
See § 357(c)(2)(A).

Example: In the previous example, if A had a
tax-avoidance purpose with respect to the transfer
of Asset # 1 (subject to the $20,000 liability), then
the entire $50,000 of liabilities relieved would be
recognized as cash boot under § 357(b), rather than
the $20,000 of excess liabilities over basis that
would have been recognized if § 357(c)(1) applied.
See Reg. § 1.357–1(c). The result would be the
same if A contributed additional cash.

(d) *Certain Liabilities Excluded.* Section 357(c)
(3) contains an exception to the rule of § 357(c)(1)
for liabilities that would have given rise to a deduction if paid directly by the transferor. If § 357(c)
(3) applies, the liability is not taken into account as
an excess liability under § 357(c)(1). Section 357(c)
(3) was intended to remedy the problem arising
when a cash-method taxpayer transfers zero-basis
receivables and accounts payable in a § 351 exchange. If the accounts payable were taken into
account as liabilities under § 357(c)(1), the transferor would recognize gain equal to their full
amount because he would have no basis in the
receivables to offset the accounts payable. The
transferor would have done better if he had received additional cash from the corporation and
used it to pay the accounts payable directly; although the additional cash would have been taxa-

ble as boot, the transferor would at least receive an offsetting deduction on paying the accounts payable. In order to mitigate the disparity in tax treatment, § 357(c)(3) avoids taxing the gain from relief of excess deductible liabilities. Courts had reached a similar result even prior to enactment of § 357(c)(3). *See, e.g.,* Bongiovanni (1972); Focht (1977). The special rule of § 357(c)(3) does not apply, however, to any liability which gave rise to or increased the transferor's basis in any property when incurred. § 357(c)(3)(B).

If only receivables and no offsetting accounts payable are transferred, the Service might assert that the transferor (rather than the corporation) should be taxed when the receivables are collected, under assignment-of-income principles. In the absence of a tax-avoidance purpose, however, the Service has ruled that it will not apply assignment-of-income principles to a cash-basis taxpayer's transfer of receivables in a § 351 transaction. Rev. Rul. 80–198. Thus, the corporation will be taxed on collection of the receivables, not the transferor. The corporation is also entitled to a deduction when it pays the accounts payable even though the transferor has already in effect received a deduction under § 357(c)(3). *Id.* As long as corporate rates remain higher than individual rates, a taxpayer may wish to retain the receivables and transfer only the accounts payable to the corporation. By analogy to Rev. Rul. 80–198, however, the Service might seek to reallocate the accounts payable to the transferor if the transfer is not for a bona fide business purpose.

§ 5. Transferor's Basis and Holding Period

(a) *General.* As a corollary to § 351(a) nonrecognition treatment, § 358(a)(1) provides that the transferor's basis in the stock or securities (the "nonrecognition property") is determined by reference to his basis in the transferred property. The transferor's substituted basis in the nonrecognition property is calculated as (i) the adjusted basis of the property transferred, (ii) decreased by the amount of cash and the fair market value of any other boot received, and (iii) increased by the amount of any gain recognized by the transferor on the exchange. The transferor's basis in nonrecognition property is allocated in proportion to fair market value. Reg. § 1.358–2(b)(2). The transferor takes a basis in boot received equal to its fair market value under § 358(a)(2); cash boot is in effect assigned a basis equal to its face amount.

Example: A transfers property with an adjusted basis of $20,000 and a fair market value of $100,000 in exchange for $75,000 worth of stock and $25,000 worth of securities. The stock and securities together will have an aggregate basis equal to A's basis in the transferred property ($20,000), allocated among the stock and securities in proportion to their relative fair market values. Since the stock accounts for 75% of the value of the consideration received, it receives a basis of $15,000 (75% of $20,000). The remaining basis of

$5,000 (25% of $20,000) is allocated to the securities.

(b) *Receipt of Boot.* If the transferor receives boot in addition to nonrecognition property, the basis computation under § 358(a)(1) will often leave the transferor with an aggregate basis in the nonrecognition property equal to his original basis in the transferred property. This is because the downward adjustment to basis for boot received is frequently offset by the upward adjustment for gain recognized. It is nevertheless important to calculate each separate step of the computation, since the recognized gain may be less than the fair market value of the boot received.

Example (1): A transfers property with an adjusted basis of $10,000 and a fair market value of $50,000 for total consideration of $50,000, consisting of stock ($20,000), securities ($10,000), cash ($5,000) and other property ($15,000). A realizes $40,000 gain, but recognizes only $20,000 of the gain (the fair market value of the boot). A's basis in the nonrecognition property (stock and securities) will be $10,000, calculated as: (i) the adjusted basis of the transferred property ($10,000), (ii) decreased by the cash and other boot received ($20,000), and (iii) increased by the gain recognized ($20,000). The $10,000 basis would be allocated ⅔ to the stock and ⅓ to the securities in proportion to their respective fair market values. Under § 358(a)(2), A's basis in the boot will be $20,000

($5,000 cash and $15,000 fair market value of the other property).

Example (2): The facts are the same as in Example (1), except that A has a basis of $35,000 in the transferred property. A will realize, and hence recognize, only $15,000 of gain, even though he receives $20,000 of boot. A's basis in the nonrecognition property will be $30,000, calculated as: (i) the adjusted basis of the transferred property ($35,000), (ii) decreased by the cash and other boot received ($20,000), and (iii) increased by the gain recognized ($15,000). A will still take a basis of $20,000 in the boot ($5,000 cash and $15,000 fair market value of the other property).

Example (3): The facts are the same as in Example (1), except that A has a basis of $55,000 in the transferred property. A will realize, but not recognize, a loss of $5,000. A's basis in the nonrecognition property will be $35,000, calculated as: (i) the adjusted basis of the transferred property ($55,000), (ii) decreased by the cash and other boot received ($20,000), and (iii) increased by the gain recognized ($0).

(c) *Effect of Liabilities.* Solely for purposes of determining the transferor's basis, liabilities relieved (other than liabilities subject to § 357(c)(3)) are treated as money received by the transferor. § 358(d). This means that the transferor's basis is adjusted downward for liabilities relieved, even if such liabilities do not give rise to recognition of gain under § 357(a). To the extent that the transferor recognizes gain under § 357(b) or § 357(c), however, the upward adjustment in the transferor's basis for the recognized gain will cancel the downward adjustment for liabilities relieved.

Example: A transfers property with an adjusted basis of $40 and a fair market value of $55, subject to a liability of $30, in exchange for all of the stock of X Corp., which has a fair market value of $25. Assuming that no gain is recognized on relief of liabilities, A's basis in the stock is $10, calculated as: (i) the adjusted basis of the property transferred ($40), (ii) decreased by liabilities relieved ($30), and (iii) increased by the gain recognized ($0). A's built-in gain of $15 in the transferred property (fair market value of $55 less adjusted basis of $40) is preserved in A's basis in the stock (the difference between the fair market value of $25 and the substituted basis of $10). If § 357(b) applied to the transaction, the $30 relief of liabilities would be treated as cash received and A's recognized gain would be $15 (amount of realized gain); A's basis in the nonrecognition property would be $25, calculated as: (i) the adjusted basis of the transferred property ($40), (ii) decreased by deemed boot received ($30 of liabilities relieved), and (iii) increased by gain recognized ($15).

In the case of liabilities subject to § 357(c)(3), § 358(d)(2) provides that such liabilities are not treated as cash received for purposes of determining the transferor's basis. Thus, no gain results from relief of such liabilities, and the transferor's basis is not adjusted downward.

Example: A, a cash-basis taxpayer, transfers receivables, with a basis of zero and a fair market value of $50, and accounts payable of $30 to X Corp. in exchange for all of its stock, which has a fair market value of $20. Under § 357(c), A recognizes no gain on the transfer even though the $30 of accounts payable transferred to X exceeds A's zero basis in the receivables. A's basis in the stock received is zero, the same as his basis in the transferred receivables.

(d) *Holding Period.* The transferor's holding period for nonrecognition property received in a § 351 transaction is determined by reference to his holding period for the transferred assets (a "tacked" holding period), provided that the transferred assets are capital gain property or § 1231 assets. § 1223(1). If a taxpayer transfers both capital gain and non-capital gain property, he might desire to assign a tacked holding period to some of the shares received in the exchange and a holding period commencing on the date of exchange to other shares received. The Service, however, has ruled that each share must be allocated a split holding period in proportion to the fair market value of the transferred assets. Rev. Rul. 85–164, amplifying Rev. Rul. 68–55. The character of the transferred assets (*i.e.,* ordinary or capital) does not determine the character of the stock or securities received; the nonrecognition property will generally be a capital asset (long-term or short-term) in the recipient's hands.

Example: A transfers a long-term capital asset (with an adjusted basis of $40 and a fair market value of $60) and inventory (with an adjusted basis of $20 and a fair market value of $40) to X Corp. in a § 351 transaction, and receives in exchange X stock with a fair market value of $100. Three months later, A sells the X stock for $120. Since the inventory is not a capital asset or a § 1231 asset, the holding period of the stock received in exchange for the inventory is not tacked. Each share of A's stock will be considered to have a split holding period based on the respective fair market values of the transferred assets. Thus, $^{60}/_{100}$ of A's stock will be treated as received in exchange for the long-term capital asset and $^{40}/_{100}$ for inventory. Of the total amount realized on the sale ($120), A will be treated as receiving 60% ($72) for a long-term capital asset (with a substituted basis of $40), and 40% ($48) for a short-term capital asset (with a substituted basis of $20). Accordingly, A will recognize a long-term capital gain of $32 ($72 less $40 basis), and a short-term capital gain of $28 ($48 less $20 basis) on the sale.

§ 6. The Transferee Corporation

(a) *Nonrecognition Treatment.* Section 1032 provides that a corporation recognizes no gain or loss on receipt of money or other property for its stock (including treasury stock). Although § 1032 refers only to receipt of "money or other property," the Regulations extend § 1032 nonrecognition treatment to an exchange of stock for services. Reg. § 1.1032–1(a). Thus, a corporation recognizes no gain when it uses its stock to pay for services; the payment (to the extent of the fair market value of the stock) may be deducted as an ordinary and necessary business expense under § 162 or treated as a capital expenditure under § 263, depending on the nature of the services. *See* Rev. Rul. 62–217, modified by Rev. Rul. 74–503.

Although the 1988 Act left § 1032 intact, it added new § 351(f) (effective for transfers occurring on or after June 21, 1988). This provision treats a transfer by the transferee corporation (referred to as the "controlled corporation") to its shareholders in a § 351 exchange (other than an exchange pursuant to a plan of reorganization) as if it were a nonliquidating distribution governed by § 311. *See* Chap. 4. Because § 311 permits nonrecognition treatment of a distribution of a corporation's own stock or securities, new § 351(f) will not trigger gain to the controlled corporation if a shareholder receives only stock or securities in the exchange, preserving the result under § 1032. If the shareholder receives boot property in an exchange to which § 351(b) applies to the shareholder, however, the controlled corporation will recognize gain (but not loss) under the recognition rules of § 311(b) for distributions of appreciated property. The exchanging shareholder may also recognize gain on receipt of the boot property under the general provision of § 351(b).

(b) *Transferee Corporation's Basis.* Under § 362(a)(1), the corporation takes a substituted basis in the assets received in a § 351 transaction, determined as (i) the transferor's basis in the transferred property, (ii) increased by any gain recognized to the transferor. This computation parallels the basis computation for nonrecognition property received by the shareholder under § 358(a)(1); liabilities relieved or boot paid, however, have no effect on the corporation's basis except indirectly to the extent that the shareholder is required to recognize gain. Under §§ 358 and 362, the transferor's basis is essentially preserved both in the property transferred to the corporation and in the stock or securities received by the shareholder; as a result, the same gain or loss may be recognized once when the corporation sells the property and again when the shareholder sells the stock or securities.

Example: A transfers property with a basis of $40 and a fair market value of $30 in exchange for $30 of stock in a transaction qualifying under § 351(a). Under § 362(a), the corporation's basis in the transferred property is $40, the same as the basis of the transferred property in the shareholder's hands. Under § 358(a), the shareholder's basis in the stock received is also $40, the same as the basis of the transferred property. If the corporation then sells the transferred property for $30, its fair market value, the corporation will recognize a loss of $10. Similarly, the shareholder will also recognize a loss of $10 if he sells his stock for its fair market value of $30.

(c) *Allocation of Transferee Corporation's Basis.* If the transferor recognizes no gain on the § 351 exchange, the corporation's basis in each asset received is the same as the transferor's basis in the particular asset. There is no indication in the Code or the Regulations, however, of how to allocate any increase in basis among the transferred assets in the hands of the corporation when the transferor recognizes gain. One possible method of allocation would be simply to increase the basis of each asset by the amount of the transferor's gain recognized on the particular asset, by analogy to the asset-by-asset allocation of boot under Rev. Rul. 68–55. For example, if the transferor were taxed on $100 of boot allocated 60% to one transferred asset and 40% to another based on the respective fair market values of the transferred assets, it seems reasonable to increase the basis of the first asset by $60 and that of the second asset by $40.

(d) *Holding Period.* The corporation may tack the transferor's holding period in each transferred asset for purposes of determining the corporation's holding period for the asset. § 1223(2). Tacking occurs regardless of the character of the asset in the transferor's hands.

§ 7. Avoiding § 351

(a) *General.* Although § 351 is nominally a mandatory provision, its effects can often be avoided by appropriate planning. For example, a taxpayer may wish to avoid § 351 by structuring a transaction as a sale of property rather than a tax-free contribution, in order to allow the transferor to recognize a loss. Alternatively, the taxpayer may desire to recognize gain on appreciated property, thereby stepping up the basis of the property in the corporation's hands. Before the 1986 Act, sale treatment was particularly useful if the transferor held undeveloped land ready for subdivision because the inherent appreciation would be taxed to the transferor as capital gain rather than ordinary income. Since the corporation would obtain a stepped-up basis, any ordinary income would be limited to the enhanced value attributable to the corporation's development activities. Moreover, an installment sale might allow the transferor to defer recognition of gain, even though the corporation received a stepped-up basis immediately.

The 1986 Act reduced the attractiveness of sales by repealing the preferential treatment of capital gains. Since the corporate tax rates are generally higher than the individual tax rates, however, sale treatment still offers the transferor an opportunity to recognize the pre-contribution gain at lower rates and avoid double taxation of the built-in gain. Also, a transferor may have offsetting capital losses against which to use the capital gain triggered by a sale.

(b) *Limitations on Sale Treatment.* Judicially-developed doctrines may be used to recast the form of a transaction structured as a sale. For example, if a major asset is transferred to a corporation for an installment note, the note may be recharacterized as stock or securities if the corporation is thinly capitalized. *See, e.g.,* Burr Oaks Corp. (1966) (treating the transaction as a contribution to capital in exchange for preferred stock). On the other hand, courts have respected sale characterization when undeveloped land was transferred to a corporation in exchange for installment notes. *See, e.g.,* Bradshaw (1982). In *Bradshaw,* the court refused to recharacterize the notes as securities or "equity," even though the corporation was concededly thinly capitalized. The taxpayer succeeded in deferring recognition of gain, despite the fact that the corporation developed and sold the property during the term of the notes.

Several Code provisions also limit the benefits of sale treatment. Section 1239 treats any gain from sale of property between related parties (*e.g.,* a corporation and a more-than-50% shareholder) as ordinary income if the property is depreciable in the hands of the related transferee. § 1239(a). Moreover, § 453(g) requires generally that gain be recognized immediately in the case of an installment sale of depreciable property between related parties; the purchaser's basis in the acquired property is not stepped up until the gain is includible in the seller's income. *See also* § 453(i) (requiring recognition of any recapture income under § 1245 or § 1250). In addition, § 453(e) limits the attractiveness of the *Bradshaw*-type transaction by treating a subsequent sale of property received in an installment sale from a related party as a "second disposition" which triggers the installment gain to the transferor. Finally, § 267 prevents recognition of loss on a sale between a corporation and a more-than-50% shareholder.

§ 8. Contributions to Capital

Section 118(a) excludes capital contributions from the gross income of a corporation. Thus, if a corporation obtains additional capital through voluntary pro-rata contributions from shareholders, the contributions do not constitute gross income, even though the outstanding shares of the corporation are not increased. Reg. § 1.118–1. In the case of pro-rata contributions, § 118(a) serves a purpose analogous to the nonrecognition provision of § 1032 when a corporation issues its stock for property. Section 118 also applies to contributions to capital by non-shareholders, such as property contributed by a governmental unit or civic group in order to induce a corporation to locate in a particular area. Reg. § 1.118–1. The exclusion from gross income does not apply, however, to payments for goods or services by customers or potential customers. *Id. See* § 118(b).

Under § 362(a)(2), the corporation's basis for contributed capital is generally the same as the transferor's basis in the contributed property. Section 362(c), however, provides a special rule for contributions to capital by non-shareholders: § 362(c)(1) gives the corporation a zero basis in property (other than cash) contributed by non-shareholders, and § 362(c)(2) requires the corporation to reduce the basis of property acquired within the 12–month period following the contribution by the amount of cash contributed by non-shareholders. If the amount of cash or property received from non-shareholders is treated as a payment for goods or services, § 362(c) does not apply and no basis adjustment is required.

A shareholder who contributes capital receives an increased basis in his stock. *See* Reg. § 1.118–1. If the shareholder contributes property rather than cash, it is unclear whether the shareholder's stock basis is increased by the basis or fair market value of the contributed property. Since gain or loss is not recognized on a voluntary contribution, the increase in stock basis should probably be limited to the basis of the contributed property.

§ 9. Midstream Income Problems

The assignment-of-income doctrine and the tax-benefit rule may apply if assets of an existing business are incorporated. The Service has indicated that the assignment-of-income doctrine generally does not apply to a transfer of receivables, unless a tax-avoidance purpose is present. *See* § 4 above. The tax-benefit rule requires a taxpayer to include in income the tax benefit received from an earlier deduction if a subsequent event is "inconsistent" with the earlier deduction. *See* Hillsboro Nat. Bank (1983). *See also* Rojas (1988) (Unpublished Case). In the § 351 context, the Service has used this doctrine to require that transferors include in income a bad debt reserve associated with transferred receivables. The Supreme Court, however, has held that if the receivables were transferred for consideration equal to their book value net of the reserve, there is no "recovery" and hence no includible income. *See* Nash (1970). By implication, *Nash* seems to require income inclusion to the extent that the transferor receives stock and other consideration worth more than the net book value of the receivables.

CHAPTER 4

NONLIQUIDATING DISTRIBUTIONS

§ 1. General

Section 301 of the Code prescribes the treatment of nonliquidating distributions of cash or other property to shareholders. Under § 301(c)(1), a § 301 distribution is included in the shareholder's gross income to the extent that it constitutes a "dividend", as defined in § 316. Section 316, in turn, defines a dividend for income tax purposes generally as a distribution out of current or accumulated earnings and profits ("e & p") of the distributing corporation. To the extent that a § 301 distribution exceeds e & p, it is treated under § 301(c)(2) as a tax-free return of the shareholder's capital and any amount in excess of basis is treated under § 301(c)(3) as gain from a sale or exchange. The character of the gain will be capital if the stock is a capital asset in the shareholder's hands. The tax definition of a "dividend" thus bears no fixed relation to a "dividend" in the corporate law context, though the two terms often overlap.

The repeal of preferential treatment for capital gains under the 1986 Act greatly reduced the tax stakes in this area. Since ordinary income and capital gains are taxed at the same rates, the primary remaining advantage of nondividend treatment is tax-free recovery of the shareholder's basis. A corporate shareholder may even prefer dividend treatment because of the dividends-received deduction of § 243.

It should be noted that § 301 applies only to payments to a shareholder in his capacity as such; payments to a shareholder in any other capacity are not treated as § 301 distributions unless such payments are excessive and are held to be disguised dividends. Reg. § 1.301–1(c). Despite the diminished practical significance of dividend versus nondividend treatment, however, it is important to understand treatment of nonliquidating distributions before approaching the topics of redemptions, stock dividends and reorganizations discussed in later chapters.

§ 2. Dividends

Under the two-part definition of § 316, a distribution is a dividend if it is out of either (i) earnings and profits of the current taxable year, computed at the end of the year without reduction for distributions during the year ("current e & p") or (ii) earnings and profits accumulated after February 28, 1913 and before the current taxable year ("accumulated e & p"). A distribution is treated as coming first from current e & p. Thus, if current e & p are sufficient to cover all distributions during the taxable year, such distributions are dividends and it is unnecessary to consider accumulated e & p. If the aggregate distributions during the taxable year exceed current e & p, a pro-rata portion of each distribution is treated as coming from current e & p. If one class of stock has priority over other classes of stock in receiving distributions, *e.g.,* preferred stock, current e & p is allocated first to distributions on such stock. *See* Rev. Rul. 69–440.

Example: M Corp. has current e & p of $3,000 and no accumulated e & p. The common shareholders receive a distribution of $1,000 on January 1 and $1,000 on April 15; the preferred shareholders receive a distribution of $2,500 on December 31. The $2,500 distribution to the preferred stockholders will be treated as a dividend, and will leave only $500 of current e & p to be allocated to the distributions to the common stockholders. One-quarter of each of the distributions on common stock ($500/$2,000) will be treated as a dividend; and the remainder of these distributions ($1,500) will be treated as tax-free return of capital or taxable gain under § 301(c)(2) and (3).

Accumulated e & p is relevant only if current e & p are insufficient to cover distributions during the year. Distributions in excess of current e & p are dividends to the extent of accumulated e & p; the balance is treated as return of capital to the extent of the shareholder's basis in his stock, and any excess is treated as taxable gain. Accumulated e & p is allocated among distributions in chronological order. Reg. § 1.316–2(b). If a corporation has a deficit in accumulated e & p, it does not reduce current e & p; thus, distributions are still treated as dividends to the extent of current e & p.

Example: X Corp. has current e & p of $20,000 and accumulated e & p of $55,000. During the taxable year, X makes quarterly cash distributions of $25,000 each to its shareholders. One-fifth ($20,000/$100,000) of each distribution ($5,000) is treated as a dividend out of current e & p. The remainder of each of the first two distributions ($20,000 each) and $15,000 of the third distribution are treated as a dividend out of accumulated e & p. As a result, $5,000 of the third distribution and $20,000 of the fourth distribution are treated as tax-free basis recovery or taxable gain. *See* Reg. § 1.316–2(c).

If a corporation has accumulated e & p and a deficit in current e & p, the deficit in current e & p reduces the amount of the accumulated e & p. The Regulations imply that the full amount of the deficit in current e & p may be taken into account if it is traceable to a period ending on or before the date of a particular distribution. Reg. § 1.316–2(b). The Service, however, appears to take the position that any deficit in current e & p must be prorated over the entire year, even if traceable to a specific period. Rev. Rul. 74–164.

Example: X Corp. has accumulated e & p of $50,000 at the beginning of the current year, and distributes $25,000 to its shareholders on July 1 of the current year. If X has a loss of $70,000 during the first half of the year but ends up with current e

& p of $5,000 at the end of the year, the entire $25,000 distribution is a dividend ($5,000 from current e & p and $20,000 from accumulated e & p). If X instead ends up with a deficit of $10,000 in current e & p for the year (with $70,000 of losses in the first half of the year), the entire $25,000 is still a dividend, assuming that the $10,000 loss is prorated over the entire year under Rev. Rul. 74–164; as of the July 1 distribution, accumulated e & p would be reduced by $5,000 (one-half of the $10,000 loss), leaving $45,000 of accumulated e & p to cover the distribution.   Under the tracing approach of the Regulations, however, the $70,000 loss allocable to the first half of the year would more than offset the $50,000 of accumulated e & p as of the July 1 distribution; thus, the entire $25,000 distribution would be treated as tax-free basis recovery to the extent of basis and then as taxable gain.

§ 3. Nondividend Distributions

To the extent that a distribution is not covered by either current e & p or accumulated e & p, it is treated as a nondividend distribution under § 301(c)(2) and (3).   Any such distribution in excess of the shareholder's basis in his stock triggers taxable gain; loss is recognized only if the stock becomes worthless or is redeemed or otherwise disposed of without full basis recovery.   If a shareholder receives nondividend distributions with respect to several blocks of shares which were acquired at different times with different bases, the distribution apparently must be allocated ratably among all the shares. Thus, a shareholder may recognize gain on certain shares before recovering all of his basis in other shares; he is not permitted to defer gain until the aggregate basis of all of his shares has been recovered. *See* Johnson (1971).

Example: X Corp. has accumulated e & p of $100,000 and no earnings or losses for the current year. X distributes $300,000 cash pro rata to its shareholders. A, an individual, has two equal blocks of shares with adjusted bases of $8,000 and $22,000, respectively, and receives a $30,000 distribution. A must report $10,000 as a dividend, representing the ratio of the total distribution ($100,000/$300,000) covered by accumulated e & p. Of the remaining $20,000, A allocates $10,000 to each block of shares. With respect to the low-basis shares, A recovers his full basis ($8,000) tax free and recognizes $2,000 of gain. With respect to the high-basis shares, A reduces his basis by $10,000 and is left with an adjusted basis of $12,000.

§ 4. Earnings and Profits

Although § 312 provides for certain adjustments to e & p, the Code does not specifically define "earnings and profits." The starting point for determining e & p is taxable income. Generally, four types of adjustments are necessary to derive e & p from taxable income:

(a) *Items Excluded From Taxable Income But Included in E & P.* Some items excluded from taxable income must be included in e & p because they increase the dividend-paying capacity of the corporation without impairing its original capital. For example, Regulations § 1.312–6(b) provide that certain tax-exempt income (*e.g.,* municipal bond interest and life insurance proceeds exempt under §§ 103 and 101(a), respectively) is included in e & p. Section 312(f)(1) provides that realized gains and losses are not included in e & p until recognized in computing taxable income. Thus, e & p is not increased by the gain on nonrecognition transactions (*e.g.,* § 1031 like-kind exchanges) until such gain is recognized.

(b) *Items That Reduce Taxable Income But do Not Reduce E & P.* Certain "artificial" deductions allowed in computing taxable income are added back in computing e & p, since they do not represent actual expenses and therefore do not impair dividend-paying capacity. For example, the full amount of dividends received is included in e & p, despite the § 243 dividends-received deduction.

(c) *Timing Differences.* Although the corporation's method of accounting normally determines when items are included in e & p, certain timing adjustments are necessary to ensure that e & p more accurately reflect economic gain or loss. For example, § 312(k) generally disallows accelerated depreciation in computing e & p and extends the recovery period applicable for this purpose. Similarly, § 312(n)(5) requires that income from installment sales must be computed for purposes of determining e & p as if the corporation did not use the

installment method, *i.e.,* such income must be included currently in e & p without regard to any
deferral under § 453. As amended by the 1987
Act, § 301(e) makes the § 312(k) and (n) adjustments generally inapplicable to certain distributions to 20%-or-more corporate shareholders, if the
distributee would otherwise be entitled to a dividends-received deduction under § 243. The significance of ignoring these timing adjustments is to
reduce the distributing corporation's e & p solely
for the purpose of determining the amount of any
dividend to a corporate distributee.

(d) *Items That Reduce E & P But do Not Reduce
Taxable Income.* Some items not allowed as deductions in computing taxable income are allowed
in computing e & p, since they clearly reduce the
corporation's dividend-paying capacity. Thus,
items disallowed by § 162(c), (f) and (g) (certain
illegal payments, fines and penalties), § 265 (expenses allocable to tax-exempt income), § 1211(a)
(excess capital losses over capital gains) and
§ 162(a)(1) (unreasonable compensation), as well as
federal taxes and dividend distributions in prior
years, are subtracted in determining e & p.

It should be noted that, for purposes of determining the amount of a dividend under § 316(a)(2),
current distributions do not reduce current e & p
(for the year in which the distribution occurs); and
that under § 312(a) distributions reduce e & p only
"to the extent thereof," *i.e.,* distributions cannot
create a deficit in current or accumulated e & p.

Thus, if a corporation has no current e & p or accumulated e & p, operating losses may further reduce e & p, but distributions to shareholders have no effect on e & p. Current income that increases e & p above zero represents a potential source of dividends.

Example: X Corp. suffers a loss of $300,000 in its first year of operations. In Year 2, X has earnings of $100,000 and distributes $50,000 to its shareholders. The $50,000 distribution is treated as a dividend because it is covered by current e & p. At the beginning of Year 3, X's accumulated e & p deficit is $250,000 ($300,000 deficit from Year 1 reduced by the $50,000 of undistributed earnings from Year 2). In Year 3, X has no current e & p and again distributes $50,000 to its shareholders. No portion of the distribution is treated as a dividend because X has neither current e & p nor accumulated e & p; the distribution has no effect on X's accumulated e & p deficit of $250,000 carried over to the beginning of Year 4. In Year 4, X has $300,000 of current e & p and makes no distributions. X's accumulated deficit of $250,000 is eliminated by the $300,000 of current e & p, leaving X with accumulated e & p of $50,000 at the beginning of Year 5. In Year 5, X has no current e & p and distributes $50,000 to its shareholders. The entire distribution is a dividend from accumulated e & p, leaving X with no accumulated e & p at the beginning of Year 6.

§ 5. Distributions in Kind

(a) *Treatment of the Distributing Corporation.*
Section 311(a) provides generally that a corporation does not recognize gain or loss on a distribution of property with respect to its stock.   This
nonrecognition rule is often called the *General
Utilities* doctrine, an allusion to a case in which
the government argued unsuccessfully that a distribution of appreciated property resulted in taxable gain to the distributing corporation.   General
Utilities & Operating Co. (1935).   In deciding *General Utilities,* however, the Supreme Court did not
consider it necessary to address this issue.   Even
before 1986, the exceptions to nonrecognition virtually swallowed up the "general rule" of § 311(a).
The 1986 Act repealed the *General Utilities* rule
with respect to distributions of appreciated property, so that in effect § 311(a) now operates only to
deny recognition of loss on nonliquidating distributions.

Section 311(b), relating to distributions of appreciated property, provides that the distributing corporation recognizes gain on a distribution of appreciated property (other than the distributing
corporation's own obligation) as if such property
were sold to the distributee at its fair market
value.   It should be noted that the distributing
corporation recognizes gain even if the appreciation is attributable to pre-incorporation increases
in value.   In addition, if property is distributed
subject to a liability or the shareholder assumes

the liability, then the fair market value of the distributed property is deemed to be not less than the amount of such liability. § 311(b)(2) (borrowing from § 336(b) the rules for distributions of property subject to liabilities in excess of basis).

It should be noted that § 311(b) applies only to distributions covered by §§ 301–304 (*e.g.,* dividends, redemptions and partial liquidations); it does not apply to distributions governed by other Code provisions (*e.g.,* tax-free reorganizations and spin-offs). Moreover, distributions in complete liquidations are governed by a special set of rules, discussed in Chapter 6.

Example: X Corp. distributes property with a basis of $100 and a fair market value of $150, subject to a liability of $200. Under § 311(b)(2), the fair market value of the distributed property is deemed to be $200 (the amount of the liabilities) and X recognizes gain of $100. This rule applies equally to recourse and nonrecourse liabilities, with the result that the corporation must recognize gain whether the shareholder assumes the liability or takes property subject to a liability.

The character of the corporation's gain is presumably determined as if the distribution were an actual sale. In the case of property (other than inventory-type property) used in the corporation's trade or business, the gain will generally be capital gain. §§ 1221 and 1231. Where property is distributed to a more-than-50% shareholder, however, § 1239(a) treats the gain recognized by the distributing corporation as ordinary income if the property is depreciable in the hands of the distributee.

Section 311(b)(3), added by the 1988 Act, authorizes the Treasury to issue Regulations to prevent a distributing corporation from reducing gain (and hence effectively recognizing a loss) on a nonliquidating distribution of an interest in a partnership. Under § 311(b)(1), the distribution will trigger gain to the distributing corporation as if the partnership interest were sold for its fair market value; the character and amount of gain recognized will be determined in accordance with §§ 741 and 751 of Subchapter K, governing sales of partnership interests. But for new § 311(b)(3), however, the distributing corporation might reduce the amount of such gain by contributing loss property to the partnership immediately prior to the distribution. The corporation would thus receive a tax-free step-up in the basis of its partnership interest equal to its basis in the contributed property, under principles analogous to § 351, and would correspondingly recognize less gain on the subsequent deemed sale of its partnership interest. *See* § 721. To prevent such artificial reduction of gain, § 311(b)(3) provides that the amount of gain recognized by the distributing corporation may be determined by disregarding any loss attributable to property contributed to the partnership for the principal purpose of recognizing such loss on the distribution. Similar rules concerning corporate distributions of partnership interests were formerly contained in § 386, repealed by the 1988 Act as "deadwood."

Prior to the 1986 Act, the corporation might have been required to recognize gain on a nonliquidating distribution under assignment-of-income principles or the tax-benefit doctrine. *See, e.g.,* First State Bank of Stratford (1948) (corporation taxed on collectibles distributed to shareholders). Under present law, § 311(b) generally reaches the same result by expressly treating a nonliquidating distribution of appreciated property as a deemed sale at fair market value. Thus, the government is less likely to invoke assignment-of-income principles or the tax-benefit doctrine. *See* Chapter 6.

Since a distribution is treated as a recognition event, a corporation may prefer to sell appreciated property to its shareholder for the shareholder's own note. If the transaction qualifies for installment sale treatment under § 453, the corporation may be able to defer gain, and the shareholder will avoid dividend treatment. *But see* § 453(g) (installment sale of depreciable property between related persons). If the shareholder later defaults on the note, the shareholder will have cancellation-of-indebtedness income, but the corporation may be entitled to a bad debt deduction under § 166. As a result, the shareholder will be left in much the same position as if he had received a dividend, but the corporation may be better off.

In the case of loss property, it is almost always more advantageous for the corporation to sell, rather than distribute, property in order to recognize the loss. If the property is sold to a shareholder who (directly or by attribution under § 267(c)), owns more than 50% of the corporation's stock, however, § 267(a)(1) disallows a deduction to the corporation for its loss. Nevertheless, any loss disallowed by § 267(a)(1) to a seller on an actual sale of property to a related purchaser is preserved and may be used by the purchaser to offset gain on a later sale of the property. § 267(d).

Example: X Corp. distributes property with a basis of $500 and a fair market value of $200, to A, a more-than-50% shareholder. Under § 311(a), X's loss of $300 is disallowed, and A takes a basis in the property equal to $200, its fair market value. If the property appreciates and A subsequently sells it for $700, A will recognize a gain of $500 ($700 minus $200). By contrast, if the original transaction had been an actual sale rather than a distribution, the $300 loss on the initial sale would still be disallowed to X but would reduce A's gain on the subsequent sale from $500 to $200 under § 267(d).

Thus, even where a corporation is unable to recognize a loss on a sale because of § 267(a)(1), the relief available to the purchaser under § 267(d) generally makes a sale more attractive than a nonliquidating distribution of the loss property under § 311(a). This is because § 311(a) flatly disallows a deduction for the loss, without providing for deemed sale treatment; the shareholder-distributee's basis in the distributed property is limited to its fair market value, with no potential relief on a subsequent sale.

Under prior law, the government sometimes argued that a transaction structured as a distribution to a shareholder followed by the shareholder's sale of the distributed property should be recast as a sale of the property by the corporation followed by a distribution of the sale proceeds to the shareholder. *See* Court Holding Co. (1945). Because the 1986 Act makes the distribution itself taxable to the corporation, the government is now likely to seek to recharacterize purported sales as distributions, permanently disallowing loss recognition in the case of loss property.

(b) *Effect of Property Distributions on E & P.* A distribution of property in kind generally reduces the distributing corporation's e & p by the adjusted basis of the distributed property in the corporation's hands, but not below zero. In the case of a distribution of appreciated property, § 312(b) reaches the same end result by requiring that the corporation's e & p be first increased by the appreciation (excess of fair market value over basis) and then decreased (but not below zero) by the fair market value of the distributed property. The purpose of the special rule of § 312(b) is to ensure that the appreciation generates positive current e & p for purposes of determining dividend treatment. *See* § 316(a) (distributions out of current e

& p, determined without reduction for distributions during the taxable year, treated as dividends).

Example: X Corp. distributes to A, an individual shareholder, property with a basis of $1,000 and a fair market value of $200. X has current e & p from other transactions of $100 and no accumulated e & p. The distribution reduces X's current e & p to zero, but A is treated as receiving a dividend of $100 (determined prior to the reduction for the current year's distributions). The remaining $100 of the distribution is treated as basis recovery or taxable gain under § 301(c)(2) and (3). If the basis of the property is $200 and its fair market value is $1,000, X's current e & p will be increased to $900 ($100 plus $800 of appreciation) and then reduced to zero. A, however, will be treated as receiving a dividend of $900 under §§ 312(b) and 316(a)(2). The remaining $100 of the distribution is treated as basis recovery or taxable gain under § 301(c)(2) and (3).

If a corporation recognizes gain on a distribution of appreciated property, the timing of the reduction in e & p for the corporate income taxes is unclear. In the case of an accrual-basis corporation, the tax liability attributable to the distribution is fixed at year-end and presumably reduces current e & p for the year of the distribution. In the case of a cash-basis corporation, however, the tax liability apparently does not reduce e & p until the following year, when the taxes are actually paid. *See* Reg. § 1.312–6(a) (e & p generally determined under taxpayer's tax accounting method). This timing mismatch may, however, overstate current e & p available to support dividend treatment and trigger a corresponding reduction in the following year's e & p.

Example: X Corp. has no accumulated e & p and current e & p consists solely of $40 of gain triggered by a distribution of property with a fair market value of $50 and a basis of $10. If X is on the accrual method and incurs $6 of tax on the $40 gain, current e & p is only $34. Of the total distribution, $34 is a dividend and the remaining $16 is a nondividend distribution. If X is on the cash method, however, the distribution comprises a $40 dividend (corresponding to current e & p of $40, unreduced by the $6 tax liability) and a $10 nondividend distribution. In the following year, X's payment of the $6 tax liability reduces its current e & p for that year by an equal amount. This timing mismatch may be advantageous for a corporate shareholder, to the extent that the portion of the distribution eligible for the dividends-received deduction of § 243 in the year of distribution is overstated.

(c) *Treatment of Shareholders.* If property is distributed to a shareholder (including a corporate shareholder), § 301(b)(1) provides that the amount of the distribution is the fair market value of the property. Section 301(b)(2) requires that the amount of the distribution be reduced (but not below zero) by any liabilities assumed by the shareholder in connection with the distribution (or subject to which the property is distributed). Under § 301(d), the basis of the distributed property in the hands of a shareholder (including a corporate shareholder) is equal to its fair market value.

Example: X Corp. distributes property with a fair market value of $4,000, subject to a liability of $3,000, to a shareholder. The amount of the distribution will be $1,000 under § 301(b)(2) (the fair market value of the property reduced by the liability), but the shareholder's basis in the property will be its fair market value of $4,000 under § 301(d). Accordingly, X's basis in the property is relevant only for purposes of determining X's gain (if any) on the distribution and the corresponding e & p adjustment under § 312(b).

Suppose instead that the liability in the above example is $6,000 and X's basis in the property is $1,000. Assuming that the property is still worth only $4,000, X recognizes gain of $5,000, since the fair market value is treated as not less than the amount of the liability. §§ 311(b)(2) and 336(b). The distribution to the shareholder, however, would be zero under § 301(b)(2), since the liability exceeds the fair market value of the property. It is not entirely clear whether the shareholder's basis under these circumstances is fair market value ($4,000) or the amount of the liability ($6,000). If the shareholder assumes personal liability for the debt, then presumably the basis should be $6,000, despite the statutory fair-market-value limitation.

If the liability is nonrecourse, however, the shareholder's basis may be limited to fair market value. *See* Estate of Franklin (1976).

(d) *Transition Rules.*   In the 1986 Act, Congress granted relief from the repeal of the *General Utilities* rule to certain corporations distributing long-term capital gain property.   To be eligible for transitional relief, the corporation's value must not exceed $10 million and more than 50% of its stock (by value) must be owned by 10 or fewer individuals who have held their stock for 5 years or longer. The transition rules generally expire at the end of 1988.

§ 6. Distribution of Corporation's Own Obligations

Some special considerations apply if a corporation makes a § 301 distribution of its bond or note to a stockholder.   Obligations of the distributing corporation are not excluded from the broad definition of "property" in § 317(a), and are therefore treated as property.   *See* § 312(a)(2).   Accordingly, both the amount of the distribution and the basis of the distributed obligation in the hands of the shareholder are equal to the fair market value of the obligation. §§ 301(b)(1) and 301(d).   The distribution of the corporation's obligation, however, does not trigger gain at the corporate level under § 311(b).   Finally, § 312(a)(2) requires that the distributing corporation's e & p be reduced by the principal amount (or the issue price, in the case of an obligation having original issue discount) of the obligation. The 1988 Act clarified that § 312(b) does not apply to a distribution of a corporation's own obligation; thus, such a distribution will not increase the corporation's e & p.

Example: X Corp., which has $10,000 of e & p, issues to its shareholders a note with a principal amount of $10,000. The note matures in 3 years and bears no interest. The note has a fair market value of $7,500, assuming an applicable discount rate of approximately 10%. X will not recognize any gain on distribution of the note under § 311(b). The shareholders are treated as receiving a distribution of $7,500 (the fair market value of the note), which is also their basis in the note. This amount is also treated as the issue price of the note and reduces X's e & p accordingly under § 312(a)(2). Since X has sufficient e & p to cover the amount of the distribution, the entire $7,500 is a dividend to X's shareholders.

§ 7. Disguised Dividends

Shareholders generally prefer to draw economic benefits out of a corporation in ways that are tax free to themselves or deductible to the corporation (or both, if possible). The problem of disguised dividends is particularly likely to arise in closely-held corporations from transactions such as the following (for example): loans made by a corporation to its shareholders under circumstances indicating there is no intention of repayment; bargain sales of property by a corporation to its shareholders; excess compensation paid by a corporation to its shareholders for goods or services provided by the shareholders in their capacity as employees, lessors or contractors; and free use by shareholders, for personal rather than business purposes, of corporate property such as yachts and automobiles.

In the case of below-market demand loans, § 7872(a) recharacterizes the "foregone" interest (determined on an annual basis) as a constructive distribution from the corporation (lender) to the shareholder (borrower) and a constructive interest payment in the same amount from the shareholder back to the corporation. As a result, the shareholder is treated as having ordinary income to the extent of the constructive dividend (possibly offset by a matching interest deduction) and the corporation is treated as having interest income (with no offsetting deduction because the constructive dividend is nondeductible). Any loan that is not transferable and is conditioned on performance of substantial services by an individual is generally treated as a demand loan. § 7872(f)(5). If the loan is not a demand loan, the difference between the amount loaned and the present value of all required payments under the terms of the loan is treated as a constructive distribution to the shareholder at the time the loan is made. *See* § 7872(b).

Although payments are most likely to be recharacterized as disguised dividends if made to shareholders on a pro-rata basis, even a non-pro-rata payment may be so treated if made to a shareholder who obtains an economic benefit that is not available to other shareholders, regardless of whether the corporation intended to distribute a dividend. *See* Honigman (1972). Occasionally, a constructive dividend to a controlling shareholder may be found if the corporation makes a payment to a third party under circumstances indicating that the corporation is acting merely to serve the controlling shareholder's personal wishes. *See* Rev. Rul. 79–9 (charitable contribution by closely-held corporation taxable as a distribution if shareholders or their families receive economic benefits from the contribution).

If a taxpayer diverts corporate funds to himself, the issue arises whether the diverted funds are taxable under § 61 or as constructive dividends under § 301. In *Truesdell* (1988), the court treated the diverted funds as constructive dividends taxable only to the extent of the corporation's e & p. The Service failed to argue that the diverted funds were a form of disguised compensation and thus fully includible in income.

CHAPTER 5

REDEMPTIONS

§ 1. General

A "redemption" occurs when a corporation acquires its stock from a shareholder in exchange for money or other property (other than stock of the corporation). § 317(b). Section 302(a) provides that a redemption will be treated as an exchange of stock for property if the requirements of § 302(b) are satisfied; § 302(d) provides that any other redemption will be treated as a nonliquidating distribution under § 301. The 1986 Act reduces but does not eliminate the significance of exchange treatment under § 302(a), which permits the shareholder to recover his basis immediately and offset capital gain on the redemption against any capital losses that the shareholder may have from other transactions. Corporate taxpayers, however, generally prefer § 301 distribution treatment rather than exchange treatment, since the amount of the distribution may be wholly or partially excluded under the dividends-received deduction of § 243.

This Chapter first considers the § 302(b) requirements for redemptions treated as exchanges, including partial liquidations and constructive ownership rules, and then describes the related provisions of § 303 (redemptions to pay death tax-

es) and § 304 (redemptions through related corporations). Redemptions in connection with sale of a
corporate business are considered separately. Finally, certain ancillary problems (computation of
the shareholder's gain or loss, basis, and corporate-
level tax consequences) are discussed.

§ 2. Substantially Disproportionate Redemptions: § 302(b)(2)

Section 302(b) contains four alternative tests for
determining whether a redemption will be treated
as an exchange. Of the four statutory tests, the
first three (§ 302(b)(1)–(3)) focus on the effect of a
redemption at the shareholder level, while the
fourth (§ 302(b)(4)) focuses on the effect at the
corporate level. Section 302(b)(1) allows exchange
treatment whenever the redemption is "not essentially equivalent to a dividend." This ill-defined
test can be better understood after considering the
mechanical "safe harbor" rules of § 302(b)(2) (substantially disproportionate redemptions) and
§ 302(b)(3) (redemptions in complete termination of
a shareholder's interest).

Section 302(b)(2) permits exchange treatment if
the distribution is "substantially disproportionate
with respect to the shareholder," *i.e.,* if the shareholder's interest in the corporation is substantially
reduced by the redemption. In order to meet this
test, the shareholder, immediately after the redemption, must: (i) own less than 50% of the
voting power of the corporation; (ii) own less than
80% of his percentage ownership of voting stock

immediately before the redemption; and (iii) own less than 80% of his percentage ownership of common stock immediately before the redemption. If the corporation has only voting common stock outstanding, both 80% tests will be satisfied if either one is met. If the corporation has more than one class of common stock outstanding (*i.e.*, both voting and nonvoting common stock), the 80% test described in clause (iii) above is applied in the aggregate, rather than on a class-by-class basis. Rev. Rul. 87–88.

Example: X Corp. has outstanding 10 shares of voting common and 30 shares of nonvoting common stock. A, an individual, owns 6 shares (60%) of the voting common and all 30 shares of the nonvoting common. Thus, A owns a total of 36 of the 40 shares of the common stock, or 90%. Each share of voting and nonvoting common stock is equal in value. If X redeems 3 of A's voting shares and 27 of A's 30 nonvoting shares, the redemption will satisfy the "substantially disproportionate" requirements of § 302(b)(2). After the redemption, A will own 3 of the 7 outstanding shares of voting common stock (42.9%) and 6 of the 10 outstanding shares of common stock in the aggregate (60%). A will own 71.5% (42.9%/60%) of his former percentage ownership of the voting common stock, and 66.7% (60%/90%) of his former percentage ownership of the common stock in the aggregate. Thus, both 80% tests of § 302(b)(2) are satisfied. In addition, A will also own less that 50% of the voting power of X (42.9%) after the redemption.

A redemption of nonvoting preferred stock from a shareholder who owns only nonvoting preferred stock will not satisfy the § 302(b)(2) test, since there is no reduction in the shareholder's voting power. If the corporation redeems sufficient voting stock from a shareholder to meet the § 302(b)(2) test independently, however, a redemption of the same shareholder's nonvoting preferred stock in the same transaction will also qualify for exchange treatment. Reg. § 1.302–3(a). In other words, the nonvoting preferred stock can be "piggybacked" onto an otherwise qualifying redemption of voting stock meeting the requirements of § 302(b)(2). A redemption of voting preferred stock from a shareholder who owns no common stock can also qualify under § 302(b)(2). *See* Rev. Rul. 81–41 (common-stock test applies only if shareholder owns common stock).

For purposes of § 302(b)(2), the shareholder whose stock is redeemed is treated as owning stock actually or constructively owned by him under the attribution rules of § 318. § 302(c). The reduction in the shareholder's percentage stock ownership is affected both by changes in the number of shares owned by the shareholder and by changes in the total number of outstanding shares, which may in turn reflect simultaneous redemptions from other shareholders.

Example: A and B, unrelated individuals, each own 60 of the 120 outstanding shares of voting common stock of X Corp., which has no other stock outstanding. Before the redemption, A owns 50% ($^{60}/_{120}$) of the voting common stock. If X redeems 20 of A's shares, A will own 40% ($^{40}/_{100}$) of the voting common stock, or exactly 80% (40%/50%) of his percentage of stock ownership before the redemption. Although the redemption will meet the less-than-50% test, it will not meet the less-than-80% tests, and thus will not satisfy the "substantially disproportionate" requirements of § 302(b)(2). If 21 of A's shares were redeemed instead, A's percentage ownership after the redemption would be slightly less than 80% of his percentage of stock ownership prior to the redemption; the redemption would thus qualify under § 302(b)(2) because A would meet the less-than-50% test and both less-than-80% tests. If X simultaneously redeemed 5 of B's shares, however, the redemption would not be substantially disproportionate with respect to either shareholder under § 302(b)(2).

A redemption will not be treated as substantially disproportionate under § 302(b)(2) if it forms part of a series of redemptions pursuant to a plan with a result that is not substantially disproportionate (in the aggregate). § 302(b)(2)(D). For example, the Service has held that § 302(b)(2) does not apply to a redemption of stock from a majority shareholder where a second redemption from another share-holder was designed to restore the majority shareholder's control. Rev. Rul. 85–14. Similarly, even if a redemption of stock from one shareholder is substantially disproportionate, when viewed by itself, it will presumably not qualify under § 302(b)(2) if other shareholders have agreed to sell sufficient shares to the first shareholder to render the redemption (viewed together with the sales as a single transaction) not substantially disproportionate.

§ 3. Termination of Shareholder's Interest: § 302(b)(3)

Section 302(b)(3) provides for exchange treatment for a "complete redemption of all of the stock of the corporation owned by the shareholder." The chief importance of the complete termination rule of § 302(b)(3) is the waiver of the § 318 family attribution rules. A complete termination may also be helpful if § 302(b)(2) is unavailable, *e.g.*, if the shareholder owns only nonvoting preferred stock.

Without the exception to the family attribution rules under § 302(c)(2), it would often be extremely difficult to obtain exchange treatment for a redemption of stock in a closely-held family corporation. For example, assume that a father and his daughter each own 50% of the stock of a family corporation, and that the corporation redeems all of the father's stock. Under the family attribution rules, discussed below, the father would be treated as owning 100% of the stock both before and after the redemption. In order to facilitate exchange treatment in such situations, § 302(c)(2)(A) provides that the family attribution rules do not apply to a shareholder whose stock is completely redeemed if each of the following requirements is met: (i) immediately after the redemption, the shareholder has no interest in the corporation (including an interest as an officer, director or employee) other than as a creditor; (ii) the redeemed shareholder does not acquire such a prohibited interest (other than stock acquired by bequest or inheritance) within 10 years from the date of the redemption; and (iii) the shareholder files an agreement to notify the Service of any prohibited interest acquired within the 10–year period. If the shareholder acquires a prohibited interest within the 10–year period, the waiver is retroactively invalidated and the statute of limitations is automatically tolled.

It should be noted that the waiver only applies to complete terminations under § 302(b)(3), and that constructive ownership rules other than the family attribution rules of § 318(a)(1) cannot be waived. If the corporation distributes its own note to a shareholder in redemption of all of the shareholder's stock, it may be unclear whether the note represents a true debt obligation or a disguised equity interest. *See* Reg. §§ 1.302–4(d) and 1.302–4(e). The Service will generally not rule on the tax consequences of a redemption if the payment period on a corporation's obligation extends beyond 15 years. Rev. Proc. 88–3. The obligation must bear a market rate of interest and should not be subordinated to other corporate debts.

In *Lynch* (1984), the Tax Court held that an interest as an independent contractor was not a prohibited interest, at least where the actual services performed were infrequent. It focused on whether the retained interest gave the shareholder a financial stake in, or continuing control of, the corporation. The Ninth Circuit, however, reversed the Tax Court's decision, reasoning that Congress intended to establish a "bright-line" test in this area. Lynch (1986). The Service takes the position that actual performance of services, whether or not compensated, constitutes a prohibited interest; but an interest as an officer or director is not a prohibited interest if the former shareholder actually performs no duties and receives no compensation. *See* Lewis (1966). The Service has also ruled that a § 302(c)(2) waiver is valid if the shareholder retains an interest as a lessor, provided that rental payments are not dependent on earnings and are determined at arm's length. Rev. Rul. 77–467. *See also* Rev. Proc. 88–3.

The waiver of family attribution rules is subject to a 10-year look-back period. § 302(c)(2)(B). The family attribution rules may not be waived if (i) any of the redeemed stock was acquired within 10 years of the redemption from a related person (within the meaning of § 318(a)), or (ii) any related person owning stock at the time of the redemption acquired such stock from the terminated shareholder within 10 years of the distribution, unless such stock is also redeemed. This limitation on waiver of the family attribution rules does not apply, however, if such acquisition of stock by or from the terminated shareholder did not have tax avoidance as one of its principal purposes. § 302(c) (2)(B) (last sentence).

For example, if a father gives part of his stock to his son for the purpose of shifting control of the corporation to the son, and then has the corporation redeem the remainder of the father's stock, tax avoidance is not a principal purpose of the transaction and the son's stock ownership is not attributed to the father for purposes of § 302(b)(3). *See* Lynch (1986). The Service has also held that a tax-avoidance purpose is not present if the transfer to a related party "was not in contemplation of redemption of the balance of the transferor's stock nor of the stock transferred to the transferee." Rev. Rul. 85–19. In Revenue Ruling 85–19, a father reacquired stock that he had previously transferred to his son and the son's remaining stock was redeemed; since the net effect was merely to restore the original pattern of stock ownership, the son's waiver of the family attribution rules was valid.

In the case of a § 302(b)(3) redemption of stock owned by an entity (*i.e.*, a corporation, partnership, estate or trust), the entity can waive the family attribution rules if the additional requirements of § 302(c)(2)(C) are met. Under § 302(c)(2)(C), each person whose stock ownership would otherwise be attributed to the entity (under § 318(a)(3)) as well as the entity itself must meet the requirements of § 302(c)(2)(A) (no interest other than as a creditor; no acquisition of a prohibited interest for 10 years; agreement to notify the Service of any prohibited interest) and must agree to be jointly and severally liable for any deficiency resulting from acquisition of a prohibited interest. A waiver by an entity serves to break the chain of attribution from a related family member to an entity's beneficial owner (and hence to the entity itself).

Example: The stock of X Corp. is owned 50% by F and 50% by T, a trust having D (F's daughter) as its sole beneficiary. If X redeems all of T's stock, the redemption will not qualify as a complete termination of T's interest. The stock owned by F is attributed to D under § 318(a)(1), and is in turn reattributed to T under § 318(a)(3)(B). *See* § 318(a) (5)(A). If T waives the family attribution link (from F to D), however, the redemption of T's stock will qualify for exchange treatment because T will no longer be treated as owning F's shares.

§ 4. Redemptions Not Essentially Equivalent to a Dividend: § 302(b)(1)

A redemption that fails to meet the mechanical "safe harbor" tests of § 302(b)(2) or (3) may nevertheless qualify for exchange treatment if it is "not essentially equivalent to a dividend." Although this test is too amorphous to be used as a planning device, its contours were clarified to some extent by the Supreme Court in the *Davis* case (1970). In *Davis*, a corporation redeemed preferred stock held by the taxpayer at a time when the taxpayer and his family owned all of the stock of the corporation. The corporation had originally issued the preferred stock to the taxpayer in exchange for a $25,000 capital contribution, which was necessary to increase the corporation's working capital in order to secure a loan from a third party to the corporation. It was understood at the time of the $25,000 capital contribution that the preferred stock would be redeemed upon repayment of the loan. The Supreme Court held that the redemption did not qualify for exchange treatment under § 302(b)(1). It held specifically that (i) the taxpayer was considered to own 100% of the corporation's stock both before and after the redemption for purposes of § 302(b)(1), by virtue of the family attribution rules; (ii) the redemption of a sole shareholder's stock is always essentially equivalent to a dividend; (iii) the corporation's business purpose is irrelevant; and (iv) exchange treatment is available only if the redemption results in a "meaningful reduction of the shareholder's proportionate interest in the corporation."

The "meaningful reduction" standard may be helpful in qualifying a redemption of nonvoting preferred stock from a shareholder owning only nonvoting preferred stock. Reg. § 1.302–2(a) (third sentence). *See also* Rev. Rul. 77–426 (redemption of even a small amount of nonvoting preferred stock qualifies, if shareholder does not own stock of any other class actually or constructively). If a shareholder owns stock of another class as well as nonvoting preferred stock, a redemption of the nonvoting preferred may not qualify if the shareholder's voting power is not reduced. *See* Rev. Rul. 85–106 (redemption of ⅔ of a trust's nonvoting preferred stock was essentially equivalent to a dividend where the trust owned constructively 18% of the voting common stock both before and after the redemption). In Revenue Ruling 85–106, the Service found dividend equivalency even though the redemption concededly resulted in a reduction in the shareholder's economic interest. This view seems inconsistent with the Second Circuit's approach in *Himmel* (1964), where the court emphasized that stock ownership involves three important rights: (i) the right to exercise control through voting rights, (ii) the right to participate in current earnings and accumulated surplus, and (iii) the right to share a distribution of assets on liquidation. Revenue Ruling 85–106 states that the Service will not follow *Himmel* to the extent inconsistent with *Davis* and subsequent developments.

If the shareholder's voting power is reduced as a result of the redemption, the crucial question is whether the reduction is meaningful. This essentially factual determination is of limited use in planning. The Service has held, however, that a meaningful reduction occurs if a shareholder goes from a position of majority control (57%) to a deadlock position (50%). Rev. Rul. 75–502. *See also* Rev. Rul. 76–364 (reduction from 27% to 22.27% meaningful where shareholder lost the ability to control the corporation in concert with only one other shareholder). A reduction in the shareholder's interest from 90% to 60% was not considered meaningful, however, where no corporate action requiring a $2/3$ vote was anticipated. Rev. Rul. 78–401. Finally, a redemption from a minority shareholder whose stock interest is minimal and who exercises no control over the corporation may be meaningful even though it results in a minimal reduction. *See, e.g.,* Rev. Rul. 76–385 (reduction of shareholder's interest from .0001118% to .0001081%). If no reduction in the minority shareholder's interest occurs, however, the distribution will be treated as essentially equivalent to a dividend. *See, e.g.,* Rev. Rul. 81–289 (minority shareholder's interest was .2% before and after the redemption).

It is not clear whether family discord should be taken into account in applying the family attribution rules under § 302(b)(1). *Compare* Metzger Trust (1982) (discord not taken into account) *with* Haft Trust (1975) (discord "might negate the presumption" of family attribution). The Tax Court has recently taken the position that family discord may be relevant at least in testing dividend equivalency after application of the family attribution rules. Cerone (1986). According to the Tax

Court's view, the attribution rules should be applied to determine whether any reduction in the taxpayer's percentage interest has occurred; evidence of family discord may be relevant in determining whether any such percentage reduction is meaningful.   In *Patterson Trust* (1984), the Sixth Circuit also found that a percentage reduction from 97% to 93% was meaningful in view of family hostility.

§ 5.   Attribution of Stock Ownership: § 318

(a) *General.*   For purposes of determining stock ownership under § 302(b)(1)–(3), the attribution rules of § 318 are generally applicable.   These rules, which fall into four categories, treat an individual as constructively owning stock that is actually owned by related parties.

(b) *Family Attribution: § 318(a)(1).*   An individual is generally treated as constructively owning the stock actually owned by his spouse, children, grandchildren or parents.   There is no attribution, however, between siblings or from a grandparent to a grandchild.

(c) *Entity-to-Beneficiary Attribution: § 318(a)(2).* Stock owned by a partnership or estate is treated as constructively owned proportionately by the partners or beneficiaries, and stock owned by a trust is attributed to the beneficiaries in proportion to their actuarial interests (in the case of a grantor trust, the grantor is treated as the sole beneficiary).   Stock actually owned by a corporation is treated as constructively owned by any shareholder owning 50% or more in value of the corporation's stock, in proportion to such shareholder's percentage stock ownership. There is no attribution from the corporation to a shareholder owning less than 50% of the corporation's stock.

Example: A, an individual, actually owns 50 of the 100 shares of the outstanding stock of X Corp., and the other 50 shares are owned by M Corp. The stock of M is owned 60% by A and 40% by B, an unrelated party. If X redeems 30 of A's 50 shares of X stock, A's actual percentage ownership is reduced from $^{50}/_{100}$ to $^{20}/_{70}$. The redemption fails to qualify under § 302(b)(2), however, because A is treated as constructively owning 60% of M's 50 shares of X stock (30 shares) both before and after the redemption. Accordingly, A's percentage ownership (both actual and constructive) of X stock falls from $^{80}/_{100}$ (80%) to $^{50}/_{70}$ (71.4%).

(d) *Beneficiary-to-Entity Attribution: § 318(a)(3).* A partnership or estate is treated as constructively owning stock actually owned by its partners or beneficiaries. Stock owned by a trust beneficiary is attributed to the trust, unless the beneficiary's interest is a "remote contingent interest." § 318(a)(3)(B)(i). Stock owned by a 50%-or-more shareholder of a corporation is attributed to the corporation. When beneficiary-to-entity attribution applies, all stock owned by a beneficiary is treated as constructively owned by the entity; this differs from the attribution of only a proportionate part of an entity's stock to its beneficiaries under the entity-to-beneficiary rules.

Example: The facts are the same as in the example above, except that A does not sell any of his stock and X redeems 30 of its shares from M. Before the redemption, M is treated as owning 100% of X's stock (50 shares directly and 50 shares constructively from A, a 60% shareholder of M). After the redemption, M continues to own 100% of X's stock (20 shares directly and 50 shares constructively from A). Accordingly, the redemption will be treated as a § 301 distribution rather than an exchange; M will be entitled to a dividends-received deduction under § 243 if X has sufficient e & p.

(e) *Option Attribution: § 318(a)(4).* A person holding an option to acquire stock is treated as owning the underlying stock. This rule may have the effect of decreasing the percentage of stock owned by all shareholders other than the owner of the option, if it increases the total number of shares considered outstanding. Thus, the option rule may actually facilitate exchange treatment for a shareholder whose percentage reduction would not be meaningful in the absence of the option rule. *See, e.g.,* Patterson Trust (1984) (applying the option rule in the context of a § 302(b)(1) redemption).

(f) *Reattribution of Stock: § 318(a)(5).* The "operating rules" of § 318(a)(5) generally provide for "chain" attribution running from the actual owner to an ultimate constructive owner by way of one or more intermediate constructive owners. In order to prevent an unduly tenuous chain of constructive ownership, the operating rules contain two important limitations. The first limitation prevents "double family attribution" by providing that stock attributed once from one individual family member to another family member (under the family attribution rules) cannot be reattributed to a third family member under the family attribution rules. § 318(a)(5)(B). The second limitation prevents "sidewise attribution" by providing that stock attributed once from a beneficiary to an entity (under the beneficiary-to-entity attribution rules) cannot be reattributed from the entity to another beneficiary under the entity-to-beneficiary rules. § 318(a)(5)(C). In addition, option attribution takes precedence over family attribution if both rules apply. § 318(a)(5)(D).

Example: F, an individual, owns 30 of the 100 shares of stock of X Corp. D (F's daughter) and S (F's son) each own directly 30 shares of X stock; the remaining 10 shares are owned by T, a trust in which D and S each have a one-half beneficial interest. Under § 318, F will be treated as owning 100 shares of X stock: 30 directly, 30 by attribution from D, 30 by attribution from S and 10 by chain attribution from T (5 by way of D and 5 by way of S). T will also be treated as owning 100 shares: 10 directly, 30 by attribution from D, 30 by attribution from S, and 30 by chain attribution from F (by way of D or S; F's stock is counted only once). D and S, however, are each treated as owning only 65 shares: 30 directly, 30 by attribution from F and 5 by attribution from T. Neither child will be treated as owning any part of the 30 shares owned directly by the other child, since § 318(a)(5)(B) prevents double family attribution by way of F and § 318(a)(5)(C) prevents sidewise attribution by way of T.

§ 6. Partial Liquidations: § 302(b)(4)

(a) *General.* Section 302(b)(4) permits exchange treatment for redemptions of stock held by noncorporate shareholders if the redemption is in "partial liquidation" of the corporation. Partial liquidations are defined in § 302(e). Under § 302(e)(1), a distribution may be treated as in partial liquidation if the distribution "is not essentially equivalent to a dividend." Unlike the identical phrase in § 302(b)(1), which refers to the effect of a redemption at the shareholder level, § 302(e)(1) focuses on the effect at the corporate level. The definition of a partial liquidation embodies the concept of a "corporate contraction," *i.e.,* a reduction in the size of the business. *See, e.g.,* Imler (1948) (distribution of fire insurance proceeds).

(b) *Termination-of-Business Safe Harbor.* The "safe-harbor" provisions of § 302(e)(2) mitigate the vagueness of the "corporate contraction" requirement by providing mechanical rules for distributions attributable to termination of an active business. To qualify under § 302(e)(2), the distribution must be attributable to the corporation's ceasing to conduct a 5–year–old active business, and immediately after the distribution the distributing corporation must be engaged in a 5–year–old active business. §§ 302(e)(2) and 302(e)(3). The 5–year–old business requirement is designed to prevent temporary investment of accumulated earnings in a business in anticipation of a bailout disguised as a corporate contraction. The additional requirement of an active business forestalls a bailout of passive investments. The requirement of two 5–year–old active businesses (one terminated and one continuing) raises problems similar to those encountered under § 355 in the context of business separations. *See* Chapter 9. *See also* Prop. Reg. §§ 1.346–1(c), 1.355–3(b)(2).

(c) *Other Requirements.* A distribution will qualify as a partial liquidation only if it is "pursuant to a plan and occurs within the taxable year in which the plan is adopted or within the succeeding taxable year." § 302(e)(1)(B). Although pro-rata distributions would preclude exchange treatment under § 302(b)(1)–(3), § 302(e)(4) specifically permits exchange treatment for a partial liquidation meeting the safe-harbor test of § 302(e), without regard to whether the distribution is pro rata. Moreover, a constructive redemption is deemed to occur where there is a genuine corporate contraction and the surrender of shares would be a "meaningless gesture" because the distribution is pro rata. Rev. Rul. 81–3. *See also* Fowler Hosiery Co.

(1962). If no shares are surrendered, the number of shares treated as redeemed is "that number of shares the total fair market value of which equals the amount of the distribution." Rev. Rul. 77–245, clarifying Rev. Rul. 56–513. Exchange treatment for distributions in partial liquidation is expressly limited to noncorporate shareholders. Stock held by so-called "passthru entities" (*i.e.,* a partnership, estate or trust) is treated as if actually held by the entity's partners or beneficiaries. § 302(e)(5).

(d) *Corporate Distributees.* A distribution in partial liquidation to a corporate shareholder will be treated as a dividend eligible for the dividends-received deduction, if the distributing corporation has sufficient e & p. This seemingly preferential treatment of corporate distributees was, in fact, originally intended to prevent corporate distributees from obtaining a stepped-up basis for selected assets without a corporate-level tax under prior law. The repeal of the *General Utilities* doctrine eliminated the underlying abuse in both liquidating and nonliquidating distributions, so that the original reason for special treatment of corporate distributees is no longer relevant. The apparent advantage of dividend treatment for corporate distributees is negated in effect, however, by the special basis reduction rules of § 1059 for redemptions in partial liquidation. *See* § 13 below. *See also* Chapter 2.

§ 7. Redemptions to Pay Death Taxes: § 303

Section 303 permits exchange treatment for a redemption of stock that is included in a decedent's gross estate, subject to certain limitations. Congress was concerned that it might be necessary to sell or liquidate a family-held business to pay death taxes and related expenses at the death of a major shareholder. Thus, § 303 offers a one-time opportunity to redeem closely-held stock with little or no tax cost, since the basis of any stock included in the decedent's gross estate will be stepped up (or down) to fair market value. Exchange treatment is available, independently of the provisions of § 302(b), up to the amount of specified death taxes and related expenses, regardless of whether the estate is illiquid or whether the proceeds of the redemption are actually used to pay such taxes and expenses.

In order to qualify under § 303, the redeemed stock must be included in determining the gross estate of the decedent for federal estate tax purposes. Thus, the stock must be owned by the decedent at the time of his death or have been transferred prior to death in such a manner that it is nevertheless includible in his gross estate. In addition, the value of the stock included in the decedent's gross estate must be at least 35% of his adjusted gross estate, *i.e.,* the value of the gross estate reduced by deductions allowable under §§ 2053 and 2054 (funeral and administration expenses, debts and losses). § 303(b)(2)(A). A special rule permits the stock of two or more corporations to be aggregated for purposes of the 35% rule, if at least 20% of the value of the total outstanding stock of each corporation is includible in the decedent's gross estate. § 302(b)(2)(B).

The amount of the distribution eligible for exchange treatment under § 303 is limited to the sum of death taxes imposed because of the decedent's death and funeral and administration expenses allowable as deductions for federal estate tax purposes. § 303(a). Moreover, § 303 treatment is generally available only for amounts distributed within 4 years (or longer, in certain cases), after the decedent's death, § 303(b)(1), and only to the extent that the interest of the shareholder receiving the distribution is reduced by payment of death taxes and funeral and administration expenses. § 303(b)(3). Thus, although the stock must be included in the decedent's gross estate to be eligible for § 303 treatment, it may be redeemed from a beneficiary who bears at least some of the burden of death taxes and funeral and administration expenses.

Section 303(c) also permits a redemption of stock ("new stock") whose basis is determined by reference to the basis of stock actually included in the decedent's gross estate ("old stock"), such as stock issued as a tax-free stock dividend or in a recapitalization. *See* Rev. Rul. 87–132 (distribution of nonvoting common stock to estate was a tax-free dividend under § 305(a); subsequent redemption qualified under § 303).

§ 8. Redemptions Through Related Corporations: § 304

(a) *General.* Section 304 is intended to prevent a shareholder from selling stock of one corporation to another related corporation in order to bail out corporate e & p at capital gain rates. Despite the intricacy of its provisions, the purpose of § 304 can be demonstrated simply. For example, assume that A, an individual shareholder, owns all of the stock of two corporations, X and Y, each having ample e & p. If X redeems some of A's stock, the distribution will be treated as a dividend under *Davis.* If A instead sells some of his X stock to Y, sale treatment should not be available because A continues, directly or constructively, to own all of the X stock. In essence, the purported sale resembles a dividend. Section 304 recasts the sale as a hypothetical distribution of cash in redemption of Y shares; dividend equivalency is determined under § 302(b), however, by reference to A's stock ownership of X.

(b) *Application of § 304.* Section 304 applies to a transfer of stock in one corporation (the "issuing corporation") to another corporation (the "acquiring corporation") in exchange for property, if one or more persons are in "control" of both the issuing corporation and the acquiring corporation (*i.e.,* own stock possessing at least 50% of total voting power or total value). For purposes of determining control, the attribution rules of § 318(a), with certain modifications, are applicable. The 50% stock ownership requirement for corporation-to-shareholder attribution and shareholder-to-corporation attribution is reduced to 5% in each case, and the amount of stock attributed to a corporation from a less-than-50% shareholder is limited to such shareholder's proportionate ownership. § 304(c)(3). If the two corporations are "brother-sister" corporations, the transaction is governed by § 304(a)(1); if the issuing corporation is in control of the acquiring corporation (a "parent-subsidiary" relationship), the transaction is governed by § 304(a)(2).

(c) *Brother-Sister Relationship.* If a brother-sister relationship exists, § 304(a)(1) treats the shareholder as receiving a distribution in redemption of his stock of the acquiring corporation (Y); the § 302(b) test for dividend equivalency, however, is applied by reference to the stock of the issuing corporation (X), *i.e.,* the corporation whose stock is sold. The attribution rules of § 318(a) (without regard to the 50% stock ownership requirement for corporation-to-shareholder attribution or shareholder-to-corporation attribution) are applicable in testing for dividend equivalency. § 304(b)(1). For purposes of determining the amount of the distribution that is a dividend, the e & p of both corporations are taken into account. § 304(b)(2). To the extent that the redemption is treated as a § 301 distribution, the sale of stock of the issuing corporation (X) to the acquiring corporation (Y) is treated as a contribution to Y's capital.

Example: Shareholder A owns 50 of the 100 outstanding shares of the stock of X Corp. and 50 of the 100 outstanding shares of the stock of Y Corp.; the remaining shareholders are unrelated to A and each other. If X redeemed half of A's X stock, A would reduce his percentage interest from $^{50}/_{100}$ to $^{25}/_{75}$, or from 50% to 33⅓%. The redemption qualifies as "substantially disproportionate" under § 302(b)(2). If A instead sells half of his X shares to Y, § 304(a)(1) applies. The transaction is treated as a redemption of A's Y stock, but the "substantially disproportionate test" is applied by looking at the percentage reduction in A's ownership of X stock. After the transaction, A owns 25 shares of X stock directly and 12.5 shares of X stock (50% of the 25 shares of X stock sold to Y) constructively. Since X's total outstanding stock is still 100 shares, A owns a total of 37.5% of X's stock, actually or constructively. Since the percentage reduction in A's ownership of X stock is still greater than 80%, the sale of X stock to Y is treated as an exchange under § 302(b)(2).

The 1986 Act clarifies that sale of the issuing corporation's stock is treated as a contribution to capital of the acquiring corporation only to the extent that the distribution is subject to § 301. § 304(a)(1). If § 301 treatment applies, the shareholder's basis in the stock transferred is added to the basis of his stock in the acquiring corporation, and the acquiring corporation takes a basis in the transferred stock equal to its basis in the shareholder's hands. If § 302(b)(2) exchange treatment applies, however, the acquiring corporation is treated as purchasing the stock transferred, and receives a cost basis in such stock. If exchange treatment applies, the shareholder will recover his basis in computing gain or loss on the transferred stock, and his basis in the acquiring corporation's stock will apparently be unaffected by the transaction.

(d) *Parent-Subsidiary Relationship.* Under § 304(a)(2), similar principles apply if a subsidiary acquires stock of its parent from a controlling shareholder. If § 304(a)(2) applies, the transaction is recharacterized as a redemption of the parent's stock for purposes of the § 302(b) dividend equivalency test, and earnings of both corporations are taken into account in determining the amount of any dividend.

The basis consequences of a deemed § 301 distribution are less clear in the parent-subsidiary context than in the brother-sister context; apparently, the shareholder's basis in the transferred parent stock will be added to his basis in his remaining stock of the parent. It should be noted that a brother-sister relationship could be converted into a parent-subsidiary relationship, by virtue of the attribution rules. The Regulations implicitly adopt the position, however, that an actual brother-sister relationship will prevail over a constructive parent-subsidiary relationship.

(e) *Definition of Property.* Section 304 applies only if stock is transferred to a related corporation in exchange for "property." Section 317(a) defines property as money, securities or other property, except stock (or stock rights) of the distributing corporation. In *Bhada* (1987), the Tax Court considered the applicability of § 304(a)(2) to a transaction in which a subsidiary transferred cash and issued its own stock to shareholders of its parent corporation in exchange for stock of the parent. The cash concededly represented property, as defined in § 317(a). The court held, however, that the subsidiary stock received by the parent's shareholders was not property because it was "stock in the corporation making the distribution," which is expressly excepted from the definition of property in § 317(a). The court rejected the government's argument that the transaction should be treated as if the parent had received a distribution from the subsidiary of cash and subsidiary stock and had then distributed the cash and subsidiary stock to the parent's shareholders in redemption of their parent stock. Instead, the court disregarded the deemed distribution in redemption by the parent under § 304(a)(2), and focused on the actual transfer by the subsidiary to the parent's shareholders. The court apparently viewed the term "distribution" in § 317(a) as having a broader meaning for purposes of § 304(a)(2) than for general purposes of

Subchapter C. As a result, the court concluded that § 304(a)(2) did not apply to the receipt of subsidiary stock by the parent's shareholders, and held that the exchange of parent stock for subsidiary stock was eligible for exchange treatment under § 1001.

(f) *Overlap With § 351.* Section 304 may overlap with § 351. For example, a shareholder may transfer stock of a brother corporation to a sister corporation in exchange for stock of the sister corporation plus cash. If the shareholder owns 80% of the sister corporation after the transfer, § 351 could apply with the result that the boot would be taxed only to the extent of the shareholder's realized gain. In 1982, Congress amended § 304 to provide that § 304 will generally prevail over § 351. § 304(b)(3)(A). Thus, in the example, the cash boot would be tested for dividend equivalency under the rules of § 302(b); the stock of the sister corporation would be received tax free, however, since it would not constitute property under § 317(a) and § 304(a)(1). In addition, § 304(b)(3)(B) contains special rules concerning assumption of liabilities if §§ 304 and 351 overlap.

(g) *Transfers of Stock Within an Affiliated Group.* The 1987 Act also added § 304(b)(4) to provide that in the case of any transfer described in § 304(a), where stock of one member of an affiliated group is transferred to another, "proper adjustments shall be made to (i) the adjusted basis of any intragroup stock, and (ii) the earnings and profits of any member of such group, to the extent necessary to carry out the purposes" of § 304. Although the statutory language is opaque, the purpose of the provision is to eliminate use of § 304 to accomplish results similar to "mirror transactions" in the context of the consolidated return regulations. *See* Chapter 6.

§ 9. Redemptions in Connection with Sale of a Corporation

(a) *Bootstrap Acquisitions.* Redemptions are frequently used to withdraw nonessential liquid assets from a closely-held corporation and permit a purchaser to acquire the remaining stock of the corporation at a reduced price. In this type of "bootstrap" acquisition, the seller may sell part of his stock to the purchaser and arrange for the corporation to redeem the remainder of his stock. Regardless whether the redemption occurs before or after the sale, the seller will be entitled to exchange treatment on the redemption if the redemption and sale are part of an integrated plan to dispose of the seller's entire interest. *See* Zenz v. Quinlivan (1954). Similarly, the Service has ruled that a sale and redemption may be combined in order to qualify the redemption under the "substantially disproportionate" test of § 302(b)(2). Rev. Rul. 75–447.

If a corporate seller is involved, dividend treatment may be more favorable than exchange treatment. In such cases, however, the Service is likely to recast the dividend to the seller as part of the purchase price, eliminating the possibility of a dividends-received deduction. *See* Waterman Steamship Corp. (1969). In *Waterman Steamship,* the purported dividend was distributed in the form of a note which was subsequently paid with funds supplied by the corporate purchaser; this offered the government a favorable opportunity to treat the dividend as part of the purchase price. In a recent case, the Tax Court distinguished *Waterman Steamship,* and held that a subsidiary's pre-sale dividend to its parent was not part of the purchase price for the subsidiary's stock. Litton Industries, Inc. (1987). The Tax Court noted the absence of a prearranged plan to sell the subsidiary's stock at the time of the dividend distribution, and distinguished the situation from *Waterman Steamship* where no dividend would have been paid unless the rest of the transaction had been prearranged.

(b) *Buy-Sell Agreements and Redemptions.* A purchaser who has entered into a binding obligation to purchase stock from an existing shareholder may arrange for the corporation to assume the obligation and redeem the shareholder's stock. The use of corporate funds to discharge the purchaser's obligation will be treated as a dividend to the purchaser. *See* Wall (1947); Sullivan (1966). If the purchaser has only an option to acquire the shareholder's stock, rather than an unconditional obligation, the purchaser does not have a dividend if he assigns the option to the corporation and the corporation redeems the seller's stock. *See* Holsey

(1958). *See also* Rev. Rul. 69–608. In *Citizens Bank & Trust Co.* (1978), the court did not find a constructive dividend where a corporation purchased property (stock of another corporation) at fair market value that its controlling shareholder was obligated to purchase. The court distinguished *Wall* and *Sullivan* by noting that the corporation did not purchase its own shares, but rather shares of another corporation; there was no constructive dividend because the corporation received property equal to the value of the consideration paid by it.

§ 10. Consequences to the Distributing Corporation

If a corporation distributes in-kind property in redemption of stock, the distributing corporation recognizes gain (but not loss), whether the shareholder receives dividend treatment under § 301 or exchange treatment under § 302(a) or § 303. Under § 312(b), the corporation's e & p will be increased by the excess (if any) of the fair market value of the distributed property over its basis in the corporation's hands. If the redemption is treated as a distribution under § 301(a), § 312(a) requires that the corporation's e & p be reduced by the adjusted basis of the distributed property (or fair market value, under § 312(b), if the property is appreciated). If the distribution is treated as an exchange under § 302(a) or § 303, the adjustment to e & p is further limited by § 312(n)(7).

Under § 312(n)(7), the part of the distribution which is properly chargeable to the corporation's e & p cannot exceed the ratable share of accumulated e & p attributable to the redeemed stock. This treatment reflects the fact that the value of the redeemed shares includes unrealized appreciation (or depreciation) in the value of corporate assets which is not reflected in e & p and therefore should not be taken into account for purposes of the § 312(a) adjustment to e & p. Furthermore, the value of the redeemed shares includes a share of accumulated profits which reduces e & p (even though the shareholder is not taxed as if he received a dividend).

Example: Assume that 50% of the stock of X Corp. is redeemed for $250,000 at a time when X's balance sheet shows a capital account of $100,000 (the amount of cash originally contributed by X's shareholders) and accumulated e & p of $225,000. If the total net fair market value of all of X's assets is $500,000, X's assets must have unrealized appreciation of $175,000, *i.e.,* the excess of net asset value ($500,000) over the sum of paid-in capital ($100,000) and accumulated e & p ($225,000). Under § 312(n)(7), the amount of the distribution charged to X's e & p is $112,500 (50% of $225,000). The remaining $137,500 of the distribution is treated as attributable to the shareholder's paid-in capital ($50,000) and unrealized appreciation ($87,500).

It may be more difficult to determine the proper charge to e & p if the corporation has more than one class of stock. Legal priorities between the different classes of stock must be taken into account in allocating e & p among classes of stock. Presumably, a redemption of preferred stock should not reduce e & p at all, except for any accumulated dividends, since a preferred stockholder is generally entitled only to a return of capital on liquidation.

Example: X Corp. has two classes of common stock, Class A and B, which are identical except that Class A has a preference over Class B in dividends and liquidating distributions in the ratio of 2:1. X has net assets worth $210,000, and accumulated e & p of $120,000. If X distributes $140,000 (⅔ of $210,000) in redemption of all of the Class A stock, § 312(n)(7) requires that X's e & p be reduced by $80,000 (⅔ of $120,000).

§ 11. Computation of Shareholder's Gain (or Loss) in Exchange

If a distribution is treated as an exchange under § 302(a) or § 303, the shareholder recognizes gain or loss on the difference between the amount of the distribution and his basis in the redeemed stock. The basis of the distributed property in the shareholder's hands will be its cost, which is equal to fair market value as a result of the taxable exchange. If the shareholder does not actually surrender any stock (as in the case of a pro-rata distribution in partial liquidation), an appropriate number of shares will be deemed to be surrendered for purposes of determining gain or loss. On an actual surrender of shares, the shareholder may be able to manipulate the amount of gain or loss by selecting shares with a high or low basis.

Example: X Corp. redeems 100 shares of its stock from shareholder A for $25,000, their fair market value. A's basis in the redeemed stock is $26,000, and he retains an additional 100 shares of stock which also have an adjusted basis of $26,000 before the redemption. If the redemption qualifies as an exchange under § 302(a), A will report a $1,000 capital loss.

§ 12. Redemptions Treated as § 301 Distributions: § 302(d)

If a redemption does not qualify for exchange treatment under § 302(a) or § 303, the shareholder's surrender of shares is ignored and he will be treated as receiving a § 301 distribution. The shareholder receives a basis in the distributed property equal to its fair market value, under the general rule of § 301(d). Under § 301(c), the distribution will be treated as a dividend to the extent of e & p, and any remaining amounts will be treated as recovery of basis or capital gain. If a distribution is treated as a dividend, the Regulations provide that "proper adjustment of the basis of the remaining stock will be made with respect to the stock redeemed." Reg. § 1.302–2(c). Thus, the shareholder's basis in the redeemed shares is added to his basis in the remaining shares.

Example: X Corp., which has ample e & p, redeems 2 out of 10 shares held by shareholder A for $30. A had an adjusted basis of $10 per share in his X stock ($100 aggregate basis) before the redemption. The entire amount received ($30) is treated as a § 301 distribution, resulting in $30 of dividend income to A since X has sufficient e & p to cover the distribution. A's adjusted basis in the 2 redeemed shares will be reallocated among the remaining 8 shares, resulting in a new basis of $12.50 per share and an unchanged aggregate basis of $100.

If the corporation lacks e & p, § 301 may still apply to a distribution in redemption of stock which is made under circumstances that would otherwise render it essentially equivalent to a dividend. Although the law is not entirely clear, the statutory language supports the view that the shareholder may apply the amount of the distribution against the basis of all of his stock (not merely the redeemed shares) and treat as capital gain only the amount in excess of his aggregate basis.

A problem of "disappearing basis" may arise if the shareholder retains no stock but the redemption is nevertheless treated as a § 301 distribution, *e.g.,* because of the constructive ownership rules. In this situation, the Regulations permit the shareholder's basis in the redeemed shares to be added to the basis of the related party. Reg. § 1.302–2(c), Example (2). *See also* Levin (1967) (basis of taxpayer's redeemed shares added to basis of shares owned by his son). In Revenue Ruling 70–496, however, the Service held on the particular facts of the transaction that the shareholder's basis was simply "lost" in a § 304/§ 301 distribution. The problem of disappearing basis does not arise with respect to a redemption treated as an exchange, since the shareholder recovers the basis of the redeemed stock in computing gain or loss.

§ 13. Special Treatment of Corporate Shareholders: § 1059

Ordinarily, a corporate shareholder prefers that a redemption be treated as a § 301 distribution because of the dividends-received deduction of § 243. If the distribution constitutes an "extraordinary dividend" under § 1059, however, the corporate distributee's basis in its remaining stock must be reduced by the amount of the dividend excluded under § 243. *See* Chapter 2. Section 1059 eliminates the abuse under prior law, in which a corporate shareholder might withdraw the value of preferred stock from the distributing corporation in the form of a dividend and then sell the preferred stock at a loss. *See* Rev. Rul. 77–226 (recasting the purported dividend as part of the sale price and treating such a transaction as a complete termination under *Zenz*). If the corporate shareholder does not intend to dispose of its remaining stock immediately, however, the impact of the basis reduction rules of § 1059 will be deferred and will be correspondingly less burdensome.

CHAPTER 6

COMPLETE LIQUIDATIONS; COLLAPSIBLE CORPORATIONS

§ 1. Introduction

When a corporation distributes its assets to shareholders in complete liquidation, the transaction is generally treated as an exchange of the distributed assets for the shareholders' stock. At the shareholder level, § 331 expressly precludes § 301 dividend treatment and provides instead that amounts received by shareholders in complete liquidation are treated as "full payment in exchange for the stock." Under the general sale or exchange rules, a shareholder determines gain or loss by subtracting his adjusted basis in the stock from the amount realized on the liquidating distribution. §§ 1001(a) and 1001(b). If the stock is a capital asset in the shareholder's hands (as is normally the case), such gain or loss will be capital in nature.

At the corporate level, § 336(a) states the general rule that a corporation recognizes gain or loss on a distribution in complete liquidation as if the distributed property were sold at fair market value. Congress amended § 336 in 1986 to provide for recognition of gain or loss at the corporate level, abandoning the rule of nonrecognition formerly codified, subject to numerous exceptions, in § 336. Prior to the 1986 Act, a corporation could distribute its assets in complete liquidation at the cost of a nominal "toll charge" tax at the corporate level; shareholders were taxed on the distribution at favorable capital gains rates and received a stepped-up basis in the distributed property equal to its fair market value. Thus, unrealized corporate gains, having escaped tax at the corporate level, were taxed only at the shareholder level, while realized corporate gains were generally subject to tax at both levels. The 1986 Act eliminates this disparity by treating a distribution to shareholders in complete liquidation as a deemed sale. Under present law, a liquidating distribution of corporate assets produces substantially the same tax consequences as an actual sale of corporate assets followed by a liquidating distribution of the after-tax sale proceeds.

The following discussion of complete liquidations covers the tax consequences to shareholders and to the liquidating corporation. Subsequent sections deal with the special rules applicable to subsidiary liquidations and certain asset purchases treated as stock sales. This Chapter concludes with an overview of the "collapsible corporation" provisions of § 341.

§ 2. Tax Treatment of Shareholders

(a) *Recognition of Gain or Loss and Basis.* Typically, in a complete liquidation, each shareholder recognizes capital gain or loss on the difference between the amount realized on surrender of his stock and the adjusted basis of his stock. §§ 331 and 1001. Each shareholder to whom property is distributed in a complete liquidation takes the property with a basis equal to its fair market value. § 334(a). In the absence of a preferential capital gains tax rate, the principal distinction between a nonliquidating distribution under § 301 and a liquidating distribution under § 331 is whether the shareholder can recover his basis. In addition, capital gain treatment may be advantageous for purposes of offsetting capital losses subject to the limitations of § 1211.

Example: An individual, A, recently inherited all of the stock of X Corp., which has a basis in A's hands of $500,000, the fair market value of the stock at the date of the previous owner's death. § 1014(a). The fair market value of X's assets is presently also $500,000. X distributes $200,000 to A as a dividend and A then sells the stock for $300,000, the net value of X's remaining assets after paying the dividend. A will have ordinary income of $200,000 (assuming X has sufficient e & p) and a capital loss of $200,000, which can be used to offset only $3,000 of ordinary income for the current year. By contrast, if X had distributed all $500,000 of its assets to A in complete liquidation, A would have had no gain or loss on surrendering his stock.

The Regulations require that the amount and character of gain or loss on a liquidating distribution be calculated separately for each block of stock. Reg. § 1.331–1(e). Thus, if a shareholder has one block of stock with a high basis and another with a low basis, he may recognize a loss on the high-basis stock and gain on the low-basis stock.

Example: In December 1988, X Corp. makes a cash distribution of $1,000 per share in complete liquidation; the shareholders surrender all of their stock for cancellation. Shareholder A surrenders 50 shares which he purchased 5 years ago for $200 per share, and 40 shares which he purchased 5 months ago for $1,500 per share. A recognizes long-term capital gain of $40,000 ($50,000 amount realized less $10,000 adjusted basis) on the 5–year–old block of stock, and short-term capital loss of $20,000 ($60,000 adjusted basis less $40,000 amount realized) on the 5–month–old block.

If the corporation makes a series of distributions to shareholders pursuant to a plan of complete liquidation, the series is treated as a single liquidating distribution under § 346(a) and shareholders are permitted to recover basis before recognizing gain or loss. *See* Rev. Rul. 85–48, amplifying Rev. Rul. 68–348.

Example: The facts are the same as in the preceding example, except that X Corp., pursuant to a plan of complete liquidation, distributes $600 per share in cash on December 1, 1988 and $400 per share as a final liquidating distribution on March 1, 1989. As of December 31, 1988, the amount of the final liquidating distribution cannot be determined with reasonable certainty. A reports long-term capital gain of $20,000 ($30,000 amount realized less $10,000 adjusted basis) for 1988 and $20,000 (amount realized) for 1989 on the 5–year-old block; he reports nothing on the 5–month–old block until 1989, when his $20,000 short-term capital loss ($60,000 adjusted basis less $40,000 amount realized) becomes ascertainable.

A liquidating corporation may distribute assets (*e.g.,* disputed claims or contingent contract rights) that are difficult to value with reasonable accuracy. Although the Service normally requires valuation of assets, the transaction may be held "open" in "rare and extraordinary" circumstances. Reg. § 1.1001–1(a). *See* Burnet v. Logan (1931). The effect of open transaction treatment is to defer the reporting of all or part of the stockholder's gain or loss. In an open liquidation, any gain or loss ultimately realized when the value of the assets becomes ascertainable will be treated as part of the capital gain or loss on the liquidation; if the transaction is treated as a closed transaction, however, any subsequent gain may be ordinary in character in the absence of a sale or exchange. *See* Waring (1969). *See also* § 453(g) (denying use of open transaction treatment in installment sales of depreciable property between related parties).

If a shareholder gives his stock to a donee (*e.g.,* a charity or a lower-bracket family member) during the liquidating process, any gain on the transferred stock will most likely be taxed to the donor on assignment-of-income principles. *See, e.g.,* Jones (1976); Hudspeth (1972). By contrast, a gift of stock prior to formal adoption of the plan of liquidation is usually effective in shifting the gain to the donee.

(b) *Special Treatment of Liabilities.* If a shareholder assumes (or takes property subject to) liabilities in connection with a liquidating distribution, the liabilities reduce the amount realized on the distribution. Contingent liabilities that cannot be valued are not taken into account; a shareholder may have a capital, rather than an ordinary loss, if he pays the contingent liability in a subsequent year, on the theory that the later payment "relates back" to the original liquidation. *See* Arrowsmith (1952).

Example: X Corp. makes a liquidating distribution to shareholder A of property with a gross value of $10,000, subject to a liability of $4,000. A has an adjusted basis of $2,000 in his stock. A will realize $6,000 (the net value of the property taking the liability into account) on the distribution, and will report a gain of $4,000 (amount realized less basis in the X stock). A's basis in the property will be $10,000, its fair market value. If the liability were contingent and could not be reasonably valued, it would be disregarded in determining the amount initially realized by A, leaving A with a recognized gain of $8,000 ($10,000 gross value less $2,000 stock basis). If A subsequently paid $4,000 in satisfaction of the liability, he would realize a capital loss of $4,000.

(c) *Installment Treatment.* Under § 453B, a corporation recognizes gain on distribution of an installment obligation if the fair market value of the installment obligation exceeds its adjusted basis. If installment obligations are distributed to shareholders (in exchange for their stock) in a § 331 liquidation, the shareholder-level gain may be deferred under § 453(h). The shareholders are not taxed upon receipt of the obligation, but instead report payments received under the obligation as received in exchange for their stock. The installment obligation must arise from sales or exchanges by the corporation during the 12–month period beginning on the date of adoption of a plan of complete liquidation and the liquidation must be completed within such 12–month period. § 453(h)(1)(A). An installment sale of inventory does not qualify for this special rule, unless it constitutes a sale of substantially all of the corporation's inventory to one person in one transaction. § 453(h)(1)(B). Moreover, if the obligor and shareholder are married to each other or are related persons (within the meaning of § 1239(b)), the shareholder must recognize gain immediately upon receipt of the obligation. § 453(h)(1)(C).

§ 3. Tax Treatment of the Liquidating Corporation

(a) *Recognition of Gain or Loss.* Under § 336(a), a corporation is generally taxed on a liquidating distribution of property as if the property had been sold to the shareholders at fair market value. Under § 336(a), a corporation generally recognizes losses as well as gains on a liquidating distribution; this treatment is distinctly more favorable than the treatment of nonliquidating distributions under § 311(a), which disallows losses while requiring recognition of gains. *See* Chapter 4. The purpose of disallowing losses on nonliquidating distributions is apparently to prevent corporations from selectively distributing loss property. In a complete liquidation, however, there is no problem of selective distribution, since the corporation must distribute all its assets. Nevertheless, § 336(d) limits losses in certain situations perceived by Congress as potentially abusive. In addition, § 336(c) provides an exception for corporate formations and reorganizations which are governed by §§ 351 to 368. Finally, § 337 provides for nonrecognition of gain or loss on certain liquidating distributions from a subsidiary corporation to an 80% parent corporation.

Because § 336(a) treats a distribution in complete liquidation as a deemed sale of the corporation's assets, gains and losses are apparently computed separately for each asset. *See* Williams v. McGowan (1945). Thus, a liquidating corporation may realize capital losses from certain assets that cannot be used to offset ordinary income from other assets. This result is generally less advantageous to the corporation than if it were permitted to report its aggregate gain or loss. Indeed, the corporation may be unable either to deduct its capital losses currently or to carry them back to previous taxable years (if there were no capital gains in such years). *See* § 1212(a)(1).

(b) *Loss Limitations.* Section 336(d) contains two separate loss limitation rules. Section 336(d)(1) absolutely disallows losses on certain liquidating distributions to a "related person." Section 336(d)(2) applies to so-called "built-in" losses (*i.e.,* losses accrued before property was transferred to the corporation) on distributions to any shareholder (whether or not a related person) as well as built-in losses on sales and exchanges.

(c) *Losses on Distributions to Related Parties:* § *336(d)(1).* Section § 336(d)(1) denies recognition of losses to a corporation on certain liquidating distributions to a "related person" (within the meaning of § 267). Typically, the related person referred to in § 336(d)(1) is a shareholder who owns, directly or indirectly, more than 50% of the stock of the liquidating corporation. Although the relationship between the corporation and the distributee is determined by reference to § 267, the treatment of losses at the corporate level is governed exclusively by § 336(d)(1). Unlike § 267(a)(1) (which by its terms does not apply to liquidating distributions), § 336(d)(1) permanently disallows recognition of the corporation's loss and makes no provision for deferred loss recognition to the distributee. Section 336(d)(1) applies if: (i) the distribution is not pro rata or (ii) the distributed property is "disqualified property" defined as property acquired by the corporation in a § 351 transaction (or as a contribution to capital) during the 5–year period ending on the date of the distribution.

Example: X Corp. has two shareholders, A and B; A owns 75% of the stock and B owns 25%. X has only two assets, both of which were contributed to X more than 5 years ago. Each asset has a fair market value of $500. Asset # 1 has a basis of $450 and Asset # 2 has a basis of $550. If X distributes a 75% interest in each asset to A and the remaining 25% to B in complete liquidation, the distribution will be pro rata. Because the distribution is pro rata and the distributed property was contributed more than 5 years ago, § 336(d) (1) does not apply, and X recognizes a $50 gain on Asset # 1 and a $50 loss on Asset # 2.

In the above example, assume instead that X distributes equal undivided interests in Asset # 1 to A and B, and distributes Asset # 2 entirely to A. (Note that A and B still receive distributions corresponding in value to their respective proportionate stock ownership.) X will recognize the $50 gain on Asset # 1, but not the $50 loss on Asset # 2 because Asset # 2 was not distributed pro rata and A is a related person. Thus, it appears that the only way that a corporation may recognize a loss on property distributed to a related shareholder in complete liquidation is to allocate the loss property ratably among all shareholders, in proportion to their respective percentages of stock ownership.

If the property is "disqualified property" within the meaning of § 336(d)(1)(B) (*i.e.*, property contributed within the 5–year period ending of the date of distribution), the loss is disallowed at the corporate level regardless of whether the property is distributed pro rata. § 336(d)(1)(A)(ii). This prohibition on loss recognition was aimed at the potential double counting of losses when property with a basis exceeding its fair market value is contributed to a corporation during the tainted 5–year period preceding the distribution. Both the corporation's basis in the contributed property and the shareholder's basis in his stock will preserve the pre-contribution loss under the rules relating to § 351 exchanges and capital contributions. *See* Chapter 3. But for § 336(d)(1), the pre-contribution loss might thus be recognized at both the corporate and shareholder level. Section 336(d)(1) denies recognition of the corporation's loss, however, even if the property has a fair market value exceeding its basis at the time of contribution but subsequently declines in value. This result may seem anomalous particularly since § 336 provides no parallel nonrecognition treatment for pre-contribution appreciation.

Example: A is the sole shareholder of X Corp. X's assets consist exclusively of two parcels of land: Parcel # 1, which X bought 3 years ago, has a fair market value of $10,000 and a basis of $5,000;

Parcel # 2, which A contributed 6 months ago, has a fair market value of $5,000 and a basis of $10,000. X distributes both parcels to A in complete liquidation. But for § 336(d)(1), X would have no net gain or loss on the distribution because the $5,000 loss on Parcel # 2 would offset the $5,000 gain on Parcel # 1. Section 336(d)(1) disallows X's $5,000 loss on Parcel # 2 because it is "disqualified property," *i.e.,* property contributed within the 5–year period preceding the distribution. X must recognize the $5,000 gain on Parcel # 1. The result would be the same even if Parcel # 2 had a fair market value of $15,000 and a basis of $10,000 at the time of the contribution, and subsequently declined in value to $5,000. Section 336(d)(1) would deny recognition of the post-incorporation loss in X's hands even though there was no tax-avoidance purpose for the contribution.

(d) *Losses With Tax-Avoidance Purpose: § 336(d) (2).* Section 336(d)(2) imposes a separate limitation on loss recognition if the distributed property was acquired in a § 351 transaction or as a contribution to capital as "part of a plan a principal purpose of which was to recognize loss by the liquidating corporation with respect to such property in connection with the liquidation." Section 336(d)(2) denies recognition only of the amount of the built-in loss (determined as the excess of the adjusted basis of the property over its fair market value immediately after the contribution). Thus, if the contributed property has built-in gain at the time of contribution, § 336(d)(2) will not apply, but § 336(d)(1) may nevertheless apply if the distribution is to a related shareholder.

Unlike § 336(d)(1)(B), which applies only to property distributed within 5 years after contribution, § 336(d)(2) potentially applies no matter how long the corporation has held the property. The required tax-avoidance purpose is presumed to be present, except as otherwise provided in Regulations, if a corporation acquires built-in loss property not more than 2 years before adopting a plan of complete liquidation. The 1988 Act clarified that any acquisition of property after the date 2 years before the corporation adopts a plan of complete liquidation (including acquisitions after adoption of the plan) is presumed to be for a tax-avoidance purpose. Thus, a contribution of property after the date of the plan's adoption will be subject to the loss limitation rules. The legislative history contemplates that the Regulations will limit the statutory tax-avoidance presumption to situations in which "there is no clear and substantial relationship" between the contributed property and the corporation's business (*e.g.*, unimproved real estate in the southwest is contributed to a manufacturing company operating exclusively in the northeast). The legislative history also indicates that a tax-avoidance purpose will be found only in rare and exceptional circumstances if the contribution occurs more than 2 years before adoption of the plan of complete liquidation.

In any sale, exchange or distribution to which § 336(d)(2) applies, the liquidating corporation is required to reduce its adjusted basis in the property, for purposes of determining the amount of loss recognized, by the amount of the built-in loss at the time of contribution. § 336(d)(2)(A). The corporation's basis for purposes of computing depreciation and gain, however, is not affected by the downward basis adjustment. If the corporation's adjusted basis in the loss property has not changed since the time of contribution, the § 336(d)(2)(A) adjustment will produce a stepped-down basis equal to the property's fair market value at the time of contribution.

Example: On September 1, 1988, X Corp. acquires property in a § 351 transfer with a fair market value of $150 and a substituted basis of $500. On August 31, 1989, X adopts a plan of complete liquidation and distributes the property which is then worth $50. If § 336(d)(2) applies, X's adjusted basis in the property for loss purposes will be reduced from $500 to $150 (the $350 difference being equal to the built-in loss at the time of contribution). Accordingly, X's recognized loss will be $100 ($150 adjusted basis less $50 fair market value). If X instead sold the property in 1989 for $50 and distributed the proceeds in liquidation, X's recognized loss would still be limited to $100 because § 336(d)(2) applies to sales and exchanges as well as distributions.

If a corporation adopts a plan of complete liquidation which causes § 336(d)(2) to become applicable to a loss on a transaction reported in an earlier
taxable year, § 336(d)(2)(C) permits the Service to
"recapture" the disallowed portion of the loss in
lieu of reopening the corporation's return for the
earlier year. In the above example, assume that X
sells the property for $50 on December 1, 1988, and
reports a loss of $450. If X then adopts a plan of
complete liquidation in 1989, the $350 portion of
the $450 loss reported in 1988 is retroactively
subject to disallowance under § 336(d)(2). Instead
of reopening X's 1988 return, the Service may
require X to report an additional $350 of gross
income in 1989.

(e) *Application of Both Loss Disallowance Rules.*
If § 336(d)(1) and (2) both apply to the same transaction, the harsher provisions of § 336(d)(1) will
prevail.

Example: Shareholders A and B own 70% and
30%, respectively, of the stock of X Corp. X's only
assets consist of two separate parcels of real property: Parcel #1 with a fair market value of
$15,000 and a basis of $30,000, and Parcel #2 with
a fair market value of $7,500 and a basis of $3,000.
Parcel #1 was contributed to X on January 1,
1989, with a fair market value of $27,000. On
December 31, 1990, X adopts a plan of complete
liquidation and distributes a 70% undivided interest in each parcel to A and the remaining 30% to
B. X will recognize a $4,500 gain on Parcel #2

($7,500 fair market value less $3,000 basis). Under
§ 336(d)(1), X's loss on the 70% share of Parcel # 1
distributed to A will be disallowed because A is a
related person and Parcel # 1 is "disqualified
property." In addition, § 336(d)(2) may limit the
remaining loss on the 30% of Parcel # 1 distributed to B, an unrelated shareholder, because Parcel
1 is built-in loss property acquired within 2
years. Thus, X's adjusted basis in Parcel # 1, for
loss purposes, will be $27,000 ($30,000 substituted
basis less $3,000 built-in loss at the time of contri-
bution). X will recognize a $3,600 loss on distribut-
ing 30% of Parcel # 1 to B ($8,100 allocable adjust-
ed basis less $4,500 allocable fair market value). If
§ 336(d)(2) did not apply, X would recognize a
$4,500 loss on distributing 30% of Parcel # 1 to B
($9,000 allocable adjusted basis less $4,500 allocable fair market value).

(f) *Assignment of Income and Related Problems.*
The hypothetical sale requirement of § 336 eliminates the need in most cases for the government to
invoke judicially-developed doctrines to ensure that
a liquidating corporation does not avoid recognizing income. Under prior law, the Supreme Court
applied the tax-benefit doctrine to require a liquidating corporation to recognize gain on an in-kind
distribution of supplies where the corporation had
already deducted the cost of the supplies in an
earlier taxable year. Hillsboro Nat. Bank (1983).
But see Rojas (1988) (Unpublished Case) (tax-benefit doctrine does not apply to expenses deducted for

materials and services which were used and con-
sumed prior to the liquidation). Since § 336 now
generally reaches this result more directly, the tax-
benefit doctrine is likely to be less significant after
the 1986 Act. Assignment-of-income problems may
still arise, however, if a corporation has potential
income that is contingent or not yet reflected under its method of accounting.

(g) *Liquidating Corporation's Deductions.* A liquidation represents the last chance for the corporation to claim a deduction for accrued but unpaid
liabilities. In the case of a cash-method taxpayer,
where payment of the liabilities would have generated a deduction at the corporate level, the question is whether a deduction should be allowed to
the corporation on liquidation when its shareholders assume the liabilities. In the context of an
actual sale, one court held that the transferor
corporation, a cash-method taxpayer, was entitled
to a deduction for accrued liabilities assumed by
the purchaser of its assets. Commercial Sec. Bank
(1981). Since § 336 analogizes a liquidation to an
actual sale, the liquidating corporation should thus
be able to deduct liabilities for ordinary and necessary business expenses when such liabilities are
assumed by shareholders.

(h) *Liabilities in Excess of Basis.* Under
§ 336(b), the value of property distributed in complete liquidation is treated as not less than the
amount of any liability to which the property is
subject or which is assumed by shareholders in

connection with the liquidation. The treatment of excess liabilities in connection with a liquidating distribution is the same as the treatment, discussed in Chapter 4, in the context of nonliquidating distributions. Read literally, § 336(b) requires the liquidating corporation to recognize gain to the extent of any liability in excess of basis. If the shareholder's assumption of the liability is treated as an additional capital contribution followed by the corporation's payment of the liability, however, there would be no excess liabilities to trigger recognition of gain at the corporate level.

Example: X Corp. purchases an asset for $500 with borrowed funds, and gives the lender a security interest in the asset. X claims $200 of depreciation deductions on the asset, reducing its adjusted basis to $300, and distributes the asset in liquidation to a shareholder. If the shareholder assumes the $500 liability, X must apparently recognize $200 gain under § 336(b). Alternatively, the shareholder could have contributed $200 to X to pay off the excess liability, and X could then have distributed the property without recognizing gain. The difference between the two situations is whether the shareholder has actually paid $200 out of pocket (as a capital contribution) or has merely assumed an additional liability of $200. If the liabilities are nonrecourse, it seems appropriate to require the corporation to recognize gain to the extent that nonrecourse liabilities exceed the corporation's adjusted basis in the distributed property, since neither the corporation nor the shareholder may ultimately pay the excess liabilities.

§ 4. Liquidation of a Subsidiary

(a) *Stock Ownership and Timing of Distributions.* When a subsidiary corporation distributes property in complete liquidation to a parent corporation, if the requirements of § 332(b) are met, §§ 332 and 337 provide that no gain or loss is recognized to the parent or the subsidiary. In order to qualify for nonrecognition treatment, § 332(b) requires that the parent corporation own a specified amount of the subsidiary's stock and that the liquidating distributions occur within a specified time period. The first requirement is met if the parent owns stock that (i) possesses at least 80% of the total voting power of the outstanding stock of the subsidiary and (ii) has a value equal to at least 80% of the total value of the stock of the subsidiary (without regard to certain nonvoting stock that is limited and preferred as to dividends). §§ 332(b)(1) and 1504(a)(2). The 80%-stock-ownership test must be met "on the date of adoption of the plan of liquidation" and continuously thereafter until the final liquidating distribution. § 332(b)(1).

Often, a subsidiary liquidation can be structured intentionally in a way that meets (or fails to meet) the stock ownership test, thereby making nonrecognition treatment optional to a certain extent, despite the mandatory language of § 332. Riggs, Inc. (1975). Thus, for example, a parent corporation having a basis in subsidiary stock exceeding the value of the subsidiary's assets may be able to recognize a loss on liquidation of the subsidiary by selling sufficient stock to reduce its ownership below the 80% requirement. Conversely, a corporation that lacks 80% ownership may be able to obtain § 332 nonrecognition treatment by acquiring additional stock (or by arranging for the redemption of stock held by others) immediately before the liquidation. In such a case, however, the government might argue that the plan of liquidation was "adopted" informally before the additional shares were acquired and that the requisite 80% stock ownership therefore did not exist on the date the plan of liquidation was adopted.

Section 332(b) also requires that the liquidating distributions occur either (i) within a single taxable year, or (ii) within a 3–year period from the close of the taxable year in which the first distribution occurs. The term "taxable year" refers to the taxable year of the subsidiary. Rev. Rul. 76–317. The single-taxable-year rule is satisfied if all liquidating distributions are completed within a single taxable year (which need not be the taxable year in which the plan of liquidation is adopted). Rev. Rul. 71–326. For purposes of the single-taxable-year rule, a resolution of the subsidiary's shareholders authorizing the distributions is treated as adoption of a plan of liquidation. Under the 3–year rule, by contrast, the plan of liquidation must specifically provide that all liquidating distributions are to be completed within the statutory period (3 years from the close of the taxable year in which the first distribution occurs), and the distributions must actually be completed within this period. It has been held, however, that the 3–year rule may be satisfied if the liquidation is completed within the statutory period, even if the plan of liquidation fails to limit the time for distribution. Burnside Veneer Co. (1948). Under the 3–year rule, the parent must file a waiver of the statute of limitations (to permit retroactive taxation of earlier distributions if the liquidating distributions are not completed within the statutory period) and may be required to post a bond. § 332(b). *See also* Reg. §§ 1.332–4(a)(2) and 1.332–4(a)(3).

(b) *Treatment of Parent.* If the requirements of § 332(b) are met, § 332(a) provides that the parent corporation recognizes no gain or loss on receipt of property distributed in complete liquidation of the subsidiary. Under § 334(b), the basis of the property distributed to the parent in a § 332 liquidation has a substituted basis in the parent's hands equal to its basis in the subsidiary's hands. In effect, the parent steps into the subsidiary's place, and will recognize gain or loss (including built-in gain or loss at the time of the liquidating distribution) on subsequent disposition of the distributed property. The parent's basis in the stock of the subsidiary (which may be higher or lower than the subsidiary's basis in its assets) is not taken into account, and any gain or loss inherent in the parent's subsidiary stock is eliminated. The nonrecognition and substituted basis provisions of §§ 332(a) and 334(b) apply only to property distributed to the parent; in the case of property distributed to any other shareholder, the general rules of § 331 (taxable exchange) and § 334(a) (basis stepped up to fair market value) are applicable.

(c) *Treatment of the Subsidiary.* In a subsidiary liquidation to which § 332 applies, the subsidiary recognizes no gain or loss on distributions to an "80% distributee" (*i.e.,* the parent corporation meeting the 80% stock ownership requirements of § 332(b)). § 337(a). Section 337 in its present form should not be confused with the provisions of prior law bearing the same section number but relating to entirely different subject matter, which were repealed by the 1986 Act. Section 337 nonrecognition treatment also applies to distributions of property to the parent in satisfaction of the subsidiary's preexisting debts owed to the parent. § 337(b). Special rules are provided to ensure that § 337 nonrecognition cannot be converted into a permanent exclusion, in the case of certain tax-exempt organizations and foreign corporations. §§ 337(b)(2) and 337(d). If the distributing corporation recognizes gain under these special rules, the 1988 Act provides that the distributee corporation takes a basis in the distributed property equal to its fair market value. *See* § 334(b)(1).

Section 337 nonrecognition treatment applies only to the subsidiary's gain or loss on the property actually distributed to the parent, as distinguished from a ratable share of the subsidiary's aggregate gain or loss. The subsidiary must recognize gain on any appreciated property distributed to shareholders other than the parent, under the general provisions of § 336. Losses, however, are subject to a special rule disallowing recognition of the subsidiary's loss on any distribution in the case of "any liquidation to which § 332 applies." § 336(d)(3). Congress may have been concerned that the liquidating subsidiary might distribute disproportionate amounts of appreciated property to a parent without recognizing gain, while recognizing loss on disproportionate distributions of loss property to other shareholders. The special disallowance provision of § 336(d)(3) in effect prevents a subsidiary from recognizing losses on distributions to minority shareholders in a § 332 liquidation. The 1988 Act clarified that the special loss disallowance provision of § 336(d)(3) only applies to distributions to an 80% distributee if the distributing corporation is entitled to nonrecognition treatment under the general rule of § 337.

Example: X Corp. owns 80% of the voting stock of Y Corp., and individual A owns the remaining 20% of Y's voting stock. X has a basis of $6,000 in its Y stock, and A has a basis of $1,000 in his Y stock. Y owns only two assets: Asset # 1 with a fair market value of $8,000 and a basis of $5,000, and Asset # 2 with a fair market value of $2,000 and a basis of $4,000. Pursuant to a liquidating plan, Y distributes the gain property (Asset # 1) to

X and the loss property (Asset # 2) to A. Under § 337(a), Y will not recognize any gain on distributing Asset # 1 to X because X is an 80% distributee. X will receive a substituted basis of $5,000 in Asset # 1. X's basis in its Y stock disappears as a result of Y's liquidation. Section 336(d)(3) prevents Y from recognizing its $2,000 loss on the distribution of Asset # 2 to A. A will realize $2,000 (the fair market value of Asset # 2) on the deemed exchange for his Y stock, producing a taxable gain of $1,000 on the liquidation ($2,000 amount realized less $1,000 basis in Y stock). §§ 331 and 334(a).

The mix of assets distributed to the parent and minority shareholders may be structured to optimize the overall situation of the shareholders. On one hand, it may be advantageous to distribute appreciated property to the parent since this permits the subsidiary to avoid recognizing gain which would ultimately reduce the net amount received by the shareholders. On the other hand, it may be advantageous to distribute loss property to the parent to preserve a high basis in the distributed assets in the parent's hands. Distributing loss property to a minority shareholder produces no tax advantage because the shareholder's basis in the distributed property is stepped down to fair market value with no corresponding loss recognized to the liquidating corporation. The parties should consider carefully the basis and gain consequences of the many different asset mixes to determine which one

produces the most favorable overall tax consequences.

§ 5. Stock Sales Treated as Asset Transfers: § 336(e)

Section 336(e), added by the 1986 Act, authorizes
the Treasury to issue Regulations that will permit
a parent corporation to elect to treat a sale (or
distribution) of subsidiary stock as a sale of the
subsidiary's assets. A parent corporation is defined by reference to the same 80% stock ownership requirements referred to in § 332(b). If the
parent elects to treat the stock sale as an asset
transfer under § 336(e), the parent's gain or loss on
the actual stock sale is simply ignored. Instead,
gain or loss is determined solely by reference to the
gain or loss that the subsidiary would have recognized on a direct sale of its assets for the amount
paid for the parent's stock. The subsidiary receives a corresponding step-up in its basis for the
assets. The purpose of § 336(e) is to put the parent and the subsidiary in the same position as if
the subsidiary had sold its assets in a taxable
transaction and then distributed the sale proceeds
tax free to the parent in a § 332 liquidation.

Example: X Corp. originally contributed $500 to
its subsidiary, Y Corp., in exchange for all of Y's
stock. Y used the $500 to purchase property that
subsequently appreciated to $1,000. X then sold
the Y stock to P Corp. for $1,000, the fair market
value of Y's assets. If X elects under § 336(e) to
treat the stock sale as an asset transfer, the

deemed asset sale will trigger a $500 gain ($1,000 amount realized less Y's $500 basis in its assets). X will recognize no gain or loss on the actual sale of its Y stock. The new basis of Y's assets will be $1,000 (the fair market value). If Y immediately sells its assets for $1,000, no further gain or loss will be recognized. This result is proper because the gain inherent in Y's assets has already been taxed to X, and there is no reason to impose an additional tax at the corporate level unless Y's assets appreciate further in value.

If X did not make a § 336(e) election, X would recognize $500 gain on the sale of its Y stock ($1,000 amount realized less $500 stock basis), but Y's basis in its assets would still be $500. Thus, Y would recognize a $500 gain on an actual sale of its assets for $1,000. The same $500 of economic gain would hence be taxed twice at the corporate level, once to X on the sale of X's Y stock and again to Y on Y's sale of its assets. Section 336(e) offers relief from this potential multiple taxation of the same economic gain by providing a corresponding step-up in the basis of the subsidiary's assets when appreciated subsidiary stock is sold.

§ 6. Sale of a Corporate Business: § 338

(a) *Overview.* Ownership of a corporate business may be sold either in the form of the shareholders' stock or in the form of the corporation's assets. A sale of corporate assets followed by a liquidating distribution to shareholders will generate gain both at the corporate level and at the shareholder level. The purchaser, of course, will have a cost basis in the assets equal to their fair market value. Alternatively, the shareholders may sell their stock at the cost of only a shareholder-level tax. The basis of the corporate assets will not be stepped up, however, and any unrealized appreciation in the assets will be preserved. From the shareholders' standpoint, a stock sale may be preferable because any contingent liabilities will become the responsibility of the purchaser. On the other hand, the purchaser may seek to shift the risk of contingent liabilities back to the selling shareholders by demanding warranties as to the corporation's financial condition or by depositing part of the purchase price in escrow pending resolution of the contingent liabilities.

Prior to the repeal of the *General Utilities* doctrine in the 1986 Act, an acquisition of a corporate business preceded or followed by a complete liquidation offered significant advantages. Section 338, originally enacted in 1982, is intended to permit equal treatment for a purchase of corporate stock and a purchase of corporate assets. Section 338 was drastically revised in 1986 to reflect the repeal of the *General Utilities* doctrine, and its attractiveness is greatly reduced under present law. Nonetheless, § 338 could become increasingly important if preferential tax rates for capital gains are reintroduced.

(b) *Mechanics of § 338.* In order to be eligible to make a § 338 election, a purchasing corporation

(P) must make a "qualified stock purchase," *i.e.*, P must purchase at least 80% of the total voting power and at least 80% of the total value of the stock of the target corporation (T) during a 12–month acquisition period. § 338(d)(3). The term "purchase" is generally defined as any acquisition of stock (other than from certain related parties) in a taxable transaction. § 338(h)(3). The 12–month acquisition period begins to run on the date of the first purchase of stock included in a qualified stock purchase. Under § 338(g), P must make the election no later than the 15th day of the ninth month beginning after the month which includes the acquisition date (*i.e.*, the date on which the 80% stock purchase requirement is met). If P makes a § 338 election, the original target corporation (old T) is deemed to sell its assets to a new corporation (new T) at fair market value. § 338(a). The deemed sale is treated as occurring at the close of the acquisition date. § 338(a)(1). New T takes a basis in the assets of old T determined by reference to the purchase price for old T's stock, appropriately adjusted for liabilities and other items. § 338(b).

Example: Assume that T owns a single asset with a basis of $500 and a fair market value of $1,000, and that T's only liability is the potential tax of $75 that would be imposed on a sale of its asset. P buys all of T's stock for $925 ($1,000 fair market value of T's asset less potential tax liability of $75). If P makes a § 338 election, T will be treated as selling its asset to new T for $1,000, triggering $500 of gain. New T will receive the asset with a basis of $1,000 ($925 stock purchase price plus the $75 tax liability on the deemed sale of the asset). Since T has only a single asset, the entire $1,000 would be allocated to the basis of that asset. The tax consequences would be identical if T actually sold its asset to P for $1,000, paid $75 tax on the asset sale, and distributed $925 ($1,000 less $75 tax) to T's former shareholders in complete liquidation.

Section 338 quickly becomes more complex if P acquires less than all of T's stock, or if P acquired some T stock before the 12–month acquisition period. In either situation, old T will still be treated as selling its assets to new T at fair market value, triggering taxable gain to old T. New T's basis in old T's assets will be determined by what the Regulations refer to as "adjusted grossed-up basis" (AGUB). This amount depends on four factors: (i) the grossed-up basis of the P's "recently purchased stock" (*i.e.,* stock purchased within the 12–month acquisition period); (ii) the basis of P's "nonrecently purchased stock" (*i.e.,* stock, other than recently purchased stock, held on the acquisition date); (iii) T's liabilities, and (iv) certain other items. Temp. Reg. § 1.338(b)–1T.

Example (1): In the previous example, assume that P purchases 80% of T's stock for $740 (80% of $925). T will still be treated as selling its asset to new T for $1,000 (fair market value), triggering a $75 tax. The basis of the asset in T's hands will be the "grossed-up basis" of P's recently purchased stock (as defined by § 338(b)(4)) plus the $75 tax liability. Under § 338(b)(4), the grossed-up basis of P's recently purchased stock will be its basis in P's hands ($740) multiplied by 100%/80%. The grossed-up basis, $925, is the amount that P would have had to pay to acquire 100% of the T stock, assuming that the 20% minority shareholders had sold their stock for the same average price as P paid for the rest of the T stock. In effect, new T is given a basis increase equal to P's purchase price for 80% of the T stock plus the fair market value of the remaining 20% of the T stock held by minority shareholders. Thus, new T's asset basis will be $1,000 ($925 grossed-up basis plus $75 tax liability), even though minority shareholders are not taxed on the unrealized appreciation in their stock. The result is less than a full double tax because new T's asset basis is stepped up to fair market value but minority shareholders are not taxed as if T actually liquidated.

Example (2): In the previous example, assume that P purchased 20% of T's stock 5 years ago for $100 and then acquired an additional 80% in a qualified stock purchase. The grossed-up basis of P's recently purchased stock, under § 338(b)(4), will be $740 multiplied by 80%/80%. The adjusted grossed-up basis will be the sum of $740 (the grossed-up basis of P's recently purchased stock) plus $100 (the basis of P's nonrecently purchased stock) plus the $75 tax liability. This amount

($915) is less than the fair market value of T's assets ($1,000). Under § 338(b)(3), new T can obtain a $1,000 basis in its assets only if P elects to recognize gain on a hypothetical sale of its nonrecently purchased stock for the average price of the recently purchased stock. The hypothetical sale price would be $185 ($740 times 20%/80%), resulting in an $85 gain to P ($185 less P's stock basis of $100). If P recognizes the $85 gain on the hypothetical sale of its nonrecently purchased T stock, new T can obtain an additional $85 basis in its asset. If P does not elect to recognize this gain, new T's asset basis will be the fair market value of old T's asset ($1,000) less the unrealized appreciation in P's nonrecently purchased stock ($85) or $915. Assuming that T then distributes its property to P in a § 332 liquidation, P will receive a substituted basis of $915 in the distributed asset, thus preserving the unrealized appreciation inherent in P's T stock. The result is two levels of corporate tax on the same $85 of gain, taxed once to T on the deemed § 338 sale and then again to T (or P) on a subsequent sale of the asset.

(c) *Consistency Requirements.* A major concern of § 338 when originally enacted in 1982 was that an acquiring corporation should not be permitted to exploit the *General Utilities* doctrine selectively to obtain a stepped-up basis in some, but not all, of the acquired assets. In addressing this concern with selectivity, § 338 takes an all-or-nothing approach and imposes an exceedingly complex set of

stock and asset consistency rules which survived
the 1986 Act. The stock consistency rules, contained in § 338(f), require that a purchasing corporation that purchases stock of two or more affiliated target corporations within a "consistency
period" treat all such purchases consistently either
as stock acquisitions or as asset acquisitions. The
consistency period is generally defined in § 338(h)
(4) as a period of up to 3 years beginning one year
before the beginning of the 12–month acquisition
period and ending one year after the acquisition
date. The asset consistency rules, contained in
§ 338(e)(1), provide that the purchasing corporation will generally be deemed to have made a
§ 338 election if it purchases the stock of a target
corporation and also acquires an asset of the target
or any target affiliate during the consistency period. The repeal of the *General Utilities* doctrine in
the 1986 Act eliminated the conceptual underpin-
ning of the consistency rules, and various proposals
have been advanced to streamline or abolish these
rules.

(d) *Protective Carryover Election and § 338(h)(10)
Election.* Because the 1986 Act reduced the advantages of § 338 elections, purchasers may wish
to avoid § 338 treatment. The Temporary Regulations permit a purchasing corporation to avoid an
inadvertent election (*i.e.,* a deemed election under
§ 338(e)(1) triggered by a tainted asset acquisition)
by filing a "protective carryover [basis] election"
which generally denies a stepped-up basis in the

purchased assets in the hands of the purchaser.
Temp. Reg. § 1.338–4T(f)(6). If a protective carryover election is not expressly made, the purchaser
will still generally be treated as making an implied
election not to step up basis; the Temporary Regulations define this implied election curiously
enough as an "affirmative action carryover [basis]
election." *Id.* The Service has broad discretion,
however, to override an affirmative action carryover election by treating the purchaser as having
made a deemed election under § 338(e)(1). *Id.*

If an acquiring corporation purchases stock of a
target corporation from the target's parent, a
§ 338(h)(10) election will often be desirable. If
§ 338(h)(10) is elected, the parent will not recognize gain or loss on the sale of the target's stock,
and the target will recognize gain or loss as if it
sold its assets. The treatment of the parent's stock
sale as an asset sale produces the same results as a
§ 336(e) election, permitting the parent to dispose
of the subsidiary with only one tax at the corporate
level tax even though the purchaser obtains a
stepped-up basis in the assets. This election is also
advantageous if the unrealized appreciation in the
subsidiary's assets is less than the unrealized appreciation in the parent's stock.

(e) *Allocation of Basis.* The Temporary Regulations provide detailed rules for allocating the acquiring corporation's basis among the target's assets. Temp. Reg. § 1.338(b)–2T. Before any basis
is allocated, the adjusted grossed-up basis (AGUB)

is first reduced by the amount of cash and similar items to which no basis is allocated. The remaining AGUB is then allocated among all other assets (except goodwill and going-concern value) in proportion to their respective fair market values; the amount of AGUB allocated to any asset may not exceed the asset's fair market value. Any residual basis is then allocated to goodwill and going concern value, which cannot be amortized. This "residual method" of valuing goodwill and going concern value is intended to assign a higher basis to these nonamortizable assets than if a lump-sum purchase price were allocated among assets in proportion to their respective fair market values.

Example: On January 1, 1989, P purchases all of the stock of T, which has assets consisting of $10,000 cash, a building with a fair market value of $100,000, machinery with a fair market value of $20,000 and goodwill of $5,000. If the AGUB is $150,000, this amount would first be reduced to $140,000 by excluding the $10,000 cash. Of the remaining $140,000, $100,000 would be allocated to the building and $20,000 to the machinery (100% of their separate fair market values); the excess, $20,000, would be assigned to goodwill. If the AGUB were only $100,000, the $90,000 remaining after excluding the cash would be allocated entirely between the building and the machinery in proportion to their respective fair market values: the building would receive a basis of $75,000 ($100,000/$120,000 times $90,000) and the machinery a basis of $15,000 ($20,000/$120,000 times $90,000). The goodwill would have a basis of zero because there is no residual basis in excess of the fair market value of the assets.

(f) *New § 1060.* In 1986, Congress enacted § 1060 which applies to any acquisition of assets which constitute a trade or business in a cost-basis transaction, *i.e.,* any transaction in which the transferee's basis in the assets is determined by reference wholly to the consideration paid for the assets. Under § 1060, both the transferee's basis for the assets and the transferor's gain or loss on the transfer will be determined by allocating the consideration received in the same manner as basis allocations under § 338(b)(5). *See* Temp. Reg. § 1.1060–1T. Thus, the residual method of valuing goodwill and going-concern value must be applied in any direct or indirect asset purchase described in § 1060. Although new § 1060 was probably not intended to apply to liquidating distributions, the requirement of § 336(a) that the distributing corporation be treated as selling its assets at fair market value would bring such distributions within the literal terms of § 1060.

§ 7. Techniques for Avoiding Repeal of *General Utilities*

The repeal of the *General Utilities* doctrine leaves several unanswered questions concerning when a corporation can or should be able to avoid gain on a transfer of appreciated property. The 1986 Act (unlike earlier proposals for repealing

General Utilities) provided relief exclusively in the form of transitional rules. Congress failed, however, to provide clear guidance on whether the repeal of *General Utilities* was intended to require recognition of corporate-level gain when appreciated assets are transferred out of an economic unit, but remain in corporate solution and retain their historic basis. Under an expansive view of the *General Utilities* repeal, it might be argued that it is necessary to tax corporate-level gain in such transactions, which combine elements both of stock sales and asset sales, in order to prevent circumvention of the general rule of gain recognition. Under a restrained view of the *General Utilities* repeal, however, it might be argued that corporate-level gain should be taxed only when the assets receive a stepped-up basis as a result of a transfer. In the 1987 Act, Congress apparently opted for the expansive view, as illustrated by the response to so-called "mirror transactions."

Example: A purchasing corporation (P) desires to acquire all of the stock of a target corporation (T) for $200. T operates two divisions, T1 and T2, each with appreciated assets worth $100. P wishes to keep T1 but plans to sell T2 to an unrelated buyer. If P purchases the assets of both T1 and T2 directly, corporate-level gain will be recognized on the assets of both divisions. If P purchases T's stock and sells the unwanted assets of T2, there will be corporate-level gain on T2's assets. In order to avoid gain on the T2 assets, P forms a subsidiary, S, capitalized with $100 to "mirror" the fair market value of the unwanted T2 assets. P and S each acquire 50% of the T stock; T then liquidates, distributing the T1 assets to P and the T2 assets to S. The liquidation of T will be tax free under § 337 if, but only if, the stock ownership of P and S can be aggregated to meet the 80% requirement of § 332. P can then sell the stock of S (now containing the unwanted T2 assets) without recognizing gain; the purchaser of the S stock will not obtain a stepped-up basis in the T2 assets, however, unless § 338 is elected, triggering recognition of the gain inherent in the T2 assets.

The 1987 Act amended § 337(c) to provide that the 80% requirement of § 332 must be met by direct ownership, without regard to certain provisions in the consolidated return regulations that arguably permitted the result described above. Since P and S each acquired only 50% of the T stock separately, § 337 will not apply to the liquidation of T, and all of T's gain on the T1 and T2 assets must be recognized under § 336. If P had acquired 80% of T's stock directly and S the remainder, P (but not S) would qualify as an 80% distributee, and only 80% of T's gain would be entitled to nonrecognition; recognition of the remaining 20% of T's gain might be deferred, however, under the consolidated return regulations until a subsequent disqualifying event (*e.g.,* a sale of the S stock outside the consolidated group).

§ 8. Liquidation-Reincorporation Problems

A complete liquidation contemplates a termination of the corporation as an entity and a winding-up of its affairs. Liquidation-reincorporation problems may arise if the corporation's assets are distributed to shareholders who then form a new corporation to carry on the old business, or if some shareholders are shareholders of another corporation which acquires the liquidating corporation's operating assets. Under prior law, the benefits of liquidation treatment consisted of a step-up in the basis of the corporate assets, the elimination of accumulated e & p, and distribution of unwanted nonoperating assets without dividend treatment. Since the liquidating corporation escaped gain on unrealized appreciation of its assets, the tax cost of a successful liquidation-reincorporation was limited to a single capital gains tax at the shareholder level. The Service employed a variety of weapons to defeat liquidation-reincorporation plans. A "failed" liquidation-reincorporation might be reclassified as a § 368 reorganization, with gain to the continuing shareholders taxable as a § 301 distribution to the extent of any "boot" received. In 1984, Congress also amended § 368 to facilitate treatment as a D-reorganization. *See* Chapter 8. Although the liquidation-reincorporation issue may not be entirely dead, the 1986 Act's imposition of a corporate-level tax on unrealized appreciation has significantly diminished its importance.

§ 9. Collapsible Corporations: § 341

(a) *Overview.* Section 341 is intended to prevent a taxpayer from converting unrealized ordinary gain at the corporate level into capital gain at the shareholder level by means of a "collapsible corporation." Although the collapsible-corporation problem arose under pre–1986 law and is effectively eliminated by other provisions of present law, § 341 survived the 1986 Act virtually intact. In a typical § 341 situation, an individual forms a corporation to build an apartment building, intending to liquidate the corporation (or sell his stock) upon completion of the construction. Under prior law (other than § 341), if the corporation distributed the improved property in liquidation, the corporation would recognize no gain on the distribution and the shareholder would be taxed on the appreciation at favorable capital gains rates. Alternatively, if the shareholder merely sold his stock without liquidating the corporation, the shareholder would also be taxed at capital gains rates. In either case, a shareholder who was a real estate dealer would avoid being taxed on the appreciation at the ordinary income rates imposed on a direct sale of the improved property.

Section 341 requires that the shareholder's gain on liquidation of a collapsible corporation (or a sale of collapsible-corporation stock) be taxed as ordinary income rather than capital gain. By repealing the preferential capital gain rates of prior law, the 1986 Act effectively neutralized the § 341 penalty (although shareholders with large capital losses may still prefer capital gain treatment in order to offset the losses currently). Even if preferential capital gains rates are reintroduced, however, the repeal of the *General Utilities* doctrine has further reduced the attractiveness of collapsible corporations: distributions of appreciated property are now subject to tax at the corporate level. Although a shareholder might nevertheless sell his stock, the purchase price would probably be reduced to reflect the built-in corporate-level tax liability. Given the diminished importance of § 341 after the 1986 Act, its provisions are discussed only briefly here.

(b) *Definition of Collapsible Corporation.* A collapsible corporation is any corporation "formed or availed of principally for the manufacture, construction or production of property" (or purchase of property under certain circumstances), "with a view to" sale, liquidation or distribution before the corporation realizes ⅔ of the taxable income to be derived from the property (and realization by shareholders of gain attributable to the property). § 341(b). If these requirements are met, shareholders must generally report as ordinary income any gain from a sale or exchange of stock, a distribution in partial or complete liquidation or a nonliquidating distribution that would otherwise be treated as long-term capital gain. § 341(a). *See also* Reg. § 1.341–4(a). Since most corporations are concededly organized and operated to manufacture, construct or produce property, the crucial issue is usually whether the corporation is formed or availed of with a view to sale, liquidation or distribution. The Regulations provide that the requisite view is present if such action was "contemplated, unconditionally, conditionally or as a recognized possibility," by those in a position to determine the policies of the corporation at any time during the manufacture, construction or production of the property. Reg. § 1.341–2(a)(2). Section 341 generally does not apply, however, if the requisite view is formed subsequently as a result of circumstances that could not reasonably have been foreseen at the time of manufacture, construction or production of the property (*e.g.,* ill health of a major shareholder arising after production of property). Reg. § 1.341–2(a)(3). *See* Computer Sciences Corp. (1974).

A corporation will also be collapsible if it is formed or availed of to purchase "§ 341 assets" with the requisite view to sale, exchange or distribution. "Section 341 assets" are defined in § 341(b)(3) to include inventory, property held for sale to customers, unrealized receivables and certain § 1231 property. The inclusion of § 1231 property is intended to prevent real estate dealers from converting ordinary income into capital gain by forming a separate corporation for each venture. Even if the shareholders are not dealers and would otherwise be entitled to capital gain, however, § 341(b)(3)(D) imposes § 341 treatment on the typical real estate holding company, subject to the "escape-hatch" provisions of § 341(e), discussed below. Regardless of the type of property involved, § 341 assets are limited to assets held for less than 3 years by the corporation. The 3–year holding period only begins to run, however, after completion of manufacture, construction, production or purchase. § 341(b)(3) (last sentence).

(c) *Presumption of Collapsibility.* Collapsibility is presumed if the fair market value of the corporation's § 341 assets is (i) 50% or more of the fair market value of total assets and (ii) 120% or more of the adjusted basis of such § 341 assets. § 341(c). To prevent circumvention of these tests, § 341(c) provides that cash, stock and certain securities may not be taken into account in determining the fair market value of the corporation's total assets.

(d) *Limitations of § 341(d).* Even if a corporation is determined to be collapsible under § 341(b), § 341(d) provides three limitations on ordinary income treatment, applied on a shareholder-by-shareholder basis. First, ordinary income treatment applies only to a shareholder who has at some time owned (actually or constructively) more than 5% in value of the corporation's stock. § 341(d)(1). Second, ordinary income treatment applies only if more than 70% of a shareholder's gain on sale, liquidation or distribution in a taxable year is attributable to collapsible property. § 341(d)(2). This rule is important if the corporation owns two or more separate properties, and has realized ⅔ of

the taxable income attributable to at least one of
the properties. If 30% of the shareholder's total
gain is attributable to property on which there has
been adequate realization (*i.e.,* noncollapsible property), then none of the shareholder's gain will
subject to § 341(a), even if the remaining 70% is
attributable to collapsible property. In order to
prevent manipulation of this rule, Congress
amended § 341(d) in 1984 to permit the Treasury
to aggregate all of the corporation's inventory assets in applying the 70% test. § 341(d) (last sentence). Finally, ordinary income treatment does
not apply to a shareholder's gain realized more
than 3 years after the corporation completes manufacture, construction, production or purchase of the
property. § 341(d)(3). This provision is potentially
risky, however, since the 3–year holding period
begins to run only upon completion and it may be
unclear whether particular property comprises a
single completed project or a series of ongoing
projects. Any portion of the shareholder's gain
attributable to property completed more than 3
years earlier should be treated as capital gain,
even if the shareholder's remaining gain is taxed
as ordinary income.

(e) *Escape Hatch of § 341(e).* Section 341(e) is
intended to permit a shareholder to receive capital
gain treatment on a sale of stock of a collapsible
corporation if the gain is attributable to property
which would be capital gain property in the hands
of the shareholder. This "escape hatch" is neces-

sary to mitigate the broad definition of § 341 assets in § 341(b)(3)(D), which includes certain § 1231 assets (*e.g.,* rental apartment buildings). Section 341(e) operates by reference to the net unrealized appreciation in the corporation's "subsection (e) assets" (roughly speaking, those assets which would produce ordinary income in the hands of the corporation or in the hands of any shareholder owning more than 20% of the corporation's stock).

If the net unrealized appreciation in the corporation's "subsection (e) assets" does not exceed 15% of the corporation's net worth, a sale of stock will result in capital gain treatment to any shareholder who owns 5% or less of the corporation's stock. If the shareholder owns more than 5% of the corporation's stock, he must take into account both the corporation's "subsection (e) assets" plus any corporate assets that would be ordinary income assets in his hands (if owned directly) in applying the 15% test. If the shareholder owns more than 20% of the corporation's stock, he must also take into account any corporate assets that would be ordinary income assets (if owned directly), assuming that he held in his individual capacity the property of certain other corporations in which he was a more-than-20% shareholder during the preceding 3 years. Moreover, if a more-than-20% shareholder would be classified as a dealer in the property in question, the character of the property in the corporation's hands will be tainted, adversely affecting all of the shareholders (regardless of their percentage of stock ownership) for purposes of § 341(e).

Example: A (an investor) and B (a real estate dealer) form X Corp. which holds an appreciated apartment building as its sole asset. If B owns 20% or less of X's stock, B's status as a dealer will not be imputed to X. The apartment building will not be a "subsection (e) asset" in X's hands, and the net unrealized appreciation under § 341(e)(1) will be zero (assuming X is not a dealer). Thus, A will receive capital gain treatment if he sells his stock; and so will B if he owns 5% or less of X's stock. If B owns more than 5% of X's stock, B will recognize ordinary income if the net unrealized appreciation in the apartment building exceeds 15% of X's net worth. If B owns more than 20% of the stock, B's status as a dealer will be attributed to the corporation and the apartment building will be treated as a "subsection (e) asset" in X's hands; both shareholders will receive ordinary income treatment, therefore, if the net unrealized appreciation in the apartment building exceeds 15% of X's net worth. (If A owns 5% or less of X's stock, he may nevertheless escape ordinary income treatment under the alternative route of § 341(d), which makes § 341(a) inapplicable to 5%-or-less shareholders.)

(f) *Amnesty of § 341(f).* Section 341(f) provides an additional escape hatch from ordinary income treatment on a sale of stock of a collapsible corporation if the corporation consents to recognize its gain on "subsection (f) assets" (primarily real estate, unrealized receivables and non-capital assets) when it disposes of them in certain transactions that would otherwise qualify for nonrecognition treatment. When § 341(f) was enacted, a corporation could escape gain by distributing its assets in complete liquidation. Because a liquidating corporation must recognize gain in any event under present law, the additional burden imposed by a § 341(f) consent is negligible. Although a § 341(f) consent thus imposes no additional burden on the corporation, it also offers less advantage than under prior law because of the elimination of the preferential capital gain on the shareholder's sale of stock.

CHAPTER 7

STOCK DIVIDENDS

§ 1. General

A stock dividend is a distribution by a corporation of its own stock to shareholders. Under § 305(a), a stock dividend is generally tax free to the recipient, unless the distribution falls within one of the exceptions in § 305(b). If § 305(b) applies, the distribution is taxed under the rules of § 301 for nonliquidating distributions discussed in Chapter 4.

In *Eisner v. Macomber* (1920), the Supreme Court held that a taxpayer did not recognize income on receipt of a common stock dividend, when the only class of stock outstanding was common stock. This result, while probably not constitutionally required, is reflected in the general rule under § 305(a) for distributions of common stock with respect to common stock. For many years after the *Macomber* decision, a stock dividend was taxable only if it increased the recipient's proportionate interest in the corporation. To provide greater certainty in applying the proportionate interest test, Congress in 1969 enacted the statutory rules of § 305(b); it also added § 305(c) to ensure that § 305(b) would not be circumvented by transactions having an effect similar to taxable stock dividends.

If a stock dividend is nontaxable under § 305(a), it may nevertheless be classified as "§ 306 stock." The principal purpose of § 306 is to prevent a "preferred stock bailout," *i.e.,* a tax-free distribution of preferred stock to a shareholder who then sells the stock to a third party at capital gain rates. When applicable, § 306 treats some or all of the gain recognized on a sale or other disposition of § 306 stock as ordinary income.

§ 2. Basis of Tax–Free Stock Dividends: § 307

A tax-free stock dividend typically represents a reallocation of the shareholders' preexisting investment among an increased number of shares; the aggregate value of the shareholders' investment does not change, but the value of each share decreases to reflect the increased number of outstanding shares. Accordingly, when a shareholder who already owns stock ("old stock") receives a distribution of additional stock ("new stock") as a tax-free § 305(a) dividend, § 307(a) requires that the shareholder allocate his aggregate adjusted basis in the old stock (determined immediately before the distribution) among the old stock and the new stock. The Regulations require that the shareholder's basis be allocated in proportion to the respective fair market values of the old and new stock on the date of the distribution. Reg. § 1.307–1(a).

Example: Assume that A owns 50 shares of common stock of X Corp., with an aggregate adjusted basis of $1,200. If A receives 10 additional shares of common stock as a tax-free stock dividend, his $1,200 basis in the old stock must be reallocated among the 60 shares of X stock owned by A after the distribution. Assuming that each share of X stock is of equal value, A will have a basis of $20 per share of X stock (both old and new) immediately after the distribution.

If different classes of stock are involved, basis is allocated in proportion to the fair market value of each class. In the example above, assume that the fair market value of A's common stock is $10,000 immediately before the distribution and A receives 10 shares of a new class of preferred stock with a fair market value of $1,000; the distribution leaves A's common stock with a value of $9,000. Of A's $1,200 aggregate basis in the old stock, 10% ($120) will be allocated to the preferred stock and 90% ($1,080) to the common stock in proportion to their respective fair market values ($1,000 and $9,000).

The holding period of new stock received tax free under § 305(a) "tacks" onto the holding period of the old stock. § 1223(5). Thus, any gain will be long or short-term capital gain, depending on the shareholder's holding period for the original shares. In keeping with the tax-free nature of the distribution, the corporation's e & p is not reduced by a § 305(a) stock dividend. § 312(d)(1)(B).

§ 3. Taxable Stock Dividends: § 305(b)

(a) *General.* A distribution of stock (or stock rights) is taxable as a § 301 distribution if, but only if, it falls within one of the exceptions of § 305(b). Under § 301(b), the amount of the distribution is the fair market value of the distributed stock. The shareholder recognizes ordinary income if the corporation has sufficient e & p to cover the distribution; the remainder is treated as basis recovery and any excess as capital gain. § 301(c). The shareholder takes a basis in the distributed stock equal to its fair market value under § 301(d); there is no tacking of holding periods. At the corporate level, a taxable stock dividend may be viewed as a distribution of cash equal to the fair market value of the distributed stock: the corporation recognizes no gain under § 311, and the corporation's e & p is reduced (but not below zero) by the fair market value of the distributed property. *See* § 312(a); Reg. § 1.312–1(d).

(b) *Optional Distributions: § 305(b)(1).* If any shareholder can elect to receive a cash distribution in lieu of a stock dividend, the distribution is taxable to all of the shareholders under § 305(b)(1), even if the shareholder actually elects to receive only stock. In the case of a § 305(b)(1) taxable stock dividend, a shareholder who receives cash is taxed directly under § 301, and a shareholder who receives stock is taxed under §§ 305(b)(1) and 301 as if he had received cash and used it to purchase additional shares. The amount of the § 301 distribution to shareholders receiving stock is the greater of the fair market value of the stock or the amount of cash which they might have received. Rev. Rul. 76–53.

Under § 305(b)(1), it does not matter whether the election to receive stock or cash is exercisable before or after the declaration of the stock dividend. Section 305(b)(1) also applies to "dividend reinvestment plans" which permit a shareholder to elect to receive stock of a greater value than the cash dividend or to purchase additional shares at a discount. Rev. Rul. 78–375. Similarly, the Service has held that a pro-rata distribution of preferred stock that is immediately redeemable at the shareholder's option is taxable under § 305(b)(1). Rev. Rul. 76–258; Rev. Rul. 83–68. *But see* Colonial Sav. Ass'n (1988) (§ 305(b)(1) inapplicable because corporation had discretion to redeem).

(c) *Disproportionate Distributions: § 305(b)(2).* Under § 305(b)(2) tax-free treatment is denied in the case of a distribution that increases the proportionate interests of some shareholders in the assets or earnings of the corporation, while other shareholders receive cash (or other property). The Regulations provide that the requirement of an accompanying distribution may be met regardless of whether "the stock distributions and cash distributions are steps in an overall plan or are independent and unrelated." Reg. § 1.305–3(b)(2). If the distribution of cash or other property occurs more than 36 months before or after the stock distribution, however, the Regulations presume that the distributions are outside § 305(b)(2), unless the distributions are part of an integrated plan. Reg. § 1.305–3(b)(4).

Example (1). X Corp. has two classes of common stock outstanding, Class A and Class B, which are identical except that the X pays stock dividends on Class A and cash dividends on Class B. The distributions of cash to the Class B shareholders are taxed under § 301. The distributions of stock to the Class A shareholders are taxed under §§ 305(b)(2) and 301, because the interest of the Class A shareholders in the assets and earnings of X has increased while the Class B shareholders have received property. Reg. 1.305–3(e), Example 1.

Example (2). X Corp. has two classes of stock outstanding, Class A common stock and Class B nonconvertible preferred stock. X pays stock dividends on Class A and cash dividends on Class B. The Class B shareholders receiving cash are taxed under § 301. The distribution of common stock on common stock to the Class A shareholders, however, is tax free under § 305(a). Since the Class A common stockholders have the entire right to the residual assets and earnings of X both before and after the distribution, there has been no increase in their proportionate interests. Reg. § 1.305–3(e), Example (2).

The outcome would be different, however, if the Class B stock were convertible preferred stock, *e.g.,* if each share of Class B preferred were convertible into one share of Class A common. In that case, the stock dividend to the Class A shareholders would increase the total number of outstanding Class A shares; unless the conversion ratio were adjusted, however, the interests of the existing Class A shareholders (who receive additional Class A shares) in X's residual earnings and assets would be increased relative to the interests of the Class B shareholders (who do not receive a right to additional Class A shares). Accordingly, if the Class B stock is convertible preferred stock with a fixed conversion ratio, the Class A shareholders should be taxed under §§ 305(b)(2) and 301 on the distribution of additional shares of common stock. Reg. § 1.305–3(e), Example (4).

Example (3). X Corp. has two classes of stock outstanding, Class A common stock and Class B nonconvertible preferred stock. X declares a stock dividend on the Class A stock, payable in Class B stock, and declares a cash dividend on the Class B stock. The distribution of cash to the Class B shareholders is taxed under § 301. The Class A shareholders have increased their proportionate interest in the assets and earnings of X, because they are now entitled to share in any future dividends and liquidating proceeds allocable to the preferred stock. Accordingly, the distribution of preferred stock to the Class A shareholders is taxed under §§ 305(b)(2) and 301.

The Regulations provide an exception to § 305(b)(2) if the corporation declares a dividend payable in stock and distributes cash in lieu of fractional shares. The stock distribution is not taxable under § 305(b)(2), provided that the purpose for the cash payment is to save the corporation the "trouble, expense, and inconvenience" of issuing fractional shares. Reg. § 1.305–3(c).

(d) *Distributions of Common and Preferred: § 305(b)(3).* A distribution of common stock to some common stockholders and preferred stock to other common stockholders is taxable under § 305(b)(3). A § 305(b)(3) distribution, like a § 305(b)(2) distribution, alters the proportionate interests within the class of common stockholders. Technically, a § 305(b)(3) distribution might fail to meet the accompanying distribution test of § 305(b)(2), however, because the definition of "property" under § 317(a) excludes stock of the distributing corporation. Section 305(b)(3) overcomes this technical difficulty by providing specifically for the taxability of such distributions.

(e) *Distributions on Preferred: § 305(b)(4).* Any distribution on preferred stock (other than certain adjustments in conversion ratios) is taxable under § 305(b)(4). The Regulations define preferred stock generally as any stock which has "limited rights and privileges (generally associated with specified dividend and liquidation priorities) but does not participate in corporate growth to any significant extent." Reg. § 1.305–5(a). Thus, stock which has a fixed priority as to dividends and liquidations will generally be preferred stock. If stock has both priority as to dividends and liquidations and, in addition, a meaningful right to participate in corporate growth, it is not preferred stock.

Example: X Corp. has two classes of stock outstanding, Class A common stock and Class B preferred stock. X distributes preferred stock to the Class A stockholders and common stock to the Class B stockholders. The distribution of common stock on the preferred stock held by the Class B stockholders is taxable under § 305(b)(4). The distribution of common stock to the Class B stockholders is therefore treated as a distribution of "property" for purposes of § 305(b), and the distribution of preferred stock on the Class A common stock increases the proportionate interest of the Class A stockholders in the assets and earnings of X. § 305(b)(2). Accordingly, the distribution to the Class A shareholders is taxed under § 305(b)(2).

The exception under § 305(b)(4) for certain adjustments in the conversion ratio of convertible preferred stock permits tax-free adjustment of conversion ratios in order to avoid dilution of the preferred stockholders' proportionate interests. The Service has held that the anti-dilution exception is limited to changes in conversion ratios, and does not apply to an actual distribution on preferred stock. Thus, if a corporation distributes common stock to holders of its convertible pre-

ferred stock to compensate for a stock dividend on
common stock into which the preferred stock is
convertible, the Service has ruled that the preferred stockholders are taxed under § 305(b)(4),
even if the distribution has the same effect as a
change in conversion ratios (which could be accomplished tax free). Rev. Rul. 83–42.

(f) *Distributions of Convertible Preferred:
§ 305(b)(5).* Distributions of convertible preferred
stock are taxable under § 305(b)(5) unless the corporation can establish that they will not result in a
disproportionate distribution within the meaning
of § 305(b)(2).   The Regulations provide further
that a distribution of convertible preferred is ordinarily not taxable if the conversion rights may be
exercised over a long period (*e.g.,* 20 years) and the
dividend rate is consistent with market rates at the
time of distribution.   Reg. § 1.305–6.   Conversely,
a distribution of convertible preferred is taxable if
the conversion period is relatively short and it may
be anticipated that some shareholders will exercise
their conversion rights while others will not.   The
likelihood that some (but not all) shareholders will
exercise their conversion rights indicates that the
end result will be a disproportionate distribution
within the meaning of § 305(b)(2).

§ 4. Deemed Distributions: § 305(c)

Under § 305(c), certain transactions are treated
as distributions of property to shareholders, even
in the absence of an actual stock dividend, if they
increase the proportionate interest of any share-

holder in earnings or assets of the corporation. The transactions covered by § 305(c) include: a change in conversion ratio or redemption price, a difference between redemption price and issue price, a redemption treated as a § 301 distribution, and any transaction (including a recapitalization) having a similar effect on the interest of any stockholder. A "deemed distribution" is taxable under § 305(c) if it has a result described in § 305(b)(2)–(5). Reg. § 1.305–7(a).

Example: X Corp. has two shareholders, A and B, each of whom owns 50 shares of X stock. If X redeems 20 of A's shares for cash, A's proportionate interest will decrease from 50% to 37.5% (satisfying the "substantially disproportionate" requirement of § 302(b)(2)), and the redemption will be treated as an exchange under § 302(a) rather than a distribution under § 301. If only 10 of A's shares were redeemed, however, the "substantially disproportionate" requirement would not be met, and the redemption would be treated as a § 301 distribution. The deemed distribution rules of § 305 would then apply, and B (the non-redeeming shareholder) would be treated as receiving a constructive dividend due to the increase in his proportionate interest (from 50% to 55.56%). Thus, any redemption to which § 301 applies could potentially trigger a deemed § 305(c) distribution to the shareholders whose stock is not redeemed.

Fortunately, the Regulations provide relief from § 305(c) treatment in this situation, restricting

such treatment to transactions that are part of a
"plan to periodically increase a shareholder's proportionate interest" in the corporation's assets or
earnings. Reg. § 1.305–7(c). The Regulations con-
firm that an isolated redemption is not taxable
under § 305(c), regardless of whether the redemption is treated as a § 301 distribution or a § 302
exchange. Reg. §§ 1.305–3(b)(3) (last sentence) and
1.305–3(e), Example (10). The result is the same
even if a stock dividend is distributed at the same
time as the isolated redemption. Reg. § 1.305–3(e),
Example (11). Similarly, typical recapitalizations
involving a transfer of control from one generation
to another are exempted from § 305(c) treatment.
Reg. § 1.305–3(e), Example 12. *See* Chapter 8.

If a corporation offers to redeem a certain percentage of its stock annually, however, the transaction may fall under § 305(c) as part of a plan for
periodic increases in the proportionate interests of
some shareholders. The Service has held, for example, that periodic redemptions taxable as § 301
distributions to the shareholders whose stock was
redeemed also triggered § 305(c) constructive dividends taxable to the other shareholders under
§§ 305(b)(2) and 301. Rev. Rul. 78–60. If the
redemptions had qualified for exchange treatment
under § 302, however, § 305(c) would not have
applied.

If a corporation issues preferred stock which
may be redeemed after a specified period of time at
a price higher than the issue price, the excess of

the redemption price over the issue price may be treated as a constructive dividend under § 305(c). Reg. § 1.305–5(b). The Regulations provide an exception, however, for "reasonable redemption premiums"; a redemption premium not in excess of 10% of the issue price of stock which is not redeemable for 5 years from the date of issuance will be considered reasonable. *Id.;* Reg. § 1.305–5(d), Example (4). *See* Rev. Rul. 83–119 (excess redemption premium taxable as constructive § 305(b)(4) dividend over life of shareholder where preferred stock not redeemable until death).

§ 5. Distribution of Stock Rights

For purposes of § 305(a), rights to acquire stock are treated as stock, and an owner of such rights is treated as a shareholder. § 305(d). The basis of stock rights, if received tax free, is determined under § 307. If the rights are exercised or sold, basis is allocated between the old stock and the new rights in accordance with their respective fair market values. Reg. § 1.307–1(a) (last sentence). If the rights expire or lapse in the shareholder's hands, no deduction is allowed and the basis of the old stock is unaffected. If the value of the rights is less than 15% of the fair market value of the stock with respect to which the rights are distributed, the shareholder takes a zero basis in the rights unless he elects to allocate basis under § 307. § 307(b). If the shareholder later exercises a right to acquire stock, his basis in the acquired stock will be the exercise price plus any basis originally allocated to the right. The holding period of the acquired stock begins on the date of exercise. § 1223(6).

§ 6. Non-pro-rata Stock Surrenders

A non-pro-rata surrender of stock does not fit easily within any of the Code provisions. It may resemble a stock dividend to the non-surrendering shareholders whose proportionate interests are increased or a contribution to capital by the surrendering shareholder. In *Fink* (1987), the Supreme Court held that no deductible loss arises when a dominant shareholder surrenders some stock non pro rata but retains voting control over the corporation after the surrender. *See also* Schleppy (1979) and Frantz (1986) (both disallowing losses on non-pro-rata surrenders). The Supreme Court treated the surrender as a nontaxable contribution to capital, even though there was no increase in the corporation's net worth. Thus, the shareholder's basis in the surrendered shares was shifted to his basis in the remaining stock, and the determination of the shareholder's economic loss was postponed until later sale or disposition.

The Supreme Court's decision in *Fink,* however, leaves open several questions of interpretation. Instead of adopting a bright-line rule that non-pro-rata stock surrenders do not give rise to a deductible loss, the Supreme Court limited its holding to surrenders by "dominant" shareholders who retain "control." A concurring opinion would have reached the same result even if the surrendering shareholder had not retained control. Moreover, the majority's opinion suggests that § 302(b)(2) may provide an appropriate analogy in determining whether the reduction in the shareholder's interest after the surrender is sufficiently substantial to warrant loss recognition.

As an alternative to issuance of stock by a corporation to a valued employee (as an incentive to continue employment), a shareholder may transfer outstanding stock to the employee. Such a transfer of stock by a shareholder to an employee is treated as a capital contribution. Reg. § 1.83–6(d); Tilford (1983). Although the Sixth Circuit's *Tilford* decision was premised on the congressional intent reflected in the Regulations under § 83(b), the Supreme Court's holding in *Fink* would seem to reach the same result in this situation.

§ 7. Non-payment of Dividends: Potential Gift

If a controlling shareholder periodically waives his right to payment of annual noncumulative dividends on preferred stock, the waiver indirectly increases the value of the common stock held by the other shareholders. In Letter Ruling 8723007, the Service held that such a waiver constituted a taxable gift to the other shareholders (trusts for the benefit of the waiving shareholder's grandchildren). The Service rejected the argument that no taxable gift should be imputed where the failure to pay dividends was based on the corporation's need to retain the funds for internal corporate purposes.

See also Letter Ruling 8726005 (failure of preferred shareholder to convert convertible preferred stock into common stock diverted earnings to common shareholders and gave rise to a taxable gift).

§ 8. Preferred Stock Bailouts: § 306

(a) *General.*   Section 306 is intended to prevent a preferred stock bailout in which shareholders receive a tax-free distribution of preferred stock on their common stock and then sell the preferred stock to a third party. A typical bailout transaction is illustrated by the facts of *Chamberlain* (1953), in which a corporation distributed a new class of preferred stock tax free to its common shareholders; the shareholders then sold the new preferred stock to an outside investor, with the expectation that the preferred stock would be redeemed over a period of several years. The end result was that the old shareholders received cash on the sale of the preferred stock, recovered their allocable basis in the preferred stock tax free while reporting capital gain on the sale proceeds in excess of basis, and retained undiminished control over the corporation. Congress responded to *Chamberlain* by enacting § 306, which characterizes certain tax-free stock dividends as "§ 306 stock" and taxes as ordinary income some or all of the proceeds received on a sale or other disposition of § 306 stock. After the 1986 Act, the problem of converting ordinary income into capital gain is attenuated as long as the rates remain identical. Nevertheless, § 306 still serves to prevent shareholders from exploiting the *Chamberlain* pattern to recover a portion of their basis tax free.

(b) *Definition of § 306 Stock.* Section 306 operates by "tainting" preferred stock received as a tax-free stock dividend. Under § 306(c)(1)(A), § 306 stock is defined to include any stock (other than common stock issued with respect to common stock) which is received wholly or partially tax free under § 305(a). Section 306 stock also includes stock (other than common stock) received in a tax-free reorganization or § 355 exchange if receipt of the stock is essentially equivalent to a stock dividend. § 306(c)(1)(B). It also generally includes stock having a basis determined by reference to the basis of § 306 stock, *e.g.,* stock received as a gift under § 1015 or in exchange for § 306 stock under § 351. § 306(c)(1)(C). *See* Reg. § 1.306–3(e). Stock having a basis stepped up (or down) under § 1014 (relating to property acquired from a decedent), however, is not § 306 stock in the hands of the transferee.

Section 306 stock does not include any stock received tax free if the distributing corporation had no earnings and profits at the time of the distribution. § 306(c)(2); Reg. § 1.306–3(a). The applicability of this exception depends essentially on whether a distribution of cash in lieu of stock would have been a dividend at the time of distribution. If the corporation lacked e & p, a cash distribution would not have been treated as a dividend, and the rationale for tainting the stock re-

ceived in lieu of cash does not apply. If the corporation had *any* e & p, however, all (not merely a
portion) of the stock received is treated as § 306
stock.

The definition of § 306 stock means that a distribution of common stock on common stock can
never be § 306 stock; thus, § 306 applies essentially to preferred stock. For this purpose, preferred
stock is stock which does not participate to a significant extent in corporate growth. *See, e.g.,* Rev.
Rul. 82–191. A distribution of common stock is not
viewed as offering the same bailout potential because a subsequent sale of the common stock would
diminish the shareholder's interest in the corporation.

In 1982, Congress added § 306(c)(3), which treats
stock (other than common stock) acquired in a
§ 351 transaction as § 306 stock if a distribution of
cash (in lieu of stock) would have been taxable as a
dividend. In determining dividend equivalency,
rules similar to those of § 304(b)(2) apply. *See*
Chapter 5. This provision prevents taxpayers from
avoiding a § 306 taint by transferring common
stock of one corporation (X) to a newly-formed,
commonly-controlled corporation (Y) with no earnings and profits, in exchange for Y preferred stock.
Under § 306(c)(3), the transfer will be tested to
determine whether the shareholders would have
had a dividend on a distribution of cash in lieu of
the Y preferred stock. Although Y has no e & p,
§ 304(b)(2) requires that X's e & p be taken into

account. If X has any e & p, the Y preferred stock will be tainted § 306 stock because a cash distribution would have resulted in a dividend under § 304.

§ 9. Operation of § 306

On redemption or other disposition of § 306 stock, the tax consequences are determined under § 306(a), subject to exceptions under § 306(b).

(a) *Redemptions: § 306(a)(2).* If § 306 stock is redeemed, the entire amount realized is treated as a § 301 distribution. § 306(a)(2). The amount received is taxable as ordinary income to the extent of e & p at the time of the redemption, and any excess is treated as basis recovery or capital gain under § 301(c). Presumably, basis recovery is allowed against the shareholder's aggregate basis, not merely the basis allocated to the redeemed § 306 stock.

(b) *Other Dispositions: § 306(a)(1).* If § 306 stock is disposed of other than by redemption, the amount realized is treated as ordinary income to the extent of the shareholder's ratable share of e & p as of the time of the distribution of the § 306 stock. § 306(a)(1)(A). The remainder of the amount realized is treated as basis recovery or capital gain. § 306(a)(1)(B). For this purpose, basis recovery is limited to the adjusted basis of the stock actually sold or otherwise disposed of. If the shareholder does not recover his entire basis in the stock sold (*e.g.,* because the entire amount realized is a dividend), then the unrecovered portion of his basis is added back to the basis of his remaining stock. Under § 306(a)(1)(C), no loss is recognized to the shareholder.

It is important to note that redemptions of § 306 stock are treated differently from other dispositions. In a disposition other than a redemption, dividend treatment is determined by reference to the corporation's e & p at the time of the distribution; by contrast, in a redemption it is necessary to look at the corporation's e & p at the time of the redemption. Moreover, § 306(a)(1) (dispositions other than redemptions) limits the amount of ordinary income to the shareholder's ratable share of e & p, but § 306(a)(2) (redemptions) contains no similar limitation. Thus, a redemption results in ordinary income to the full extent (not merely a ratable portion) of the corporation's e & p. Since a redemption is treated as a § 301 distribution, it reduces corporate e & p by the amount of the distribution. § 312(a). By contrast, in the case of a disposition other than a redemption, there is no distribution from the corporation and e & p is unchanged.

Example (1): X Corp. issues a new class of preferred stock as a tax-free stock dividend with respect to common stock, at a time when X has $100,000 e & p. The preferred stock is § 306 stock. Shareholder A, who owns 10% of X's stock, receives 100 shares of new preferred stock; his allocable basis in the preferred stock is $90,000. A

sells the preferred stock two years later for
$92,000. Under § 306(a)(1)(A), A recognizes ordi-
nary income on the sale to the extent of his ratable
share of X's e & p as of the time when the preferred stock was distributed ($10,000). The re-
mainder of the sales price ($82,000) is treated as
basis recovery, leaving A with $8,000 of unrecov-
ered basis in the stock sold. A's $8,000 unrecov-
ered basis is added back to the basis of his remaining common stock. Reg. § 1.306–1(b)(2), Example
(2). If A instead sold the preferred stock for
$102,000, A would still have $10,000 ordinary income. Since the remainder of the sales price
($92,000) exceeds A's $90,000 basis in the stock
sold, A would treat the amount in excess of basis
($2,000) as capital gain.

Example (2): The facts are the same as in Example (1), except that X redeems A's preferred stock
for $100,000 at a time when X has e & p of
$150,000. Under § 306(a)(2), the entire amount
realized ($100,000) is treated as a § 301 distribu-
tion. Since the amount of the distribution does not
exceed X's e & p at the time of the redemption, A
must report $100,000 ordinary income. It is un-
clear whether A's unrecovered basis of $90,000 in
the redeemed stock may be added back to the basis
of A's remaining common stock or whether this
basis simply disappears. Under the general rule
for redemptions treated as § 301 distributions, reallocation of the unrecovered basis may be permitted. *See* Reg. § 1.302–2(c).

§ 10. Exceptions: § 306(b)

Section 306(b) provides four exceptions to the
application of § 306(a). The first three exceptions
are mechanical safe-harbor rules, and the fourth is
a subjective test.

(a) *Termination of Shareholder Interest.* If a
shareholder disposes of all of his common and
preferred stock in a transaction (other than a redemption) that terminates the shareholder's interest (actual and constructive) in the corporation,
§ 306(a) does not apply. § 306(b)(1)(A). If the
shareholder completely terminates his interest,
there is no bailout potential. Similarly, if the
shareholder's § 306 stock is redeemed in a transaction that qualifies for exchange treatment under
§ 302(b)(3) or (4) (complete termination or partial
liquidation), § 306(a) does not apply. § 306(b)(1)(B).
In the case of a redemption in complete termination of the shareholder's interest, the shareholder
may waive the family attribution rules under
§ 302(c)(2) to facilitate safe-harbor treatment. The
family attribution rules may not be waived, however, in a non-redemption transaction that completely terminates the shareholder's actual (but not his
constructive) ownership, *e.g.,* a sale to a related
family member. In this situation, the shareholder
would have to rely on the subjective test of § 306(b)
(4).

(b) *Liquidation.* Section 306(a) does not apply if
the shareholder's § 306 stock is redeemed in a
complete liquidation. § 306(b)(2). Since § 331 al-

lows capital gain treatment to shareholders whose stock is redeemed in a complete liquidation, there is no reason to treat § 306 stock differently in this context.

(c) *Nonrecognition Transactions.* If a shareholder transfers his § 306 stock in a nonrecognition transaction, § 306(a) does not apply to the transfer. § 306(b)(3). The § 306 taint, however, carries over to any stock acquired in the nonrecognition transaction. § 306(c)(1)(C). Thus, if a transferor gives § 306 stock to his children, the transferor is not taxed under § 306(a) but the stock remains tainted § 306 stock in the children's hands. Similarly, if a shareholder transfers § 306 stock to a controlled corporation in exchange for common stock, in a § 351 transaction, the common stock will be § 306 stock in the shareholder's hands. *But see* § 306(e) (common stock is not § 306 stock if exchanged tax free for § 306 stock of the same corporation).

(d) *Transactions Not in Avoidance.* Under the subjective test of § 306(b)(4), § 306(a) does not apply if the taxpayer satisfies the Service that the transaction was not part of a plan having tax avoidance as "one of its principal purposes." The shareholder must demonstrate a non-tax-avoidance purpose both for the distribution and for the disposition; except that only the disposition is considered if the shareholder, in a prior or simultaneous transaction, disposes of the underlying stock with respect to which the § 306 stock was issued.

In *Fireoved* (1972), the court addressed the question of whether a prior sale of a portion of the taxpayer's underlying common stock removed the § 306 taint from an equivalent portion of the taxpayer's § 306 stock, in the context of a redemption. The court held that § 306(b)(4) was inapplicable, in part because the taxpayer retained effective control of the corporation despite the prior sale of common stock. *Fireoved* leaves open the question whether a combined redemption of common and preferred stock that is not substantially equivalent to a dividend under the tests of § 302(b)(1) or (2) might be sufficient to meet the requirements of § 306(b)(4). *See also* Pescosolido (1988) (Unpublished Case) (rejecting argument that § 306(b)(4) applies only to minority shareholders who are not in control of the distributing corporation).

It may be difficult for the taxpayer to demonstrate a non-tax-avoidance purpose for a distribution of the § 306 stock. The Service has ruled that even if a valid business purpose exists, the distribution may still be considered part of a tax-avoidance plan if the corporation could have achieved the same business result by some other means. *See, e.g.*, Rev. Rul. 80–33 (taxable distribution of corporate debt would have accomplished same business result as distribution of preferred stock).

§ 11. Uses of § 306 Stock

Despite the § 306 taint, a distribution of § 306 stock may still be useful for tax planning purposes. For example, an older-generation family member may receive common and preferred stock in exchange for common stock in a tax-free recapitalization. If the older-generation family member retains the preferred stock until death, the § 306 taint will be removed when the basis is stepped up (or down) in the recipient's hands under § 1014. This type of recapitalization might also be useful in limiting the value of the older-generation family member's interest in the corporation, for estate tax purposes, while providing fixed dividend income. The 1987 Act substantially reduces the attractiveness of such an "estate freeze," however, if part of the common stock is transferred to younger-generation family members. In general, such a transfer will be ineffective for purposes of reducing the value of the stock included in the older-generation family member's estate. *See* Chapter 8.

CHAPTER 8

REORGANIZATIONS

§ 1. Introduction

If a transaction qualifies as a "reorganization" within the meaning of § 368, the Code provides generally for nonrecognition of gain or loss at both the shareholder level (§§ 354 and 356) and the corporate level (§ 361); any unrecognized gain or loss is reflected in the substituted basis of qualifying property received by a shareholder (§ 358) or a corporation (§ 362), and is preserved for recognition in a subsequent taxable disposition.

Tax-free treatment of reorganizations is premised on the notion of "continuity of investment": investors are viewed as preserving their interest in a business enterprise through continuing stock ownership, notwithstanding the change in corporate form. In order to qualify as a reorganization, a transaction must fall within one of the categories defined in § 368(a)(1). In addition, the Regulations require continuity of proprietary interest, business purpose and continuity of business enterprise.

This Chapter discusses amalgamating reorganizations ("A," "B," "C," and some "D" reorganizations) and single-corporation reorganizations ("E" and "F" reorganizations). Divisive "D" reorganizations are discussed separately in Chapter 9.

§ 2. "A" Reorganizations

(a) *General.* An "A" reorganization, as defined in § 368(a)(1)(A), is a merger (or consolidation) under state law. In a typical statutory merger, one corporation (the "acquiring corporation") acquires the assets of another corporation (the "acquired corporation"), in exchange for assumption of the acquired corporation's liabilities (by operation of law) and for stock of the acquiring corporation; the shareholders of the acquired corporation may also receive additional consideration. The acquired corporation disappears as a legal entity, and its shareholders and creditors become shareholders and creditors of the acquiring corporation.

(b) *Continuity of Proprietary Interest.* Although § 368 contains no express restriction on the type of consideration that may be received in an A reorganization, a transaction will be treated as a taxable sale rather than a tax-free reorganization unless the shareholders of the acquired corporation maintain sufficient continuity of proprietary interest. Generally, for advance ruling purposes, the Service requires at least 50% continuity of interest by value, *i.e.,* shareholders of the acquired corporation in the aggregate must receive stock of the acquiring corporation equal in value to at least 50% of the acquired corporation's stock. Sales or redemptions made pursuant to a plan of reorganization are considered in determining whether the 50% continuity-of-interest requirement is met. Rev. Proc. 77–37. Courts have found continuity of interest where shareholders of the acquired corporation received less than 50% in value of the acquired corporation's stock. *See, e.g.,* John A. Nelson Co. (1935) (38% continuity sufficient). Although there is no fixed minimum required percentage of continuing stock ownership, less than 20% continuity is likely to preclude reorganization treatment. *See, e.g.,* May B. Kass (1973) (16% insufficient); Yoc Heating Corp. (1973) (15% insufficient). The continuity-of-interest test applies to the shareholders in the aggregate rather than to each separate shareholder of the acquired corporation. If some shareholders receive cash while others receive stock, the transaction as a whole may still qualify as a reorganization; the shareholders who receive cash, however, will recognize gain under §§ 354(a)(2) and 356. *See* § 9 below.

In order to establish continuity of proprietary interest, the shareholders of the acquired corporation must receive an equity interest in the acquiring corporation. Thus, stock of any class (common or preferred, voting or nonvoting) counts toward continuity; cash and cash equivalents (*e.g.,* short-term notes) do not count toward continuity of interest. An early line of cases established that consideration consisting of debt securities does not count toward continuity, because shareholders receiving such consideration are viewed as terminating their investment as shareholders to become creditors. Pinellas Ice & Cold Storage Co. (1933); Letulle v. Scofield (1940). These cases indicate that stock is the only type of consideration embodying a proprietary interest, even though the economic position of a preferred shareholder may be closer to that of a creditor than that of a common shareholder.

More recently, the Supreme Court held that continuity of interest was lacking in a merger of two savings and loan associations (one authorized to issue "guaranty stock" to its shareholders and the other having no capital stock), where shareholders of the acquired corporation gave up their guaranty stock in exchange for passbook accounts and certificates of deposit in the surviving corporation. Paulsen (1985). The passbook accounts and certificates of deposit had several equity characteristics (including the right to vote on association matters and participate in liquidation proceeds), but the debt characteristics were predominant. The result was perhaps not surprising, since the consideration could be viewed as essentially a cash equivalent without significant equity features. The taxpayer argued, however, that the continuity-of-interest test should focus on the nature of the consideration received rather than the relative change in proprietary interest. If this is the appropriate test, it is difficult to distinguish the *Paulsen* situation from a merger of two non-stock savings and loan associations, which has been held to constitute a tax-free reorganization. Rev. Rul. 69–3. Although the Supreme Court sought to distinguish Revenue Ruling

69–3, the *Paulsen* decision leaves some uncertainty concerning the appropriate standard.

Continuity of interest must also be maintained for a sufficient period to show a definite and substantial ownership interest. Rev. Rul. 66–23 (5 years unrestricted ownership sufficient). A prearranged plan to sell stock received in the reorganization may render the entire transaction taxable. *See* McDonald's of Illinois, Inc. (1982) (step-transaction doctrine applied to post-merger sales; transaction treated as a taxable sale rather than a tax-free reorganization). If the subsequent sales are not contemplated as part of the plan of reorganization, however, continuity of interest is not broken. *See* Penrod (1987).

(c) *Continuity of Business Enterprise.* The Regulations also require continuity of business enterprise at the corporate level. Under Reg. § 1.368–1(d), the acquiring corporation must either continue the acquired corporation's "historic business" or use a significant portion of the acquired corporation's "historic business assets" in another business. If an acquired corporation has more than one line of business, continuity of business enterprise requires only that the acquiring corporation continue a significant line of business. Reg. § 1.368–1(d)(3)(ii). The Regulations warn, however, that a corporation's historic business is "not one the corporation enters into as part of a plan of reorganization." Reg. § 1.368–1(d)(3)(iii). Thus, the continuity-of-business-enterprise requirement is not met if the acquired corporation sells all of its historic business assets and reinvests the proceeds in a new business immediately prior to the reorganization, even though the acquiring corporation continues to conduct the new business. *See* Rev. Rul. 87–76 (continuity not satisfied where acquired corporation sold its historic business assets, consisting of investment portfolio of corporate stocks and bonds, and bought municipal bonds).

§ 3. "B" Reorganizations

(a) *General.* A "B" reorganization is defined in § 368(a)(1)(B) as the acquisition of stock of one corporation in exchange solely for voting stock of the acquiring corporation (or its parent), provided that the acquiring corporation has control of the acquired corporation immediately after the transaction. "Control" means ownership of at least 80% of the total combined voting power of voting stock and at least 80% of the total number of shares of all other classes of stock. § 368(c). Although the acquiring corporation must have control immediately after the transaction, it does not matter whether the acquiring corporation gains control in the reorganization exchange or in a previous transaction (or series of transactions). Thus, an acquiring corporation owning 79% of the acquired corporation may acquire an additional 1% in a "creeping B" reorganization.

(b) *Solely for Voting Stock.* The requirement that the acquiring corporation use solely voting stock means that there will generally be continuity of interest in a B reorganization. Redemptions and other dispositions pursuant to the plan of reorganization must be considered in applying the 50% continuity-of-interest test. Permissible consideration includes voting stock of either the acquiring corporation or (under the parenthetical provisions of § 368(a)(1)(B)) its parent, but not a combination thereof. A reorganization in which the acquiring corporation uses its parent's stock as consideration (often referred to as a "parenthetical B") is considered below with triangular reorganizations.

The term "solely" has been strictly interpreted to preclude the use of any amount of consideration other than voting stock in a B reorganization. *See, e.g.,* Turnbow (1961). This restriction does not prevent the acquiring corporation from paying cash in lieu of issuing fractional shares, provided that such cash is incidental to the exchange and not separately bargained for. Rev. Rul. 66–365, amplified by Rev. Rul. 81–81. In addition, the acquiring corporation may pay cash to the acquired corporation's shareholders (other than in their capacity as shareholders) in a separate transaction without disqualifying the stock-for-stock exchange as a B reorganization. For example, simultaneously with a B reorganization, the acquiring corporation may pay cash to a majority shareholder for entering into a non-competition agreement in a separate transaction, provided that the cash is not in reality paid as additional consideration for the stock acquired in the B reorganization.

The receipt of anti-takeover "poison pill rights" by shareholders of the acquired corporation may violate the "solely" requirement in a B reorganization. Typically, a poison pill gives shareholders a right to acquire additional stock of the issuing corporation (or any acquiring corporation) at a bargain price, in the event of a hostile takeover. In Letter Ruling 8808081, the Service held that poison pill rights constituted "other property" (boot) for purposes of § 356. Although the Service's ruling did not affect qualification of the transaction as a reverse triangular A reorganization, boot treatment would spoil a B reorganization.

(c) *Series of Transactions.* The requirement that the acquiring corporation use solely voting stock may cause problems if a series of transactions are collapsed into a single transaction for tax purposes. The Regulations indicate that a series of transactions taking place over a relatively short period of time (*e.g.,* 12 months) may qualify as a B reorganization. Reg. § 1.368–2(c). For example, if the acquiring corporation acquires 20% of the acquired corporation's stock and then acquires an additional 60% six months later solely for its voting stock, the exchanges will be viewed together as a single B reorganization.

Acquisition of 80% control solely for voting stock may qualify as a B reorganization even if the acquiring corporation purchased some stock in an earlier, unrelated taxable transaction. *See* Chapman (1980). In *Chapman,* the acquiring corporation purchased 8% of the acquired corporation's stock for cash, and then exchanged its voting stock for the remaining voting stock of the acquired corporation. For purposes of the summary judgment motion at issue in *Chapman,* the taxpayer conceded that the initial cash purchases were intended to further its acquisition of the acquired corporation. The court held that if the 8% stock purchase and the later stock-for-stock exchange were viewed as part of a single transaction, the cash boot would disqualify the entire transaction as a B reorganization. This would be so even if the acquiring corporation acquired 80% of the acquired corporation's stock solely for voting stock, since the "solely" requirement applies to the total consideration received in the exchange. If the 8% stock purchase were unrelated or sufficiently remote in time ("old and cold"), however, it would not violate the "solely" requirement of § 368(a)(1) (B).

§ 4. "C" Reorganizations

(a) *General.* In a "C" reorganization, as defined in § 368(a)(1)(C), one corporation acquires "substantially all" of the assets of another corporation in exchange for voting stock of the acquiring corporation (or its parent). For advance ruling purposes, the requirement that the acquired corporation transfer "substantially all" of its assets is deemed to be satisfied only if the transferred assets constitute at least 90% of the fair market value of the net assets and at least 70% of the gross assets held by the acquired corporation immediately before the transfer. Rev. Proc. 77–37. Threshold redemptions, extraordinary dividends and payments to dissenters made pursuant to the plan of reorganization are taken into account.

The purpose of the "substantially all" requirement is to ensure that a transaction which is divisive in nature will not qualify as a C reorganization, but instead will be subject to the rules for divisive D reorganizations. *See* Rev. Rul. 57–518. *See also* Chapter 9. If an acquired corporation sells 50% of its business assets and immediately thereafter transfers all of its assets (including the cash from the sale) to the acquiring corporation, the Service has held that the "substantially all" requirement is satisfied. Rev. Rul. 88–48. The Service emphasized that the transaction was not divisive in nature because the former business was sold to an unrelated party and the sale proceeds were not retained by the acquired corporation or its shareholders. Under prior law, a transferor corporation might retain operating assets for the purpose of continuing in business after the reorganization. Under present law, however, if the transferor corporation continues in existence, the transaction will fail to qualify as a C reorganization, as discussed below. Thus, the Service may be inclined to interpret the "substantially all" requirement less restrictively than under prior law.

(b) *Liabilities; Boot Relaxation.* Section 368(a)(1)(C) requires that the consideration for the acquired corporation's assets consist "solely" of voting stock of the acquiring corporation (or its parent). "Triangular" reorganizations are discussed in § 5 below. As in a B reorganization, the requirement that voting stock be used generally ensures that there will be continuity of interest; in a C reorganization, however, the "solely" requirement is subject to two important exceptions. First, § 368(a)(1)(C) permits the acquiring corporation to assume liabilities of the acquired corporation (or acquire property subject to liabilities) in any amount if the other consideration consists exclusively of voting stock of the acquiring corporation. Second, the boot relaxation rules of § 368(a)(2)(B) permit the use of cash or other boot (*i.e.,* property other than voting stock of the acquiring corporation), provided that at least 80% of the acquired corporation's assets (by gross fair market value) are acquired solely for voting stock.

For the limited purpose of applying the 80% requirement of § 368(a)(2)(B)(iii), liabilities assumed (or taken subject to) are treated as cash. Under § 368(a)(2)(B), the sum of (i) any liabilities assumed (or taken subject to), (ii) the fair market value of other boot consideration, and (iii) the fair market value of any assets retained by the acquired corporation may not exceed 20% of the gross fair market value of the acquired corporation's assets. Thus, if no liabilities are assumed and the acquired corporation transfers all of its assets, up to 20% of the consideration for the assets may consist of cash or other boot. The amount of permissible boot will be reduced, however, to the extent that liabilities are assumed or less than all of the acquired corporation's assets are transferred. For purposes of § 368(a)(2)(B), if voting stock of both the acquiring corporation and its parent is used as consideration, the parent stock is treated as boot.

A liability created in the reorganization and assumed by the acquiring corporation (*e.g.,* an obligation to pay cash to dissenting shareholders of the acquired corporation) may be treated as boot for purposes of § 368(a)(2)(B). Rev. Rul. 73–102. The payment by the acquiring corporation of the acquired corporation's share of reorganization expenses (*e.g.,* legal and accounting fees) is not considered boot if such expenses were directly and solely related to the reorganization; but the payment of unrelated expenses (*e.g.,* investment and estate planning advice to shareholders) is treated as boot. Rev. Rul. 73–54.

Example (1): X Corp. has assets with a fair market value of $100,000 and liabilities of $25,000. Y Corp. may acquire all of X's assets in a C reorganization by issuing solely Y voting stock worth $75,000 and assuming X's liabilities of $25,000. The assumption of liabilities is disregarded for purposes of § 368(a)(1)(C) because the other consideration consists solely of voting stock.

Example (2): The facts are the same as in the preceding example, except that X has only $15,000 of liabilities. Under § 368(a)(2)(B), Y may issue $80,000 of its voting stock, assume the $15,000 liabilities, and pay up to $5,000 cash without disqualifying the transaction as a C reorganization. If X retains an additional $1,000 of assets (or Y pays an additional $1,000 cash) and Y issues only $79,000 of voting stock, however, the transaction will fail as a C reorganization, because the sum of the liabilities ($15,000) and the cash paid and assets retained ($6,000) exceeds 20% of the fair market value of X's assets ($20,000). The provision of § 368(a)(1)(C) permitting liabilities to be disregarded does not apply if any cash or other boot is paid.

(c) *Liquidation of Transferor.* A corporation that transfers its assets in a C reorganization (the "transferor corporation") must distribute all of the stock, securities and other property received in the reorganization, as well as any retained assets, pursuant to the reorganization plan. § 368(a)(2)(G)(i). This provision furthers the underlying objective of preventing a divisive C reorganization. If the transferor corporation fails to make the required distributions, the transaction will be treated as a taxable exchange.

(d) *Overlapping Provisions.* Except for the requirement that the consideration consist of voting stock, a C reorganization resembles an A reorganization. In addition, a transaction that would otherwise qualify as a B reorganization will be treated instead as a C reorganization if the stock-for-stock exchange is followed promptly by a prearranged liquidation of the acquired corporation. *See* Rev. Rul. 67–274. A failed B reorganization (*e.g.,* in which a limited amount of boot is paid by the acquiring corporation) may still qualify as a Type C reorganization if the asset transfer and liquidation requirements are complied with.

§ 5. Triangular Reorganizations

A "triangular" reorganization generally refers to an A, B, or C reorganization in which the consideration for the stock or assets of the acquired corporation includes stock of a parent corporation (the "controlling corporation") in control of the acquiring corporation. The transaction could be structured as a normal A, B, or C reorganization in which the controlling corporation acquired the stock or assets of the acquired corporation in exchange for its own stock followed by a distribution of the stock or assets to the controlling corporation's subsidiary, under the "drop down" provisions of § 368(a)(2)(C). A triangular reorganization achieves the same end result in a single step.

Sections 368(a)(1)(B) and 368(a)(1)(C) expressly permit a B or C reorganization, respectively, to be structured as a direct acquisition of the acquired corporation's stock or assets in exchange for voting stock of the acquiring corporation's parent. In an A reorganization, two types of triangular structures are permitted under § 368(a)(2)(D) ("forward subsidiary merger") and § 368(a)(2)(E) ("reverse subsidiary merger"), respectively.

A forward subsidiary merger is an A reorganization in which the acquired corporation merges into the acquiring corporation and the former shareholders of the acquired corporation receive stock of the controlling corporation; additional consideration may also be used, subject to the continuity-of-interest requirement, but no stock of the acquiring corporation may be used. § 368(a)(2)(D)(i). A further provision of § 368(a)(2)(D) which distinguishes forward subsidiary mergers from normal A reorganizations requires that the acquiring corporation receive "substantially all" of the acquired corporation's assets. This requirement is analogous to the corresponding requirement for C reorganizations.

A reverse subsidiary merger is an A reorganization in which the acquiring corporation's controlled subsidiary merges into the acquired corporation; the acquired corporation survives, and its shareholders exchange controlling stock of the acquired corporation for voting stock of the acquiring corporation (*i.e.*, the merged subsidiary's parent). For this purpose, controlling stock means 80% of the voting power of the voting stock, and 80% of the total number of shares of the other stock, of the acquired corporation. Although up to 20% boot consideration may be used in a reverse subsidiary merger, the requirement that the acquiring parent obtain control of the acquired corporation in the transaction generally precludes the possibility of a "creeping" reverse subsidiary merger.

§ 6. Non-divisive "D" Reorganizations

A "D" reorganization, as defined in § 368(a)(1)(D), requires that one corporation (the "transferor") transfer all or part of its assets to another "controlled" corporation (the "transferee"), and that the transferor then distribute stock or securities of the controlled corporation either in a non-divisive § 354 transaction or in a "divisive" § 355 transaction. The present discussion focuses on non-divisive D reorganizations; divisive transactions are dealt with in Chapter 9.

The "control" requirement of § 368(a)(1)(D) is satisfied if, immediately after the transfer, the transferee corporation is controlled by the transferor or by one or more of its shareholders (including persons who were shareholders immediately before the transfer). For purposes of non-divisive D reorganizations, control is defined in the same manner as under § 304(c), *i.e.,* 50% of the voting stock or 50% of the fair market value of all classes of stock (applying modified § 318 attribution rules). § 368(a)(2)(H).

A transaction will qualify as a non-divisive D reorganization only if (i) the transferee corporation acquires "substantially all" of the assets of the transferor corporation and (ii) the transferor distributes any retained assets, as well as the stock and securities (and other consideration, if any) received from the transferee, pursuant to the plan of reorganization. § 354(b)(1). If these requirements are met, the transferor corporation disappears, leaving some or all of its shareholders in control of the transferee corporation. Thus, in a non-divisive D reorganization, the assets of the transferor and transferee are combined in the hands of the transferee; in this respect, a non-divisive D reorganization resembles a C reorganization. Under § 368(a)(2)(A), however, a transaction described in both § 368(a)(1)(C) and § 368(a)(1)(D) is treated exclusively as a D reorganization.

Example: A transferor corporation (T) transfers all of its assets (with a fair market value of $1,000,000) to its newly-formed subsidiary (S) in exchange for all of the S stock (with a fair market value of $700,000) and $300,000 of S bonds; T then liquidates and distributes the S stock and bonds to its shareholders; some T shareholders receive exclusively S stock, while others receive a combination of stock and bonds. The end result at the corporate level is that S takes over T's continuing business enterprise; at the shareholder level, there is continuity, but not identity, of stock ownership. Any assets retained by T could be used to satisfy preexisting liabilities without violating the "substantially all" requirement. *See* Reg. § 1.354–1(a) (2) (second sentence); *see also* Rev. Proc. 77–37 (retention of 30% of gross assets violates "substantially all" requirement). T must distribute any retained assets, together with all of the property received from S, to its shareholders in complete liquidation. The tax treatment of T's shareholders is determined under §§ 354 and 356, discussed in § 9 below.

§ 7. "E" Reorganizations

(a) *General.* Section 368(a)(1)(E) defines an "E" reorganization simply as a "recapitalization." The Supreme Court has described a recapitalization as a "reshuffling of a capital structure within the framework of an existing corporation." Southwest Consol. Corp. (1942). The Regulations offer several examples of "recapitalizations." Reg. § 1.368–2(e). The Service ordinarily will not issue an advance ruling on whether a transaction involving a closely-held corporation constitutes an E reorganization. Rev. Proc. 88–25.

(b) *Exchanges of Stock for New Stock.* An exchange of stock for stock (preferred for common or common for preferred) qualifies as an E reorganization. Reg. §§ 1.368–2(e)(3) and 1.368–2(e)(4). If a corporation issues new preferred stock in exchange for its outstanding common stock, the new preferred stock may be § 306 stock. § 306(c)(1)(B). *See* Chapter 7. An exchange of common for common or preferred for preferred will also qualify; such an exchange would also be tax free under § 1036 even if it occurred directly between two shareholders. If cumulative preferred stock with dividend arrearages is exchanged for other stock, however, the transaction will be taxable under § 305(b)(4) (distributions on preferred stock) to the extent of the dividend arrearages. Regs. §§ 1.305–5(d), Example (1) and 1.368–2(e), Example (5). A recapitalization which is part of a plan to produce periodic increases in a shareholder's proportionate interest may also be treated as a taxable stock dividend under § 305.

In a typical "estate freeze" recapitalization involving a corporation with a single class of stock, younger-generation family members exchange part or all of their stock for new common stock while older-generation family members exchange their stock for new preferred stock. The usual reason for such a recapitalization is to establish a low value (for estate tax purposes) for the older generation's interest, based on the limited participation of the preferred stock in assets and earnings, while transferring a greater share of potential equity growth to the younger generation. The Regulations provide that such a recapitalization is outside the purview of § 305 if it is a "single and isolated transaction." Reg. § 1.305–3(e), Example 12. Although the new preferred stock is ordinarily § 306 stock, the § 306 taint is removed at the death of the older-generation family member. *See* § 306(c)(1)(C). In the 1987 Act, Congress curtailed the estate tax advantages of such a preferred stock recapitalization. *See* § 2036(c).

(c) *Exchanges of Bonds for New Stock.* If a shareholder exchanges bonds for new stock, the exchange is ordinarily tax free, except to the extent of any interest arrearages discharged in the exchange. If bonds with accrued market discount are exchanged for stock, such discount will carry over to the new stock received and will be taxable as ordinary income upon subsequent disposition of the stock. § 1276(c)(2). If a corporation issues stock with a fair market value smaller than that of the surrendered bonds, the corporation recognizes cancellation of indebtedness income. *See* § 108(e) (10). The 1986 Act eliminated the debt cancellation provisions of §§ 108 and 1017 with respect to solvent corporations, thus requiring immediate taxation of such gains.

(d) *Exchanges of Bonds for New Bonds.* An exchange of old bonds for new bonds is generally tax free, except to the extent that the principal amount of the new bonds exceeds that of the surrendered bonds. *See* § 9 below. The original issue discount rules of §§ 1272 to 1275 may also apply to reorganization exchanges, whether or not the bonds are publicly traded.

(e) *Exchanges of Stock for New Bonds.* An exchange of stock for new bonds (or other securities) raises a potential bailout problem. In *Bazley* (1947), shareholders exchanged their stock for a combination of stock and securities in a purported recapitalization. Under then existing law, the receipt of the securities pursuant to a recapitalization would have been entirely tax free. The Supreme Court, however, recharacterized the distribution of the securities as a taxable dividend under § 301 equal to the fair market value of the securities received in the exchange. This type of bailout is now foreclosed by § 354(a)(2) which treats the receipt of securities as boot, if no securities are surrendered in the reorganization.

§ 8. "F" Reorganizations

An "F" reorganization is defined in § 368(a)(1)(F) as a "mere change in identity, form, or place of organization of one corporation, however effected." The words "of one corporation" were added to this definition in 1982 to prevent the use of F reorganizations to amalgamate multiple operating corporations owned by the same shareholders; this limitation, however, does not preclude the use of F reorganizations if multiple corporations are combined but only one of them is an operating company. The 1982 amendment substantially reduced the attractiveness of F reorganizations.

§ 9. Treatment of Stockholders and Security Holders

(a) *Nonrecognition Property and Boot: §§ 354 and 356.* Under § 354(a)(1), no gain or loss is recognized if stock or securities of one corporate party to a reorganization are exchanged solely for stock or securities of the same corporation or another corporate party to the reorganization, pursuant to the plan of reorganization. Permissible consideration under § 354(a)(1) consists of stock, securities or a combination of both. Reg. § 1.368–2(h). Securities received in a reorganization, however, are nonrecognition property only to the extent that their principal amount does not exceed that of the securities surrendered. § 354(a)(2). The fair market value of any excess principal amount is treated as "other property," *i.e.*, boot. § 356(d)(2) (B). Thus, an exchange will be wholly tax free only if (i) stock or securities are exchanged solely for stock, or (ii) securities are exchanged for securities of a lesser or equal principal amount (with or without additional stock). If a creditor receives only stock (or stock and a limited amount of securities), nonrecognition is available because the creditor has increased his equity investment by becoming a shareholder. On the other hand, if a shareholder receives only securities, thereby upgrading his position to that of a security holder, the exchange is fully taxable.

If a taxpayer receives boot in addition to property permitted to be received tax free under § 354(a) (1), the exchange is partly taxable under § 356. The shareholder receiving boot must recognize any realized gain to the extent of the sum of any cash and the fair market value of any other property constituting boot. § 356(a)(1). No loss is recognized. § 356(c).

Example: Shareholders A, B and C each exchange 100 shares of stock, pursuant to a reorganization, for stock (with a fair market value of $1,500) and securities (with a fair market value of $800). The basis of A, B, and C, respectively, in the surrendered stock is $1,000, $2,000 and $3,000. A's realized gain of $1,300 ($2,300 amount realized less $1,000 basis) is recognized to the extent of the boot received ($800) and the remaining gain ($500) is deferred. B's realized gain of $300 ($2,300 amount realized less $2,000 basis) is less than the amount of boot received; accordingly, B's entire gain of $300 is recognized. C's realized loss of $700 ($3,000 basis less $2,300 amount realized) is not recognized.

(b) *Dividend Within Gain:* § *356(a)(2).* The character of any recognized gain may be ordinary or capital, depending on the effect of the transaction at the shareholder level. Under § 356(a)(2), if the exchange has the effect of a dividend, the shareholder's recognized gain is treated as a dividend to the extent of his ratable share of e & p (dividend "within gain" limitation); any remaining gain is treated as capital gain. The 1986 Act's repeal of preferential treatment for capital gain has greatly reduced the significance of dividend versus capital gain treatment of boot. A shareholder with capital losses may prefer capital gain treatment, of course, since capital gains can be used to offset capital losses. A corporate shareholder will almost always prefer dividend treatment under § 356(a)(2), however, because of the § 243 exclusion for dividends received.

The test for dividend equivalency is based on § 302 (with application of the § 318 attribution rules). In a recent case, the Service argued that § 302 should be limited to redemptions involving a single corporation rather than multi-party reorganizations. Clark (1987). The Fourth Circuit rejected the Service's approach, however, based on the Service's own position in Revenue Ruling 75–83 that "it is appropriate to look to principles developed under section 302 for determining dividend equivalency" under § 356(a)(2). The crucial issue in *Clark* was how the reduction in the shareholder's interest should be measured. Because the taxpayer was the sole shareholder of the acquired corporation, the Service argued that any gain should automatically be treated as a dividend based on a hypothetical redemption by the acquired corporation of a portion of the taxpayer's stock immediately before the reorganization. *See also* Shimberg (1978).

Following *Wright* (1973), however, the Fourth Circuit analyzed the transaction as (i) a hypothetical exchange by the taxpayer of his stock in the acquired corporation solely for stock of the acquiring corporation and (ii) a hypothetical redemption by the acquiring corporation of part of the taxpayer's stock received in the reorganization for cash. Since the hypothetical redemption reduced the taxpayer's holdings in the acquiring corporation by more than 20% and left the taxpayer with less than 50% of the stock of the acquiring corporation, the court found that the boot qualified for capital gain treatment.

Example: Shareholders A, B, C and D each own 25% of the stock of X Corp. X is acquired by Y Corp. in a statutory merger, in which A, B, and C

each receive Y stock worth $10,000 and cash of
$2,000; D receives Y stock worth $1,000 and cash
of $11,000. Assume that the cash received by A, B
and C has the effect of a dividend but the cash
received by D does not, and that each shareholder's
ratable share of accumulated e & p is $1,500.
Assume further that the shareholders have the
following adjusted bases in their respective X
stock: $9,000 (A), $11,000 (B), $13,000 (C) and
$10,000 (D). A's realized gain of $3,000 ($12,000 less
$9,000) is recognized to the extent of boot received
($2,000); $1,500 of the recognized gain is treated as
a dividend under § 356(a)(2) and the remainder
($500) as capital gain. B's realized gain of $1,000
($12,000 less $11,000) is treated entirely as a dividend under § 356(a)(2). C has a realized but unrecognized loss of $1,000; none of the boot is treated
as a dividend because of the "within gain" limitation of § 356(a)(2). All of D's realized gain of
$2,000 ($12,000 less $10,000) is taxed as capital
gain under § 356(a)(1) because it does not have the
effect of a dividend.

Apart from the issue of the appropriate test for
dividend equivalency, the further question remains
whether the amount of the dividend, if any, should
be limited to e & p of the acquiring corporation.
Perhaps the e & p of both corporations might be
considered in measuring the amount of the dividend, by analogy to § 304.

(c) *Basis: § 358.* The basis of property received
in a reorganization is determined under § 358.

Under § 358(a)(2), boot (except cash) takes a basis equal to its fair market value. Under § 358(a)(1), nonrecognition property takes a substituted basis equal to the shareholder's original basis in the stock surrendered, decreased by the amount of cash and the fair market value of any other boot received and increased by the amount of any dividend or other recognized gain. The basis of multiple classes of nonrecognition property received must be allocated in proportion to their respective fair market values. § 358(b)(1); Reg. §§ 1.358-2(a)(2) and 1.358-2(a)(3).

Example: In a reorganization, shareholder A exchanges his stock in X Corp. (with an adjusted basis of $10,000) for stock in Y Corp. worth $11,000, Y securities worth $3,000 and cash of $1,000. A's realized gain of $5,000 ($15,000 less $10,000) is recognized to the extent of the boot received of $4,000 ($3,000 of securities plus $1,000 cash). A's basis in the Y stock will be equal to his original basis in the X stock ($10,000), decreased by the cash and fair market value of other boot property ($4,000) and increased by the amount treated as a dividend or capital gain ($4,000). A's basis in the boot securities will be equal to their fair market value ($3,000), under § 356(a)(2). A's realized but unrecognized gain of $1,000 is reflected in the basis of the Y stock (fair market value of $11,000 and basis of $10,000). If A's basis in the X stock were instead $16,000, A would have an unrecognized loss of $1,000, which would be reflected in his basis of $12,000 in the Y stock ($16,000 less $4,000), under § 358(a).

§ 10. Treatment of the Corporate Transferor

Section 361 provides generally for nonrecognition of gain or loss to the corporate transferor on an exchange of property pursuant to a reorganization. In order to correct numerous technical problems in § 361 as enacted by the 1986 Act, the 1988 Act essentially reinstated the pre–1986 version of § 361, with a few modifications.

(a) *Property Exchanged or Received in Reorganization.* A corporate party to a reorganization recognizes no gain or loss on an exchange of property, pursuant to the reorganization, solely for stock or securities of another corporate party to the reorganization. § 361(a). The transferor (acquired) corporation also recognizes no gain on loss on any other consideration (boot) permitted to be received in addition to stock and securities, as long as the transferor distributes the boot pursuant to the reorganization. § 361(b)(1)(A). Generally, no issue arises in connection with the distribution of boot in a C reorganization, since the transferor is required to liquidate under § 368(a)(2)(G)(i).

The acquiring corporation may also assume (or take property subject to) some or all of the acquired corporation's liabilities. Liabilities relieved are part of the amount realized by the acquired corporation, but the acquired corporation normally recognizes no gain because the liabilities relieved are generally not treated as boot for purposes of § 361. *See* § 357(a). If relief of liabilities is for a tax avoidance or non-business purpose under § 357(b), however, the total liabilities relieved are treated as boot; because there is no way to "distribute" liabilities relieved, the acquired corporation is required to recognize its gain to the extent of the liabilities.

(b) *Distribution of Property.* Under § 361(c)(1), a corporate transferor generally recognizes no gain or loss on a distribution of property to its shareholders pursuant to a plan of reorganization; the provisions of § 311 and §§ 336–338 (relating to nonliquidating and liquidating distributions, respectively) are expressly made inapplicable to distributions under § 361. § 361(c)(4). If the acquired corporation distributes appreciated property other than stock or securities of another corporate party, however, gain is recognized as if such property had been sold to the distributee at its fair market value. §§ 361(c)(2)(A) and 361(c)(2)(B). Moreover, if the acquired corporation distributes property subject to a liability in excess of basis (or if its shareholders take such property subject to the liability), § 361(c)(2)(C) treats the fair market value of the property as not less than the amount of the liability.

Example: P Corp. acquires all of the assets of T Corp. for consideration consisting of P voting stock worth $1.7 million, P securities worth $200,000 and gold bars with a fair market value of $100,000.

Under the boot relaxation provisions of § 368(a)(2)
(B), the acquisition is a valid C reorganization. T
recognizes no gain or loss on exchange of its assets
under § 361(a). The P voting stock and securities
are nonrecognition property, and T takes a substituted basis in such property under § 358(a)(1), *i.e.,*
T's original basis in the assets transferred, decreased by the amount of cash and the fair market
value of any other boot received. The basis of the
nonrecognition property in T's hands is generally
irrelevant, since T may distribute the nonrecognition property tax free under § 361(c). Moreover, T
recognizes no gain on the distribution of the gold
bars to its shareholders, even though the gold bars
are boot, because they take a basis in T's hands
equal to their fair market value under § 358(a)(2).
The substituted-basis provisions of § 358(a)(1) do
not apply to boot, even if the boot may be received
tax free in a reorganization. § 358(f) (limiting substituted-basis treatment to stock or securities of a
corporate party to the reorganization).

(c) *Retained Assets.* The "fresh start" basis rule
for boot received in a reorganization generally prevents the acquired corporation from recognizing
gain on distribution of such boot. Thus, only post-
acquisition appreciation in the boot property will
trigger gain under § 361(c)(2). Similarly, § 361(c)
(2) prevents the acquired corporation from recognizing gain on distribution of stock or securities
received in the reorganization, even if such property is appreciated. If the acquired corporation

transfers less than all of its assets in the reorganization, § 361(c)(2) will trigger gain (but not loss) on the distribution of the retained assets.

Example: T Corp. transfers 80% of its assets to P Corp. in a valid C reorganization; the remaining 20% of T's assets not transferred in the reorganization consists of appreciated real property with a basis of $100 and a fair market value of $200. Under § 368(a)(2)(G)(i), T is required to distribute any retained assets as well as the consideration received in the reorganization in order to qualify the transaction as a C reorganization. Although T recognizes no gain on distributing the property received in the reorganization, T recognizes $100 of gain on distributing the retained asset ($200 fair market value less $100 basis). If T's basis in the retained asset exceeded its fair market value, T would recognize no loss on the distribution. § 361(c)(1).

(d) *Distributions to Creditors.* If an acquired corporation liquidates and distributes stock, securities or other property received in the reorganization to creditors, such distributions are treated as pursuant to the plan of reorganization for purposes of determining whether the transaction qualifies as a C reorganization. § 368(a)(2)(G)(i). The acquired corporation generally recognizes no gain or loss when it distributes property received in the reorganization to creditors. §§ 361(b)(3) and 361(c)(3). These provisions essentially overrule the holding in *Minnesota Tea Co.* (1938), where the court treated the acquired corporation as recognizing gain on a distribution to its shareholders of cash received in the reorganization coupled with the shareholders' assumption of the acquired corporation's liabilities. If the acquired corporation holds back appreciated property for distribution to creditors in satisfaction of liabilities, it will recognize gain to the same extent as if it had sold such property. The acquired corporation may also be able to recognize a loss if it distributes retained assets to its creditors, since such a distribution is technically outside the plan of reorganization under § 361(c)(3).

Example: T Corp. has assets with a fair market value of $100, subject to liabilities of $20. In a valid C reorganization, T transfers all of its assets to P Corp. in exchange for P stock worth $100, but P does not assume T's liabilities. T distributes $20 worth of the P stock to its creditor (C) in satisfaction of T's liabilities. T recognizes no gain on the distribution of the P stock to C, even if the P stock is appreciated in T's hands. §§ 361(b)(3) and 361(c)(3). If T instead sells the P stock and uses the sale proceeds to pay C, T may recognize gain, since T's substituted basis in the P stock is likely to be less than its fair market value.

§ 11. Treatment of the Corporate Transferee

(a) *Nonrecognition Treatment.* If the consideration given by a transferee (acquiring) corporation consists exclusively of its own stock (whether newly-issued or treasury stock), the acquiring corporation recognizes no gain or loss under § 1032. If the acquiring corporation issues its own securities in addition to stock, it essentially purchases property with its debt obligation and accordingly recognizes no gain or loss. If the acquiring corporation transfers some boot (property other than stock or securities), it recognizes any gain or loss realized on such property under § 1001, but does not receive any increase in the basis of the acquired property as a result of the gain recognized. § 362(b).

In a triangular A, B or C reorganization, the acquiring corporation may use stock or securities of its parent as consideration. Although § 1032 technically applies only to an exchange of a corporation's own stock, the subsidiary will recognize no gain or loss on an exchange of its parent's stock. *See* Rev. Rul. 57–278; Prop. Reg. § 1.1032–2. The subsidiary may nevertheless recognize gain or loss if it transfers boot. *See* Prop. Reg. § 1.1032–2(c), Example (1).

(b) *Corporate Transferee's Basis.* Under § 362(b), the acquiring corporation generally takes a basis in property acquired in the reorganization equal to its basis in the hands of the acquired corporation, increased by any gain recognized by the acquired corporation on the exchange. Normally, the acquired corporation recognizes no gain when it transfers its assets under § 361, unless liabilities are relieved for a tax-avoidance or nonbusiness purpose. If the acquired corporation fails to liquidate, however, the transaction may be denied C reorganization status under § 368(a)(2)(G)(i). In this case, the transaction will be a taxable purchase, and the acquiring corporation may be entitled to a cost basis in the acquired property under § 1012.

Even if the shareholders of the acquired corporation recognize gain on the exchange of their stock for stock and securities of the acquiring corporation (together with any boot), the acquiring corporation will not obtain a basis increase in the acquired property. Similarly, the acquiring corporation's basis is not affected by any gain that the acquired corporation may recognize on distributing appreciated property under § 361(c), since such gain is recognized on the distribution rather than in the reorganization exchange. Moreover, the acquiring corporation's basis is not affected by relief of the acquired corporation's liabilities, unless such relief of liabilities is treated as cash and triggers gain due to a tax-avoidance or non-business purpose.

Section 362(b) (second sentence) makes the substituted-basis provisions of § 362(b) inapplicable to stock or securities in a corporate party to a reorganization unless such stock or securities are acquired (in whole or in part) in exchange for stock or securities of the corporate transferee (or its parent). Together with § 358(e), this sentence merely ensures that § 362(b) substituted-basis treatment will apply to the corporate transferee in an asset acquisition, but not to the corporate transferor (whose basis in the corporate transferee's stock is determined under § 358).

CHAPTER 9

CORPORATE DIVISIONS

§ 1. Introduction

Section 355 permits a tax-free division of a corporate enterprise into two separate corporations, each owned by shareholders of the original corporation. A § 355 transaction may take the form of a "spin-off", a "split-off" or a "split-up". A spin-off consists of a distribution by a corporation to its shareholders of stock in a controlled subsidiary; by analogy to a dividend, the shareholders of the distributing corporation do not surrender anything in exchange for the distributed stock. A split-off is identical to a spin-off, except that the shareholders of the distributing corporation surrender part of their stock in the distributing corporation for stock in the controlled subsidiary; in this respect, a split-off is analogous to a redemption. In a split-up, the distributing corporation distributes stock in two or more controlled subsidiaries to its shareholders in complete liquidation. Although each of these three patterns may qualify as a tax-free division under § 355, the form of the transaction may have significance with respect to taxation of boot and other matters.

The underlying premise of § 355 is that nonrecognition treatment should be available when the owners of a business merely change the form of the business while continuing to operate it. In a qualifying transaction, § 355 provides that no gain or loss is recognized on the receipt of stock or securities of the controlled corporation. If shareholders receive any other property in addition to such nonrecognition property, however, the boot provisions of § 356 are applicable. Finally, the distributing corporation generally recognizes no gain or loss on a distribution of stock or securities of the controlled corporation, although it may recognize gain (but not loss) on a distribution of boot.

§ 2. General Requirements

The three types of qualifying transactions have several elements in common. First, the distributing corporation must be in "control" of at least one subsidiary ("controlled corporation") immediately before the transaction. § 355(a)(1)(A). Control means ownership of stock possessing at least 80% of the total voting power and at least 80% of the total number of shares of all other classes of stock. § 368(c). The controlled corporation may be either a preexisting or a newly-created subsidiary. Second, both the distributing corporation and the controlled corporation (or, if the distributing corporation is a holding company, each of the controlled corporations) must be engaged in the "active conduct of a trade or business" immediately after the distribution. § 355(b)(1). Third, the active business test must also be satisfied for a 5–year period preceding the transaction. § 355(b)(2). Fourth, the distributing corporation must distribute all of the stock or securities of the controlled corporation (or sufficient stock to constitute control under § 368(c), if the remaining stock or securities are not retained as part of a tax-avoidance plan). § 355(a)(1)(D). Fifth, the distribution must not be used principally as a "device" for distributing earnings and profits. § 355(a)(1)(B).

As a result of the qualifying transaction, the shareholders of the distributing corporation will have control of two separate corporations. If the distribution is pro rata, as is the case in most spin-offs, the two corporations will be "brother-sister" corporations owned by the same group of shareholders. A non-pro-rata distribution is often used in split-offs and split-ups, for example, to resolve a dispute among shareholders. Section 355 treatment is available whether or not the distribution is pro-rata. § 355(a)(2)(A).

Example: A and B, equal shareholders of X Corp., decide to separate their business interests. Assuming that X has conducted two active businesses for at least 5 years, a tax-free § 355 transaction may be structured as a non-pro-rata split-off or split-up. In a split-off, X would transfer the assets of one business to a new subsidiary (S), in exchange for all of S's stock, and would then distribute the S stock to A in exchange for all of A's stock in X, leaving B as the sole owner of X (with the assets of the second business). In a split-up, X would form two new subsidiaries (S1 and S2), transfer the assets of one business to S1 and those of the other to S2 (leaving X a mere holding company), and finally distribute the S1 stock to A and the S2 stock to B.

§ 3. Relationship to Divisive D Reorganizations

A § 355 transaction need not be part of a reorganization. § 355(a)(2)(C). If the parent corporation distributes stock of an existing subsidiary in a spin-off, for example, the transaction is governed entirely by § 355. If the parent transfers part of its assets to a newly-formed subsidiary and then distributes the subsidiary stock in a spin-off, however, the transaction as a whole will constitute a divisive D reorganization under § 368(a)(1)(D). Under § 361, the parent will recognize no gain or loss on the initial asset transfer, and the new subsidiary will have a substituted basis under § 362(b). The distribution of the subsidiary's stock must qualify under § 355 in order to meet the distribution requirement of § 368(a)(1)(D). Although a § 354 exchange satisfies the distribution requirement in non-divisive D reorganizations, § 354 is not applicable to divisive D reorganizations; thus, the requirements of § 355 are, in effect, mandatory for all divisive D reorganizations. *See* §§ 354(b) and 368(a)(1)(D).

§ 4. Divisive Bailout Problem

The elaborate anti-avoidance provisions of § 355 were originally enacted in response to a bailout problem illustrated by the facts of *Gregory* (1935). In *Gregory,* the taxpayer owned all of the shares of a corporation (United Mortgage), which in turn owned highly appreciated shares of another corporation (Monitor Securities). In order to dispose of the Monitor shares without triggering a corporate-level tax, the taxpayer caused United Mortgage to form a subsidiary (Averill), transfer the Monitor stock to Averill in a § 351 transaction, and then spin off the Averill stock to her. Immediately thereafter, Averill was liquidated and distributed the Monitor stock to the taxpayer. If the transaction had been successful, the taxpayer would have obtained a basis in the Monitor shares equal to their fair market value (thus allowing her to sell the Monitor shares with no additional gain), without any corporate-level tax and at the cost of only a capital gain tax at the shareholder level. The Supreme Court, however, found that the transaction had "no business or corporate purpose" and was a "mere device", masquerading as a corporate reorganization, to avoid tax.

To prevent such tax-avoidance schemes, Congress repealed the tax-free spin-off provisions in 1934, only to reinstate them in substantially their present form in 1954. Present § 355 contains a set of rules designed to prevent bailouts. To some extent, however, the elimination of preferential capital gain rates in the 1986 Act has lessened the need for these anti-bailout rules as originally conceived.

§ 5. Active Business Requirement

The principal anti-bailout provision of § 355 is the active business test. § 355(b). The requirement that both the distributing corporation and the controlled corporation must actively conduct businesses immediately after the distribution is sufficient to block a transaction like the one in *Gregory*, because the controlled corporation would fail to meet this requirement if it held only cash or investment assets. In addition, § 355(b)(2)(B) requires that both corporations must have conducted active businesses for the 5–year period immediately preceding the distribution. The 5–year requirement is designed to prevent a temporary investment of liquid assets in a new business in preparation for a spin-off. If the 5–year requirement is met, then the controlled corporation was presumably not created for the purpose of tax avoidance with respect to the subsequent corporate division.

Two additional requirements must also be considered. Under § 355(b)(2)(C), the active business requirement is not satisfied if any of the businesses was acquired within the preceding 5–year period in a taxable transaction. Moreover, § 355(b)(2)(D) provides that the active business requirement is not satisfied if the distributing corporation or the distributee corporation acquired control (directly or indirectly) of a corporation conducting an active business within the preceding 5–year period in a taxable transaction. Control means ownership of stock possessing at least 80% of the total voting power and 80% of the total number of shares of all other classes of stock. § 368(c).

Example: P Corp. purchases all of the stock of T, and then distributes the T stock to P's shareholders in a spin-off. Since P acquired control of T in a taxable transaction within the preceding 5–year period, P's distribution of the T stock fails the requirement of § 355(b)(2)(D) and constitutes a taxable dividend to the P shareholders. Alternatively, if P purchases all of the stock of T, liquidates T tax free under § 332, and then distributes the stock of S Corp. (formerly a subsidiary of T, now a subsidiary of P) to P's shareholders, the transaction will fail the requirement of § 355(b)(2)(D), because P indirectly acquired control of S in a taxable transaction during the preceding 5–year period.

Section 355(b)(2)(D) also denies tax-free treatment of the distribution if the distributee corporation acquires control of the distributing corporation in a taxable transaction during the 5–year period. For example, if P acquires control of T in a taxable transaction, T's distribution of the stock of S (T's subsidiary) to P cannot qualify as a tax-free distribution under § 355 until 5 years after P's acquisition of T, regardless of how long S has conducted an active trade or business. Such a transaction literally met the requirements for a tax-free spin-off under the pre–1987 version of § 355(b)(2)(D). *See* Rev. Rul. 74–5 (valid § 355 transaction because no bailout of earnings where distributee purchased distributing corporation). Congress was concerned that such a transaction would permit the acquiring corporation (distributee) to achieve a step-up in the basis of the distributed subsidiary stock by allocating its cost basis in the target stock partly to stock of the subsidiary. By expanding § 355(b)(2)(D) to include an acquisition of control by the distributee corporation, Congress eliminated this potential abuse. If the distributee corporation acquires less than 80% of the stock of the distributing corporation, however, § 355(b)(2)(D) does not apply because the distributee corporation has not acquired "control."

§ 6. Definition of Active Business

Section 355 does not define the term "active business," but the Regulations provide some guidelines. A corporation is engaged in an active business if it carries on a specific group of activities for income-producing purposes, including every step in the income-earning process from such activities. Prop. Reg. § 1.355–3(b)(2). Two types of assets that are likely to cause problems under this definition are investment assets (*e.g.*, stock, securities, land or other property held for investment) and owner-occupied or leased real property with respect to which the owner does not provide significant services. *Id.* The Service has indicated that an active business requires substantial managerial and operational activities conducted directly by the corporation. *See* Rev. Rul. 88–19; Rev. Rul. 73–234. Rental of property has been held not to constitute an active trade or business where the corporation's activities were merely supervisory and advisory, or management services were provided by a third party. *See* Rev. Rul. 85–125; Rev. Rul. 85–126. Similarly, if a parent corporation leases real property used in its trade or business from a newly spun-off subsidiary, the subsidiary's leasing of the property may be treated as a mere investment activity rather than an active trade or business. *See* Rafferty (1967); Prop. Reg. § 1.355–3(c), Example (5). Rental activities may constitute an active trade or business, however, if the owner directly provides sufficient management and maintenance services. Prop. Reg. § 1.355–3(c), Example (4).

The Service formerly insisted that there must be two separate active businesses, each with a separate 5–year history. After taxpayer victories in *Coady* (1961) and *Marett* (1963) on this issue, the Treasury issued new Proposed Regulations in 1977 (not yet final) which explicitly permit a "vertical" division of a single preexisting business into two separate, independent businesses. Prop. Reg. § 1.355–3(c), Examples (10)-(12). For example, two equal shareholders of a construction business may divide the business in half by forming a new corporation (with part of the old corporation's construction contracts, equipment and cash) and distributing the stock of the new corporation tax free to one of them. Prop. Reg. § 1.355–3(c), Example (10). A tax-free "horizontal" division of an integrated business along functional lines is also permitted, at least if each separate function is economically viable. For example, an integrated steel company may spin-off its coal-mining activities to a separate corporation which continues to supply coal to the steel company. Even if the coal-mining business has no customers other than the original steel company, a tax-free horizontal division may be permitted. Prop. Reg. § 1.55–3(c), Example 9 (captive coal mine). If there is still a close business relationship between the two corporations, however, the transaction may be challenged as a bailout device or as lacking a business purpose, as discussed in §§ 7 and 8 below.

§ 7. Device

The "device" restriction of § 355(a)(1)(B) reinforces the active business requirement. Standing alone, the active business requirement would not prevent a tax-free spin-off even if 95% of the assets of a subsidiary were not 5–year business assets (or were liquid assets), as long as the remaining 5% of the subsidiary's assets constituted an active 5–year trade or business. The 1977 Proposed Regulations clarify the circumstances in which a distribution will be viewed as a "device for the distribution of earnings and profits" of the distributing corporation or the controlled corporation.

(a) *Stock Sales.* Section 355(a)(1)(B) provides that the mere fact that, after the distribution, stock or securities of either corporation are sold or exchanged (other than pursuant to a prearranged plan) will not be construed to mean that the transaction was used principally as a device. The Proposed Regulations interpret this language narrowly, indicating that any sale (whether or not prearranged) is evidence of an impermissible purpose. Prop. Reg. § 1.355–2(c)(2). Moreover, a prearranged sale of 20% or more of the stock of either corporation will automatically violate the device restriction. *Id.* A prearranged sale of less than 20% of the stock will be considered "substantial evidence" that the transaction was used principally as a device. *Id.* A sale is prearranged if actually negotiated before the distribution or, generally, if discussed by the buyer and seller before the distribution and "reasonably to be anticipated by both parties." *Id.*

The restriction on prearranged sales is intended to ensure continuity of interest, *i.e.,* to prevent an immediate cashing out of the shareholders' investment at capital gain rates. If stock is transferred in a tax-free exchange following a § 355 distribution, continuity of interest will also generally be preserved. The issue thus arises whether a § 355 transaction can be combined with a tax-free reorganization. The Proposed Regulations specifically permit such a combined transaction. Prop. Reg. § 1.355–(c)(2). *See also* Morris Trust (1966). In such cases, the shareholders merely maintain their proprietary interest through stock in the acquiring corporation.

Since the device test focuses on the distributee's ability to extract e & p at capital gain rates by selling stock, it should not preclude § 355 treatment for a distribution, regardless of how promptly the distributed stock is sold, if the distributee would have been entitled to capital gain treatment on the actual distribution in the absence of § 355. The Proposed Regulations seem to adopt this approach, stating that a distribution is "ordinarily not to be considered a device" if the distribution would otherwise have qualified for exchange treatment with respect to each distributee under § 302 (presumably with application of § 318) or if neither corporation had e & p at the time of the distribution. Prop. Reg. § 1.355–2(c)(1). In a typical split-off where a shareholder exchanges all of his parent stock for subsidiary stock, resulting in a complete termination of his interest in the parent, the device restriction of § 355 would thus appear to be inapplicable.

(b) *Other Factors.* The Proposed Regulations provide that other factors may also be considered in determining whether a transaction is principally a device. A pro-rata distribution, which normally provides the greatest potential for a bailout of e & p (unless neither corporation has e & p), may be subject to particularly close scrutiny. Prop. Reg. § 1.355–2(c)(1). The existence of excess liquid assets in either corporation may also be indicative of a device. The Proposed Regulations indicate that all facts and circumstances will be considered, including the "nature, kind and amount of the assets of both corporations" and their use immediately after the transaction. Prop. Reg. § 1.355–2(c)(3)(i). If two separate businesses exist, and the earnings of one have been used to finance expansion of the other within 5 years of the distribution, § 355 treatment may be inapplicable. Rev. Rul. 59–400 (earnings of hotel business used to expand rental business). Similarly, creation of a new business, as opposed to mere expansion of an existing business, may prevent a tax-free spin-off if the new business is not sufficiently "seasoned." Finally, a device may be inferred from post-distribution dealings between the distributing corporation and the controlled corporation, although the issues raised by such dealings may relate primarily to the active business test. Prop. Reg. § 1.355–2(c)(3)(iv).

§ 8. Business Purpose

The Proposed Regulations also require a substantial non-tax business purpose for a § 355 transaction, restricting tax-free treatment to "such readjustment of corporate structures as is required by business exigencies." Prop. Reg. § 1.355–2(b)(1). A shareholder purpose (as distinguished from a corporate business purpose) will suffice only if it is "so nearly coextensive with a corporate business purpose as to preclude any distinction between them." *Id.* If the transaction is motivated solely by a personal purpose of the shareholder (*e.g.,* estate planning), it will not qualify under § 355. *Id. See also* Rafferty (1971). A disagreement on major operating decisions between two managing shareholders is a sufficient business purpose for a non-pro-rata split-off.   Prop. Reg. § 1.355–2(b)(2), Example (2).

The required business purpose must relate to the distribution rather than merely the incorporation of a separate business.   Estate of Parshelsky (1962); Wilson (1965).   Thus, the desire to protect one business from the risks of another may justify the incorporation of a subsidiary to operate a risky business but does not constitute an adequate business purpose for distributing the subsidiary's stock. Prop. Reg. § 1.355–2(b)(2), Example (3).   Nevertheless, if a lender to the more stable business requires "as a matter of customary business practice" that the subsidiary stock be distributed "to prevent the potential diversion of funds" to the riskier business, there is a sufficient business purpose for the distribution.   Prop. Reg. § 1.355–2(b) (2), Example (4).   Similarly, the business purpose requirement is satisfied if stock of a controlled corporation is distributed in order to reduce substantially the amount of administrative time and expense necessary to comply with state regulatory requirements.   Rev. Rul. 88–33.   *See also* Rev. Rul. 88–34 (business purpose satisfied where distribution enabled subsidiary to hire key employee).

§ 9. Continuity of Interest

Section 355 contemplates "continuing interests in property under modified corporate forms" and "continuity of interest in all or part of the business enterprise" by persons who, directly or indirectly, owned the enterprise prior to the § 355 transaction. Prop. Reg. § 1.355–2(b)(1). The continuity-of-interest requirement, which is applicable to reorganizations generally as discussed in Chapter 8, is intended to prevent tax-free treatment of transactions that are substantially equivalent to sales. The continuity-of-interest requirement is not violated by a non-pro-rata distribution which leaves some shareholders owning the distributing corporation and other shareholders owning the controlled corporation. *See* § 355(a)(2)(A). If the shareholders immediately sell their stock in either the distributing corporation or the controlled corporation, however, the transaction may violate the continuity-of-interest requirement or the overlapping device restriction.

§ 10. Treatment of Boot

Section 355(a) provides that no gain or loss is recognized on receipt of stock or securities of the controlled corporation, if the other requirements of § 355 are satisfied. The boot rules of § 356 will apply if any other property is distributed. For this purpose, boot includes (i) cash or other property, (ii) the fair market value of the excess principal amount of any securities or, if no securities are surrendered, the fair market value of any securities received, and (iii) stock of the controlled corporation if acquired within 5 years of the distribution in a taxable transaction. §§ 355(a)(3), 356(a) and 356(b). The special rule concerning recently-ac-

quired stock of the controlled corporation is intended to prevent the distributing corporation from
investing excess funds in stock of the controlled
corporation in preparation for a tax-free spin-off.
For example, if the distributing corporation has
owned 85% of the stock of a controlled subsidiary
for more than 5 years and acquires the remaining
15% six months before a spin-off of all the subsidiary stock, the recently-acquired stock will be treated as boot in the distribution. Prop. Reg. § 1.355–
2(f)(2).

The governing provision for exchanges (split-offs
and split-ups) is § 356(a). Under the normal rules
of § 356(a)(1), any realized gain is recognized to the
extent of the boot received. If the exchange has
the effect of a dividend (applying the rules of
§§ 302 and 318), however, such recognized gain is
treated as a dividend under § 356(a)(2) to the extent of the shareholder's ratable share of e & p,
and the balance is treated as capital gain. In a
split-off, dividend equivalence is tested by determining the percentage decrease that would have
occurred had the shareholder received only the
boot in redemption of part of his parent stock and
retained the rest of his parent stock. Rev. Rul. 74–
516. If the aggregate fair market value of the
distributed property (stock, securities and boot) is
less than the adjusted basis of stock and securities
surrendered, § 356(c) prevents recognition of loss.

The governing provision for distributions (spin-
offs) is § 356(b). Under § 356(b), receipt of boot is

treated as a distribution of property under § 301; this result is appropriate since a spin-off is essentially analogous to a dividend distribution. Unlike § 356(a), § 356(b) treats the entire amount of the boot as a dividend to the extent of the corporation's e & p (without regard to the amount of realized gain or the distributee's ratable share of e & p).

§ 11. Basis to Distributee

The basis of property received by a distributee shareholder in a § 355 transaction is determined under § 358. If the distributee receives no boot, the aggregate basis of his original stock (or securities) will be allocated among the stock (or securities) received or retained in proportion to their respective fair market values. If boot is received, the boot will take a basis equal to its fair market value under § 358(a)(2), and the basis of the nonrecognition property must be decreased by the amount of any boot received and increased by the amount of any dividend or gain recognized. § 358(a)(1).

Example: X Corp. distributes stock and securities of Y, a controlled subsidiary, to X's sole shareholder A in a § 355 spinoff. Immediately before the transaction, A's X stock had a basis of $4,200 and a fair market value of $22,000; immediately after the transaction, the fair market value of A's retained X stock is $11,000. In the distribution, A receives Y stock worth $10,000 and Y securities worth $1,000. The receipt of the securities is taxed as boot to A, resulting in a $1,000 dividend under

§ 356(b), and A takes a $1,000 basis in the securities under § 358(a)(2). A's original basis in his X stock ($4,200), increased by the amount of boot received ($1,000) and decreased by the amount taxed as a dividend ($1,000), must be allocated in proportion to fair market value between the retained X stock ($11,000) and the Y stock received ($10,000). Thus, the basis of the retained X stock will be $2,200 ($4,200 x $^{11}/_{21}$), and that of the Y stock will be $2,000 ($4,200 x $^{10}/_{21}$). *See* § 358(c); Reg. § 1.358–2(c), Example (4).

§ 12. Tax Treatment of Distributing Corporation

Historically, § 355 prescribed only the tax consequences to the distributee shareholder; the treatment of the distributing corporation was governed by other provisions. The 1988 Act added new § 355(c) to clarify the tax treatment of the distributing corporation. Under § 355(c), § 311 will apply to any § 355 distribution that is not pursuant to a plan of reorganization to the same extent as if the distribution were described in §§ 301–307. The effect of this provision is that such a distribution will generally be subject to § 311(b), which requires corporate-level recognition of gain (but not loss) on nonliquidating distributions of appreciated property. The recognition rules of § 311(b) will not apply, however, to the distribution of qualifying stock or securities of the controlled corporation. No gain will be recognized at the corporate-level even if all or part of any securities distributed are treated as boot under § 356(d). Corporate-level gain will be recognized, however, on a distribution of recently-acquired stock of the controlled corporation which is not permitted to be received tax free under § 355(a)(3)(B).

New § 355(c) applies only to distributions not pursuant to a plan of reorganization. If a § 355 transaction included a D reorganization as a preliminary step (*e.g.,* if the distributing corporation initially transferred assets to a newly-formed subsidiary in preparation for a spin-off of the subsidiary's stock), then § 361 would control the treatment of the distributing corporation. Under § 361(c), the distributing corporation would recognize gain on a distribution of appreciated property (other than its own stock or securities or those of another corporate party to the reorganization received in the reorganization).

Example: A and B, equal shareholders of T Corp., receive stock of T's existing subsidiary (S) in a pro-rata spin-off. Under new § 355(c), the distribution of the S stock would be tax free to T. If T also distributed appreciated property in addition to the S stock, T would recognize gain on the distribution. If S were a newly-formed subsidiary instead of a preexisting one, T's initial transfer of assets to S would constitute part of a D reorganization. Accordingly, the tax treatment of T would be governed by § 361(c) rather than § 355(c), but the results would be identical.

§ 13. Failed Divisions

Although § 355 generally prescribes similar treatment for spin-offs, split-offs and split-ups, the consequences of a failed § 355 transaction may depend on the form of the division. A spin-off that fails to qualify under § 355 will be taxed as a § 301 distribution (dividend to the extent of e & p, balance treated as basis recovery or capital gain). A failed split-off will presumably be tested under the rules of § 302, and treated accordingly either as a § 302(a) exchange (*e.g.*, a non-pro-rata split-off resulting in a complete termination) or as a § 301 distribution (*e.g.*, a pro-rata split-off). The tax consequences of a failed split-up are less clear. On one hand, a failed split-up might be treated as a complete liquidation under § 331, allowing the shareholders to recognize capital gain or loss. On the other hand, if the split-up represents a segregation of liquid assets in preparation for a stock sale, § 301 treatment may be more appropriate. The Regulations provide that § 301 may apply to a distribution which takes place at the same time as another transaction if it is in substance a separate transaction. Reg. § 1.301–1(*l*). If the failed split-up is preceded by a § 351 transfer, the Service is likely to seek dividend treatment under a liquidation-reincorporation theory. *See* Telephone Answering Service Co., Inc. (1974). *See* Chapter 6.

§ 14. Future of Corporate Divisions

In light of the 1986 Act and subsequent developments, the future of § 355 is uncertain. The repeal of the *General Utilities* doctrine has placed great stress on § 355. A tax-free division of a corporate business in preparation for a sale of the stock of the distributing corporation or controlled corporation may contravene the policy underlying the repeal of *General Utilities,* if that policy is interpreted broadly as calling for imposition of a tax at the corporate level when assets are transferred outside an economic group while remaining in corporate solution. The 1987 Act tightened the restrictions on such transactions, while leaving considerable room for planning under § 355. Section 337(d) authorizes Regulations to prevent circumvention of the purpose of the 1986 Act (*e.g.,* the repeal of *General Utilities*) by the use of § 355 or otherwise. Thus, § 355 appears to be a likely target for further statutory and administrative measures to curb potential abuses.

CHAPTER 10

CARRYOVER OF CORPORATE ATTRIBUTES

§ 1. Introduction

When one corporation acquires another corporation's assets in certain tax-free transactions, § 381(a) provides generally that the acquiring corporation "shall succeed to and take into account" certain tax attributes of the acquired corporation specified in § 381(c). Section 381 applies to asset acquisitions under § 332 (subsidiary liquidations) and to A, C, non-divisive D and F reorganizations under § 368(a)(1). The corporate tax attributes enumerated in § 381(c) include net operating loss carryovers, earnings and profits, capital loss carryovers and accounting methods. Special operating rules are contained in § 381(b).

One of the most significant carryover tax attributes of the acquired corporation tends to be its net operating loss (NOL). Section 382, which restricts the use of NOLs in certain circumstances, originated in the 1954 Code as a response to a perceived problem of "trafficking" in NOLs, *i.e.*, the tax-motivated acquisition of a corporation in order to take advantage of its NOLs. As a policy matter, it may be argued that NOLs should be freely transferable, without restriction on the availability of these attributes to the acquiring corporation. If free trading were permitted, taxpayers who could not use their NOLs could derive the full economic benefit of the NOLs by selling their assets to a purchaser at an increased price reflecting the tax value of the NOLs. On the other hand, free trading in tax attributes may be viewed as a windfall to the purchaser because the increase in the purchase price attributable to the NOLs would presumably be less than the tax savings generated by the NOLs. The 1986 Act completely rewrote § 382 in an attempt to ensure that a change of ownership or combination affecting a loss corporation would neither enhance nor impair the value of its carry-overs.

§ 2. Overview of § 382

The provisions of § 382 come into play only if a loss corporation undergoes a significant change of ownership. After an ownership change, § 382 limits the amount of the old loss corporation's "pre-change losses" that may be used to offset post-change taxable income of the new loss corporation for any subsequent taxable year. The term "pre-change loss" includes NOL carryforwards that arose before the year of the ownership change, an allocable portion of the NOLs incurred during the year of the ownership change, and certain unrealized built-in losses and deductions. §§ 382(d) and 382(h)(1)(B). The statute uses the terms "old loss corporation" and "new loss corporation" to refer to a loss corporation before and after the ownership change, respectively. §§ 382(k)(2) and 382(k)(3). The same corporation may be both the old loss corporation and the new loss corporation, *e.g.,* if the ownership change that triggers § 382 involves a shift in the stock ownership of a single corporation.

Section 382(b) defines the annual limitation generally as equal to the value of the old loss corporation multiplied by the long-term tax-exempt rate (published monthly by the Service). The annual § 382 limitation is intended to approximate the amount of income that the loss corporation could have earned, absent an ownership change, if it had invested its equity in tax-exempt securities. This "limitation on earnings" approach contrasts markedly with the old § 382 rules which reduced or eliminated the amount of losses that could be carried over.

Example: A loss corporation (L) is merged into a profitable corporation (P) in a transaction which triggers § 382. Immediately before the merger, the value of L's stock is $900 and the tax-exempt rate is 10%. The annual limit under § 382(b) will be $90 (10% of $900). To the extent that there is insufficient income to absorb the entire $90 of available losses in any year, the excess amount of the loss will be carried forward to the next year. § 382(b)(2). The higher the loss in relationship to the loss corporation's value, the longer the period over which use of the losses will be spread.

§ 3. Definition of Ownership Change

(a) *General.* The triggering event under § 382 is an "ownership change," as defined in § 382(g). An ownership change requires two components. The first component may consist of either (i) an "owner shift" involving a 5% shareholder or (ii) an "equity structure shift" (referred to as "testing events"). The second component is an increase of more than 50 percentage points in the stock ownership of the loss corporation by one or more 5% shareholders (referred to as a "triggering event") within a 3–year testing period. Temporary Regulations § 1.382–2T contain an exhaustive discussion of ownership changes.

(b) *Owner Shift.* An owner shift is defined as any change in the ownership of stock in a loss corporation which affects the holdings of a 5% shareholder (generally, any person owning 5% or more of the loss corporation's stock, directly or by attribution, during the testing period). The percentage of stock owned is based on fair market value. An owner shift may be triggered by a stock purchase, issuance of stock, § 351 exchange or redemption. Certain transfers, however, cannot give rise to an owner shift: transfers between an individual and family members, gifts, bequests, transfers incident to divorce, and certain purchases by an employee stock option plan (ESOP). § 381(*l*)(3)(A)–(C).

(c) *Equity Structure Shift.* An equity structure shift includes any A, B, C, non-divisive D, or E reorganization.   Section 382(g)(3)(B) contemplates Regulations that may treat taxable reorganizations, public offerings and similar transactions as equity structure shifts.   Any equity structure shift that affects the holdings of a 5% shareholder will also constitute an owner shift; the overlap, however, has no substantive consequences other than a difference in statutory effective dates.

(d) *Ownership Change.*   After each testing event, *i.e.,* owner shift or equity structure shift, the loss corporation must determine whether there has been an increase of more than 50 percentage points in the stock ownership of a 5% shareholder within the 3–year testing period immediately preceding the testing event.   Thus, a series of unrelated transfers within the 3–year period may trigger § 382.   Each testing event gives rise to a separate 3–year testing period ending on the date of such testing event, but no testing period extends back further than the most recent preceding ownership change.

(e) *Examples.*   The types of transactions that trigger § 382 are best illustrated by the extreme cases of closely-held and publicly-held loss corporations.

Example (1).   Three unrelated individuals, A, B, and C, each own 50 of the 150 shares of outstanding stock of loss corporation L. Any change in stock ownership will be an owner shift because A, B, and C are all 5% shareholders.   Assume that A sells his ⅓ stock interest to D (an unrelated individual) on January 1, 1989. D's acquisition of A's stock will be an owner shift involving a 5% shareholder, but will not trigger an ownership change because D's percentage ownership increases only $33\frac{1}{3}$ percentage points (from 0 to $33\frac{1}{3}\%$). If B sells his $\frac{1}{3}$ stock interest to E (another unrelated individual) on January 1, 1990, there will be a second testing event. Since D and E together have increased their percentage ownership in L by more than 50 percentage points (from 0 to $66\frac{2}{3}\%$), there will be an ownership change on January 1, 1990. If C sells his $\frac{1}{3}$ stock interest to E on February 1, 1990, there will not be a second ownership change on that date because the testing period for the February 1 transfer extends back only to January 2, 1990 (the day following the most recent preceding ownership change).

Example (2). The facts are the same as in Example (1), except that L makes a public offering of its stock on January 1, 1989. Pursuant to the public offering, an additional 150 shares of L stock are sold to investors, none of whom acquires as much as 5% of L's stock. Rather than ignore the less than 5% shareholders, § 382(g)(4)(A) aggregates such shareholders and treats them as a single hypothetical shareholder: thus, the group of new investors (Public L) will be treated as a single 5% shareholder. Because Public L's stock ownership has increased exactly 50 percentage points (from 0 to 150 shares of 300 total outstanding), there is an owner shift but not an ownership change. After the public offering, L will have four 5% shareholders, A, B, C and Public L.

Example (3). Loss corporation L is a publicly-owned corporation. All 1,000 shares of L's stock are owned by 100 unrelated shareholders, none of whom owns as much as 5% of the L stock (Public L). If various members of Public L sell 30% of L's stock to individual A on January 1, 1989, there will be an owner shift (but not an ownership change) because A's stock ownership increases from 0 to 30%. After the transfer to A, L will have two 5% shareholders, A (who owns 30% individually) and Public L (which owns the remaining 70%). Assume that during 1990 each of the remaining individuals in Public L sells his stock to other unrelated individuals, none of whom acquires as much as 5%. Since public trading among non–5% shareholders is disregarded, the sales by members of Public L will not constitute an ownership change. *See* Temp. Reg. § 1.382–2T(e)(1)(iii), Example (3).

Example (4). The facts are the same as in Example (3), except that L makes a public offering of its stock on January 1, 1989. Pursuant to the public offering, 1,000 additional shares of L stock are sold to new investors, none of whom acquires as much as 5% of L's stock. L appears to have only a single 5% shareholder (Public L) before and after the public offering. Section 382(g)(3)(B), however, permits the Treasury to treat a public offering as an equity structure shift. Without exercising this authority, the Temporary Regulations achieve the

same result by dividing L's stockholders into two
public ownership groups, the pre-public offering
group (Public L) and the new investors acquiring L
stock pursuant to the public offering (New Public
L). Temp. Reg. § 1.382–2T(e)(1)(iii), Example (5).
Accordingly, the public offering is treated as an
owner shift because New Public L is a 5% shareholder. There is no ownership change, however,
because New Public L's stock ownership has increased by only 50 percentage points. After the
public offering, L will have two hypothetical 5%
shareholders, Public L and New Public L.

Example (5). Loss corporation L is merged into
profitable corporation P in an A reorganization.
Before the merger, shareholder A owns all the
stock of L and shareholder B owns all the stock of
P. As a result of the merger, A receives 25% of P's
stock, with B retaining the rest of P's stock. The
merger is an equity structure shift which is also an
owner shift. There is also a triggering ownership
change because B is deemed to have acquired 75%
of L in the merger. *See* Temp. Reg. § 1.382–2T(j)
(2)(iii)(B)(2), Example (1). The result is the same as
if the old loss corporation had remained in existence and issued its stock to the existing shareholders of the acquiring corporation. Since the old loss
corporation disappears as a result of the merger,
the acquiring corporation is regarded as the new
loss corporation and becomes entitled to the old
loss corporation's pre-change losses, subject to the
§ 382 limitation. To avoid an ownership change,

A must receive at least 50% of the P stock in the merger, because this would prevent B's deemed increased ownership from exceeding 50 percentage points.

Example (6). The facts are the same as in Example (5) except that L and P are both publicly-held corporations, and no single shareholder of either corporation (Public L and Public P) owns 5% of L or P stock. On January 1, 1989, L is merged into P in an A reorganization, and the L shareholders receive 50% of P's stock. The merger is an equity structure shift which is also an owner shift. Section 382(g)(4)(B)(i) requires that Public L and Public P be treated as separate hypothetical 5% shareholders. Since Public P has increased its percentage ownership in L by just 50 percentage points, the equity structure shift does not constitute an ownership change. After the merger, Public P and Public L will continue to be treated as two separate 5% shareholders.

§ 4. Attribution and Tracing Rules

In determining stock ownership, the attribution rules of § 318 generally apply with the following modifications (unless otherwise provided by Regulations). First, an individual and all family members (as defined in § 318(a)(1)) are aggregated and treated as one individual. § 382(*l*)(3)(A)(i). Thus, if a father sells stock to his daughter, the sale is disregarded and does not cause an owner shift. Second, stock owned by various entities (corporations, partnerships, trusts or estates) is attributed to the beneficial owners in proportion to their beneficial interests, regardless of the size of such interests, and is not treated as owned by the entity. § 382(*l*)(3)(A)(ii). Third, stock is not attributed from a beneficial owner to an entity. § 382(*l*)(3)(A)(iii). Fourth, an option to acquire stock is treated as exercised if such exercise would cause an ownership change. § 382(*l*)(3)(A)(iv); Temp. Reg. 1.382–2T(h)(4). The Temporary Regulations treat an entity that owns less than 5% of the loss corporation's stock as an unrelated individual, *i.e.*, stock owned by such an entity will not be attributed from the entity to its beneficial owners. See Temp. Reg. § 1.382–2(T)(h)(2)(iii). The purpose of these rules is to track the ultimate beneficial ownership of stock.

Example. A, who owns all of the stock of a loss corporation (L), creates a new corporation (X) to which A contributes his L stock in exchange for all of X's stock. There is no owner shift because all of X's L stock is treated as owned by A, not X. In effect, X is "looked through" for purposes of determining beneficial ownership of the L stock.

A loss corporation may generally rely on required filings under the Securities and Exchange Act of 1934 to determine the identity of 5% or more shareholders. Temp. Reg. § 1.382–2T(k)(1)(i). To the extent that the loss corporation has actual knowledge of stock ownership, it must take such actual knowledge into account. Temp. Reg. § 1.382–2T(k)(2). The Temporary Regulations do not define "actual knowledge" or provide any guidance as to when a loss corporation will be deemed to have actual knowledge concerning stock ownership. Although mere negligence clearly should not trigger this provision, "reckless disregard" of the facts might be sufficient. The loss corporation must also file annual statements with its tax return which identify any testing events and ownership changes during the year. Temp. Reg. § 1.382–2T(a)(2)(ii).

§ 5. Definition of Stock

The term "stock" generally includes any type of equity interest, except straight preferred stock (*i.e.*, nonvoting, nonconvertible stock which is limited and preferred as to dividends, does not participate in corporate growth to any significant extent and does not have an unreasonable liquidation or redemption premium). §§ 382(k)(6)(A) and 1504(a)(4). Thus, straight preferred stock is disregarded in testing ownership changes, but is included in determining the value of the loss corporation. Furthermore, Treasury is authorized to disregard certain equity interests that nominally constitute stock (*e.g.*, voting preferred stock) and to treat certain "non-stock" interests (*e.g.*, options and convertible debt) as "stock." § 382(k)(6)(B). *See also* Temp. Reg. § 1.382–2T(f)(18).

§ 6. Value After Redemptions and Bankruptcy Proceedings

Generally, the value of the old loss corporation is determined immediately before an ownership change. § 382(e)(1). In the case of redemptions and similar transactions, however, the value is determined immediately after the ownership change. § 382(e)(2). Thus, if a loss corporation is acquired in a "bootstrap" acquisition, distributions to redeemed shareholders will reduce the value of the loss corporation (and hence the annual loss limitation).

In the case of insolvency, a loss corporation's value will generally be $0. If the general rules of § 382 applied, this would effectively eliminate all NOLs after an ownership change. Section 382(*l*) (5), however, provides special rules for loss corporations involved in bankruptcy or similar proceedings. The effect of these special rules is generally that losses will not be limited after an ownership change, if at least 50% of the loss corporation's stock immediately after the change is owned by former shareholders and certain long-term creditors. § 382(*l*)(5)(A). The loss corporation's NOLs may, nevertheless, be reduced to reflect debt cancellation income under § 108(e) and other items. §§ 382(*l*)(5)(B) and 382(*l*)(5)(C). If a second ownership change occurs within 2 years after the initial ownership change, the § 382 loss limitation is reduced to zero for any year ending after the second ownership change. § 382(*l*)(5)(D).

§ 7. Anti-stuffing Rules

Congress was concerned that a loss corporation's value might be artificially inflated by additional capital contributions prior to the ownership change. Under the anti-stuffing rules, any capital contribution made as part of a plan with a principal purpose of avoiding or increasing the § 382 loss limitation is disregarded in determining the value of the loss corporation. § 382(*l*)(1)(A). For this purpose, any capital contribution made within 2 years before the ownership change is presumed to be part of such a plan. § 382(*l*)(1)(B). The legislative history provides that Regulations may exempt certain contributions made for business purposes.

§ 8. Reduction of Value for Investment Assets

If ⅓ or more of a corporation's assets are "nonbusiness" assets (*i.e.*, cash and investment assets), the value of the loss corporation is reduced by the value of those assets (net of any allocable debt) for § 382 loss limitation purposes. § 382(*l*)(4). A corporation that owns at least 50% of the stock of a subsidiary, however, is treated as owning its ratable share of the subsidiary's assets rather than the subsidiary's stock. § 382(*l*)(4)(E). In some instances, it may be unclear whether certain types of assets (*e.g.*, real estate) are passive investment assets or operating assets.

§ 9. Increase for Recognized Built-In Gains

If a loss corporation has a substantial "net unrealized built-in gain" at the time of an ownership change, the § 382 loss limitation is increased by the "recognized built-in gain" for any taxable year within a 5–year "recognition period" following the ownership change. § 382(h). The § 382 loss limitation is also increased by gain triggered under § 338. § 382(h)(1)(C). Since the old loss corporation could have used its losses to offset such gains in the absence of the ownership change, it is appropriate to allow the new loss corporation to use such losses similarly.

Net unrealized built-in gain is defined as the amount by which the aggregate fair market value of the corporation's assets (other than cash and certain marketable securities) exceed their aggregate basis immediately before the ownership change. § 382(h)(3). If the net unrealized built-in gain is 25% or less of the fair market value of such assets, however, the net built-in gain is deemed to be zero. For example, the 25% threshold requirement is met if the corporation has assets with an aggregate fair market value of $136 and an aggregate basis of $100, because the appreciation ($36) exceeds 25% of $136 ($34). Recognized built-in gain is any gain attributable to disposition of an asset held by the old loss corporation, to the extent that such gain does not exceed the unrealized built-in gain attributable to the asset on the date of the ownership change. § 382(h)(2). The total increase in the § 382 loss limitation for recognized built-in gain during the 5–year recognition period may not exceed the net unrealized built-in gain immediately before the ownership change. § 382(h)(1)(A)(ii).

§ 10. Limit on Net Built-In Losses

Section 382 limits the recognition of net built-in losses as well as NOLs. If a corporation has net unrealized built-in losses, § 382(h) subjects those losses to the § 382 limitation if they are realized within a 5–year recognition period following the ownership change. § 382(h)(1)(B). As in the case of built-in gains, built-in losses are determined immediately before the ownership change and must meet a 25% threshold requirement. § 382(h)(3). If a corporation has a built-in gain of $50 for one asset and a built-in loss of $100 for another asset, the net unrealized built-in loss is $50. If a built-in loss is disallowed under § 382 for a taxable year, that loss may be carried over and used in a later year, subject to the § 382 limit. § 382(h)(4). The 1987 Act amended § 382(h)(2)(B) to provide that built-in depreciation deductions are generally treated as built-in losses.

§ 11. Continuity of Business Enterprise

Under § 382(c), loss carryovers are retroactively reduced to zero if the new loss corporation fails to continue the business enterprise of the old loss corporation for the 2–year period beginning on the ownership change. The business continuity test is the same as for tax-free reorganizations under Regulations § 1.368–1(d), i.e., the new loss corporation must either continue the old loss corporation's business or must use a significant portion of the old loss corporation's assets in a business. If the business continuity test is not met, § 382(c)(2) nevertheless allows loss carryforwards to the extent of recognized built-in gains and § 338 gains.

§ 12. Section 383 Limit on Other Items

Upon an ownership change with respect to a loss corporation, § 383 limits certain other items (unused general business credits, unused minimum tax credits, capital loss carryforwards and foreign tax credits) under rules similar to those of § 382.

§ 13. Section 384 Limit on Sheltering Built-In Gains

In 1987, Congress enacted § 384 to limit a corporation's ability to offset built-in gains against "preacquisition losses" (*i.e.,* NOLs and built-in losses) of another corporation during a 5–year recognition period following certain stock or asset acquisitions. § 384. The stock acquisition rule applies if one corporation acquires "control" of another corporation and either corporation is a gain corporation (*i.e.,* a corporation with a net unrealized built-in gain at the time of acquisition). Control is defined as stock representing 80% of the voting power and value of a corporation within the meaning of § 1504(a)(2). The asset acquisition rules apply to any tax-free A, C or D reorganization if either the acquired or acquiring corporation is a gain corporation. A special rule for successor corporations ensures that the § 384 limitation remains applicable if one corporation is liquidated tax-free into another corporation under § 332. Section 384 does not apply if both corporations were members of the same controlled group under § 1563(a) (using a 50% ownership test) during the previous 5–year period (or the entire period of the gain or loss corporation's existence, if shorter). If § 384 applies, preacquisition losses may be used to offset only non-built-in gains or built-in gains which are recognized more than 5 years after the acquisition.

Example. Gain corporation G is acquired by loss corporation L in a transaction which is subject to § 384. G has a net unrealized built-in gain of $200,000 and L has an NOL of $500,000. In the first post-acquisition year, G recognizes a $50,000 built-in gain. L's loss carryforward cannot be used to offset any portion of G's gain. In the second post-acquisition year, G realizes a gain of $200,000. Only $150,000 ($200,000 net unrealized built-in gain less $50,000 previously recognized built-in gain) of the $200,000 gain is treated as a recognized built-in gain subject to § 384. Since G has recognized its entire net unrealized built-in gain, L's $500,000 NOL may be used to offset G's remaining $50,000 of gain (and any subsequent gains) until the NOL is used up or expires.

§ 14. Relationship of § 269 and §§ 382–384

Under prior law, the Service was authorized under § 269 to deny certain tax benefits following an acquisition of control of a corporation or a tax-free acquisition of a corporation's assets, if the principal purpose of the acquisition was tax evasion or avoidance. Although § 269 remains in full force, its role is greatly reduced because new §§ 382–384 automatically limit the desired tax benefits in nearly all transactions within the scope of § 269. The legislative history of the 1986 Act also notes specifically that the judicially-developed doctrine of *Libson Shops* (1954) (limiting use of loss carryovers to income of the same business that generated the losses) does not apply to transactions covered by § 382.

CHAPTER 11

SUBCHAPTER S

§ 1. General

Subchapter S (now §§ 1361–1379), originally added to the Code in 1958 and amended in 1982, is intended to minimize federal income tax considerations in deciding whether to conduct a business in the form of a corporation, partnership or other entity. A corporation that elects Subchapter S treatment (an "S corporation") is roughly comparable to a partnership for federal income tax purposes: in each case, the entity's income (whether actually distributed or not) and losses generally pass through directly to shareholders, without being separately taxed at the entity level. The analogy between the "pass-through" treatment of S corporations under Subchapter S and partnerships under Subchapter K, however, is imperfect. An S corporation represents a hybrid of corporate and partnership-type characteristics, and remains subject to the rules of Subchapter C except to the extent preempted by those of Subchapter S or otherwise made inapplicable. § 1371(a).

The 1986 Act encourages increased use of S corporations, which combine the advantages of corporate business form with those of a single-level income tax. Income from an S corporation's business operations will generally be subject to a single shareholder-level tax at a maximum rate of 28%, which is less burdensome than the double-level tax (including a 34% maximum rate at the corporate level) imposed on C corporations. Even if a corporation retains its earnings for its own growth, an S corporation will generally bear a lower tax burden in the long run because its retained earnings can be distributed tax free in a liquidation or on a sale of the shareholder's stock.

§ 2. Eligibility

An S corporation is defined as a "small business corporation" for which a Subchapter S election is in effect. § 1361(a)(1). A small business corporation is a domestic corporation with only one class of stock and no more than 35 shareholders; each shareholder must be an individual (other than a nonresident alien), an estate or an eligible trust. § 1362(b)(1). Moreover, an S corporation must not be an "ineligible corporation," defined in § 1362(b)(2) to include members of an affiliated group, financial institutions and certain other entities. For purposes of the 35–shareholder limit, a husband and wife (and their respective estates) are treated as a single shareholder, regardless of whether they hold stock jointly or separately. § 1361(c)(1). All other co-owners are treated as separate shareholders. Prop. Reg. § 1.1361–1A(e).

Eligible trusts include grantor-type trusts treated under §§ 671–678 as owned by an individual who is a United States citizen or resident. § 1361(c)

(2)(A). In addition, eligible trusts include "qualified Subchapter S trusts," essentially trusts having a single current income beneficiary who makes a timely election to have the provisions of § 1361(d) apply. A typical trust of this sort is a "qualified terminable interest property" trust established for the benefit of a decedent's surviving spouse and qualifying for the estate-tax marital deduction.

The one-class-of-stock rule is designed to ensure that each share of stock represents an equal share in the profits and assets of the corporation, and obviates the need to allocate income among different classes of stock. A corporation will not be treated as having more than one class of stock merely because of differences in voting rights among the shares of common stock. § 1361(c)(4). Also, preferred stock that is authorized but unissued does not violate the one-class-of-stock rule. A shareholder agreement restricting the transferability of stock is generally not viewed as creating a second class of stock. Rev. Rul. 85–161.

Under prior law, the Service often litigated unsuccessfully the issue of whether corporate debt owed to shareholders, if reclassified as equity, counted as a second class of stock. A safe harbor now exists for so-called "straight debt," which will not be treated as a second class of stock for purposes of the one-class-of-stock requirement. § 1361(c)(5). The safe-harbor rules require a written unconditional promise to pay a sum certain in money on demand or a specified date; the interest rate must not be contingent on profits or the borrower's discretion; the debt cannot be convertible into stock; and the creditor must be an individual or entity eligible to own stock in an S corporation. If debt is held in substantially the same proportion as nominal stock, even if not within the safe harbor, such debt presumably should not be treated as a second class of stock. *See* Reg. § 1.1371–1(g) (pre–1983 law).

§ 3. Election, Revocation and Termination

(a) *Election.* An S election for any taxable year may be made during such taxable year on or before the 15th day of the third month thereof or at any time during the preceding taxable year. § 1362(b)(1). The timing requirement must be strictly observed: an S election that is filed late is treated as being made for the following taxable year. A corporation's first taxable year does not begin until the corporation has shareholders, acquires assets or begins doing business, whichever occurs first. Reg. § 1.1372–2(b)(1) (pre–1983 law). All persons who are shareholders on the day of the election (and former shareholders, in some cases) must consent. § 1362(a)(2); Temp. Reg. § 18.1362–2(b)(1). Once made, an S election remains effective until revoked or terminated.

The Service has generally been lenient in permitting technical defects to be cured, despite the absence of statutory discretion. In *Smith* (1988) (Unpublished Case), however, the court indicated that the failure of a qualified corporate officer to sign the election form was not "substantial compliance." Accordingly, the court held that the S election was invalid even though the Service had permitted refiling of the election with a proper signature after the statutory period for making the election expired.

(b) *Revocation.* An S election may be revoked only with the consent of shareholders owning more than half of the corporation's stock on the day of the revocation. § 1362(d)(1)(B). Generally, a revocation takes effect as of the first day of the corporation's current taxable year if made on or before the 15th day of the third month thereof, or as of the first day of the following taxable year if made after the 15th day of the third month. The revocation may, however, specify any prospective effective date. §§ 1362(d)(1)(C) and 1362(d)(1)(D). For example, a revocation filed on April 1 for a calendar-year S corporation will generally be effective on the following January 1; if the revocation specifies April 15 as the effective date, however, it will be effective as of that date.

(c) *Involuntary Termination.* An S election may also be terminated involuntarily if the corporation ceases to be a "small business corporation," *e.g.,* because stock is transferred to a nonresident alien or a partnership. § 1362(d)(2). An inadvertent termination may be disregarded if action is promptly taken to requalify the corporation as a small business corporation and the shareholders agree to make any required adjustments. § 1362(f); Rev.

Rul. 86–110. An involuntary termination may also occur if an S corporation (with accumulated e & p from operations as a C corporation) for 3 consecutive taxable years has passive investment income exceeding 25% of gross receipts. § 1362(d)(3). In addition to automatic termination, the corporation is subject to a penalty tax on "excess net passive income" under § 1375, discussed in § 7 below.

(d) *Effect of Termination.* If a revocation or involuntary termination takes effect in mid-year, the corporation's taxable year is divided into 2 short years, representing the portion of the year preceding the effective date (the "S short year") and the portion of the year beginning on the effective date (the "C short year"), respectively. § 1362(e). Generally, items of income, loss, deduction and credit are allocated between the S short year and C short year in proportion to the number of days in the respective short years (the daily allocation rule). § 1362(e)(2). Alternatively, if all persons who were shareholders at any time during the S short year and on the first day of the C short year so elect, items may be allocated to the respective short years based on normal tax accounting rules (the specific allocation rule). § 1362(e)(3). If more than 50% of the corporation's stock is sold or exchanged during the termination year, then the specific allocation rule is mandatory. § 1362(e)(6)(D). The corporation's tax liability for the C short year must be computed on an annualized basis, thereby preventing the corporation from exploiting the low corporate tax brackets. § 1362(e)(5)(A).

(e) *Election After Termination.* After revocation or involuntary termination of an S election, the corporation is ineligible to make a new election for a 5–year period, without the consent of the Service. § 1362(g).

§ 4. Taxable Year and Accounting Methods

An S corporation's income or loss flows through to a shareholder in his taxable year in which (or with which) the corporation's taxable year ends. § 1366(a). For example, if the S corporation's first taxable year begins on February 1, 1989 and ends on January 31, 1990, an individual shareholder will report income for that period in his individual return for calendar year 1990. In effect, the corporation's fiscal year permits a deferral of tax at the shareholder level on the first 11 months of the corporation's income.

To eliminate such deferral, § 1378 requires that an S corporation use a calendar year unless it establishes a business purpose (other than deferral of income to shareholders) for a different fiscal year. *See* Rev. Proc. 87–32 (guidelines for requests to adopt, retain or change taxable years). The 1987 Act left § 1378 unchanged, but added two new provisions, §§ 444 and 7519. Under § 444, an existing S corporation may elect to retain its pre–1987 fiscal year and a new S corporation may elect a fiscal year that results in no more than 3 months of deferral at the shareholder level (generally, a taxable year ending in September, October or November). *See* Temp. Reg. § 1.444–1T–3T. The price of the election is that the entity must pay a tax under new § 7519 intended to compensate for the shareholder-level deferral attributable to the § 444 election. *See* Temp. Reg. § 1.7519–1T–3T.

An S corporation is generally not subject to the mandatory accrual accounting method under § 448. Moreover, under § 267(e)(1), an S corporation and any person who owns (directly or indirectly) any of its stock are treated as related parties within the meaning of § 267(b). As a result, an S corporation is not permitted to deduct salary payments to a shareholder until such payments are includible in the shareholder's income. *See* § 267(a)(2).

§ 5. Pass–Through of Income or Loss

(a) *General.* Generally, an S corporation is treated as a conduit, and is not subject to corporate-level tax except for special taxes imposed under §§ 1374 and 1375. Taxable income of an S corporation, which flows through to the shareholders, is computed in the same manner as that of an individual with certain modifications. § 1363(b). Under § 1366(a)(1), each shareholder must report his pro-rata share of the corporation's separately and non-separately stated items of income, loss, deduction or credit. Separately-stated items are those which could affect the tax liability of different shareholders differently depending on their particular tax situations, *e.g.,* capital gain, § 1231 gain, charitable contributions, and tax-exempt income. All other items (*e.g.,* operating income) are combined at the corporate level, and passed through to shareholders as an item of non-separately stated net income or loss. Each item included in a shareholder's pro-rata share has the same character as in the hands of the corporation. § 1366(b).

(b) *Basis Adjustments.* A shareholder's basis in stock and debt of an S corporation is important in determining the amount of losses and deductions that can be passed through, as well as the tax treatment of corporate distributions, sales or exchanges of stock, and repayment or retirement of debt. Initially, a shareholder's basis in stock acquired in a § 351 transaction is the amount of cash or the adjusted basis of any property contributed to the S corporation, adjusted for any liabilities assumed or taken subject to. § 358. Under § 1367(a)(1), a shareholder's stock basis is increased by separately and non-separately stated items of income. Under § 1367(a)(2), stock basis is decreased by separately and non-separately stated items of loss and deduction, tax-free § 1368 corporate distributions, and items of expense which are neither deductible to the corporation in computing its income nor properly capitalized (*e.g.,* a bribe or illegal payment).

Example: A, an individual, contributes $10,000 to X, a newly-formed calendar-year S corporation, in exchange for all of its stock. In Year 1, X earns $5,000 of taxable income and distributes $1,000 to A on December 31. Under § 1363(a), X is not taxed; under § 1366(a), the $5,000 of income passes through and is taxed directly to A. A's original basis in his X stock ($10,000) is first increased by $5,000 under § 1367(a)(1), and then reduced by $1,000 under § 1367(a)(2)(A) to reflect the tax-free distribution to A. *See* § 1368(b). If X instead distributed the $1,000 to A in Year 2 (and had no taxable income that year), the result would be the same. If X had an operating loss rather than operating income of $5,000 in Year 1, the loss would reduce A's basis in his stock from $10,000 to $5,000 under § 1367(a)(2)(B), and A could use the $5,000 deduction to offset $5,000 of otherwise taxable income, subject to the at-risk and passive loss limitations of §§ 465 and 469.

(c) *Limitation on Losses.* Section 1366(d)(1) limits the amount of losses or deductions passing through to a shareholder for any taxable year to the sum of the shareholder's aggregate basis in stock of the corporation and debt owed by the corporation to the shareholder. The purpose of § 1366(d)(1) is to limit the allowable pass-through losses and deductions to the amount of the shareholder's actual investment in the corporation. Any disallowed loss or deduction is carried over indefinitely to subsequent years and may be used when the shareholder's basis is increased through additional capital contributions, loans or net operating income. § 1366(d)(2). Under § 1367(b)(2)(A), items of loss and deduction are applied first against the shareholder's stock basis and then against the basis of any indebtedness. Under § 1367(b)(2)(B), any net increase in basis is applied first to restore any reduction in the basis of debt for taxable years beginning after December 31, 1982, and then to increase the shareholder's stock basis; any pre–1983 basis reduction in corporate debt is not restored.

Example: A, an individual, contributes $2,000 to X, a calendar-year S corporation, in exchange for all of its stock, and simultaneously lends $5,000 to X. In Year 1 (after 1982), X has an operating loss of $3,000. Under § 1367(b)(2)(A), A's basis in his stock is first reduced from $2,000 to zero, and the remaining $1,000 of loss is applied to reduce A's basis in the debt from $5,000 to $4,000. In Year 2, X has operating income of $4,000. Under § 1367(b)(2)(B), A's basis in the debt is first increased from $4,000 to $5,000, and A's stock basis is then increased from zero to $3,000. If X instead had an operating loss of $8,000 in Year 1, A's basis in the stock ($2,000) and the debt ($5,000) would be reduced to zero; the remaining $1,000 of loss would be disallowed under § 1366(d)(1) and carried over to a subsequent year. If X had operating income of $4,000 in Year 2, A's basis in the debt would first be restored to $4,000; A could then use the $1,000 carryover loss to offset $1,000 of the Year 2 income, and A's basis in the debt would be decreased to $3,000.

(d) *Basis in Corporate Debt.* Corporate debt generally creates basis in the hands of a shareholder only if it runs directly from the corporation to the shareholder. Moreover, the shareholder must make an actual economic outlay; for example, a shareholder who merely delivers his promissory note to the corporation receives no basis. Rev. Rul. 81–187. An S shareholder, unlike a partner, does not receive basis for debts incurred by the corporation to third-party lenders. A shareholder guarantee of third-party debt ordinarily does not provide basis until the shareholder actually makes payments under the guarantee, or shareholder notes are substituted for corporate notes to the lender. *See, e.g.,* Rev. Rul. 75–144; Leavitt Estate (1988) (Unpublished Case). Some courts, however, have permitted a basis increase in the guarantee context if the particular facts demonstrate that the lender looks primarily to the shareholder for repayment and the S corporation is thinly capitalized. *See* Selfe (1985).

(e) *At-Risk and Passive Loss Limitations.* Individual S shareholders are subject to the at-risk rules of § 465 which limit the amount of loss from certain activities (expanded by the 1986 Act to include real estate activities) allowable as deductions to the aggregate amount the taxpayer has "at risk" in the activity at the close of the taxable year. An S shareholder's amount at risk is initially equal to the amount of personal funds and the adjusted basis of unencumbered property which he contributes to the activity. § 465(b)(1). *See* Prop. Reg. §§ 1.465–22(a) and 1.465–23(a). Amounts borrowed for use in the activity (*e.g.*, funds borrowed by an S shareholder and lent to the corporation) increase the shareholder's amount at risk only to the extent that he is personally liable for repayment of the borrowed amount or has pledged property not used in the activity as security. § 465(b)(2). An S shareholder is generally not considered at risk for debt owed by the corporation to third parties, even if the shareholder guarantees the debt. Prop. Reg. §§ 1.465–24(a) and 1.465–6(d). Under a special rule applicable to the activity of holding real property, a taxpayer may be considered at risk to the extent of his share of "qualified nonrecourse financing" (*e.g.*, a commercial loan) which is secured by real property used in the activity. § 465(b)(6). Absent a specific S corporation pass-through rule, however, it is unclear whether this special rule applies to S shareholders. An S shareholder's amount at risk is increased by any pass-through income (including tax-exempt income), and correspondingly decreased by any pass-through losses, distributions and repayment of debt. Prop. Reg. §§ 1.465–22(b), 1.465–22(c), and 1.465–23(c). If losses exceed the S shareholder's amount at risk at the end of the taxable year, such excess losses are suspended and carried over indefinitely until the shareholder's amount at risk is increased. § 465(a)(2); Prop. Reg. § 1.465–2.

Individual S shareholders are also subject to the passive activity loss limitations of § 469. A passive activity generally includes any rental activity and any other trade or business in which the taxpayer (S corporation shareholder) does not "materially participate"; rental activities are treated as passive activities without regard to material participation. § 469(c). Under the Temporary Regulations, a taxpayer is treated as "materially participating" if he satisfies any one of 7 alternative tests (including participation in the activity for more than 500 hours in the year). Temp. Reg. § 1.469–5T(a). Passive activity losses may generally be used only to offset income from passive activities, not income from active sources or portfolio income (*e.g.*, dividends, interest and royalties). A special rule, however, permits an individual to offset non-passive income by up to $25,000 of losses from rental real estate activities in which the individual "actively participates." § 469(i). Passive losses and credits that cannot be used for the current taxable year are "suspended" and carried over indefinitely to subsequent years. Suspended passive losses are recognized and may be used to offset any other income on a fully taxable disposition of the taxpayer's entire interest in the activity. § 469(g)(1)(A).

The at-risk and passive loss rules serve as additional limitations on an S shareholder's ability to deduct losses passed through from the S corporation. The shareholder's basis is reduced under

§ 1367 regardless of whether the loss is subject to further limitation under § 465 or § 469. Similarly, the shareholder's amount at risk under § 465 is reduced regardless of whether the loss is suspended under § 469. The shareholder's basis and amount at risk are not further reduced, however, when the loss is ultimately allowed under § 469.

Example: A contributed $20,000 to X (a calendar-year S corporation) in exchange for X stock. X is engaged in an at-risk activity in which A does not materially participate. In Year 1, A's share of X's operating loss is $50,000. Since the loss ($50,000) exceeds A's amount at risk ($20,000), A may deduct only $20,000 of loss currently. Even if the $20,000 loss is subject to further limitation under § 469, A's stock basis and amount at risk are reduced to zero at the end of Year 1.

§ 6. Distributions

(a) *General.* Distributions made by an S corporation with respect to its stock that would otherwise (if made by a C corporation) be taxed under § 301(c) are instead taxed under § 1368. Such distributions may be attributable to original shareholder capital contributions, borrowed funds, S earnings, or e & p accumulated while the corporation was a C corporation.

(b) *No Accumulated E & P.* If an S corporation has no accumulated e & p from any source, a distribution of cash will be tax free to a shareholder to the extent that it does not exceed the shareholder's stock basis. § 1368(b)(1). Any excess will be treated as gain from a sale or exchange of property. § 1368(b)(2). This simplified treatment applies to all distributions from S corporations formed after 1982 for which an S election has been in effect since inception; such corporations will never have accumulated e & p (unless a former C corporation is acquired in a tax-free reorganization).

Example: A, the sole shareholder of X (a calendar-year S corporation) has a basis in his X stock of $5,000. In Year 1, X distributes $2,000 to A. The $2,000 distribution is treated as a tax-free recovery of basis under § 1368(b)(1), reducing A's stock basis from $5,000 to $3,000 under § 1367(a)(2)(A). In Year 2, X has operating income of $3,000 and borrows $10,000 from a third party. At the end of Year 2, X distributes the $3,000 of operating income and also distributes $5,000 of the borrowed funds. A's stock basis is first increased from $3,000 to $6,000 under § 1367(a)(1), and then decreased to zero by the tax-free $6,000 portion of the $8,000 distribution. §§ 1368(b)(1) and 1367(a)(2)(A). Under § 1368(b)(2), the remaining portion of the distribution ($2,000) is treated as gain from sale or exchange of property.

(c) *Accumulated E & P.* The distribution rules are considerably more complex if an S corporation has accumulated e & p from its previous existence as a C corporation. Under § 1368(c)(1), a distribution from an S corporation with accumulated e & p is treated the same as a § 1368(b) distribution (basis recovery or gain from a sale or exchange) to the extent of the S corporation's "accumulated adjustments account" (AAA). The AAA represents essentially the post–1982 undistributed net income of the S corporation; it is a corporate-level account which begins at zero and is adjusted for the S corporation's income or loss in a manner similar to the basis adjustments of § 1367. § 1368(e)(1)(A). Unlike basis adjustments, however, the AAA is not increased by tax-exempt income and may be reduced below zero. If the AAA is reduced below zero, it must first be restored to a positive balance before tax-free distributions may be made to shareholders. Any distribution in excess of the AAA is taxed as a dividend to the extent of the S corporation's accumulated e & p. § 1368(c)(2). Once distributions have exhausted accumulated e & p, any further distributions will be nontaxable to the extent of the shareholder's remaining stock basis and any excess will be taxed as proceeds from a sale or exchange. § 1368(c)(3).

Example: A, an individual, is the sole shareholder of X, a calendar-year S corporation. At the end of Year 1, A has a basis of $70,000 in his X stock; and X has accumulated e & p of $10,000 and an AAA of $50,000. On December 31, X distributes $100,000 to A. The $100,000 distribution is nontaxable to the extent of X's AAA ($50,000), and reduces A's basis in his stock from $70,000 to $20,000. §§ 1368(c)(1) and 1368(b)(1). Of the remaining distribution, $10,000 is attributed to X's accumulated e & p, and is taxed as a dividend to A under § 1368(c)(2). The portion taxed as a dividend has no effect on A's stock basis, because basis is reduced under § 1367(b)(2)(A) only by tax-free § 1368 distributions. Once X's accumulated e & p is exhausted, the remaining $40,000 is treated as tax-free basis recovery to the extent of A's remaining basis ($20,000) and the balance ($20,000) is taxed as gain from a sale or exchange under § 1368(c)(3).

The AAA must be adjusted downward by the amount of any distribution which is treated as tax-free to the shareholder. §§ 1368(e)(1)(A) and 1367(a)(2)(A). In the case of a redemption of stock which is treated as an exchange, a special rule provides that the AAA is reduced by a percentage equal to the percentage of stock redeemed. § 1368(e)(1)(B). The corporation's accumulated e & p is adjusted downward by the amount of a distribution treated as a taxable dividend under § 1368(c)(2). § 1371(c)(3). A special rule also permits an S corporation, with the consent of all affected shareholders, to elect to treat distributions as attributable first to accumulated e & p. § 1368(e)(3). This election may be useful if a corporation wishes to purge itself of accumulated e & p.

(d) *Timing of Adjustments.* The tax treatment of distributions is normally determined at the end of the S corporation's taxable year, regardless of when the distributions are actually made. Stock basis is increased by pass-through items of income, and decreased by pass-through items of loss or deduction, before the tax treatment of distributions. § 1368(d).

Example: A, an individual, is the sole shareholder of X, a calendar-year S corporation. At the beginning of Year 1, A has a basis of $50,000 in his X stock. X has net operating income of $25,000 during the first 3 months of Year 1, and a net operating loss of $75,000 during the last 9 months of the year. On April 1, X distributes $25,000 cash to A. The taxability of the distribution will be determined at the end of the year. Under § 1367(a)(2)(B), A's stock basis will first be decreased from $50,000 to zero to reflect the net loss for the year ($50,000). Since A's stock basis is now zero, the entire $25,000 distribution will be taxed as gain from a sale or exchange under § 1368(b)(2), even though A had sufficient stock basis on April 1 to absorb the entire distribution.

§ 7. Treatment of the S Corporation

(a) *General.* An S corporation without accumulated e & p is generally not subject to corporate-level tax. Under §§ 1374 and 1375, however, special penalty taxes are levied on S corporations that have prior operating histories as C corporations.

(b) *Excess Net Passive Income.* Under § 1375(a), an S corporation may be subject to a corporate-level tax if it has accumulated e & p at the end of the year and its passive investment income exceeds 25% of its gross receipts. For this purpose, gross receipts are defined as the "total amount received or accrued" under the corporation's accounting method. Reg. § 1.1372–4(b)(5)(iv) (pre–1983 law). To prevent easy manipulation of the gross receipts test, only the excess of gains over losses from disposition of capital assets (other than stock and securities) is included in gross receipts; gross receipts from sales or exchanges of stock or securities are taken into account only to the extent of gains, without netting for losses. §§ 1375(b)(3) and 1362(d) (3)(C); Reg. § 1.1372–4(b)(5)(x) (pre–1983 law). The term passive investment income includes gross receipts from royalties, rents, dividends, interest, annuities and gains from the sale or exchange of stock or securities. § 1362(d)(3)(D). Rental income does not constitute passive investment income, however, if "significant services" are rendered to the lessee. *See* Reg. § 1.1372–4(b)(5)(vi) (pre–1983 law).

Total passive investment income must exceed 25% of gross receipts to trigger the § 1375 tax. The § 1375 tax is imposed, however, only on "excess net passive income" (ENPI). To determine ENPI, the total passive investment income must first be reduced by directly attributable expenses to arrive at net passive income (NPI). NPI is then multiplied by the amount of passive investment income which exceeds 25% of gross receipts, and divided by passive investment income for the year.

The result is ENPI, subject to tax at the highest corporate tax rate of 34%. *See* Reg. § 1.1375–1A. The amount subject to tax is limited, however, to the corporation's total taxable income for the taxable year. For example, if a corporation has net passive income of $20,000, gross passive income of $25,000 and gross receipts of $40,000, the excess net passive income is $12,000 ($20,000 x $15,000/ $25,000).

(c) *Built-In Gain Tax.* Section 1374, as amended by the 1986 Act, is intended to prevent C corporations from avoiding the repeal of *General Utilities* by converting to S status prior to a liquidation. The § 1374 tax applies to built-in gains recognized on the disposition of assets during a 10–year recognition period after S status takes effect. This provision generally applies to corporations converting from C status to S status after 1986; under § 1374(c)(1), the built-in gain tax generally does not apply to a corporation that has been an S corporation since inception. *See also* Rev. Rul. 86–141 (transitional rules of 1986 Act).

Under § 1374(b), the built-in gain tax is imposed at the highest corporate rate on the corporation's "net recognized built-in gain," reduced by certain net operating loss carryforwards and capital loss carryforwards. An overall limitation restricts the amount of the net recognized built-in gain to the excess of the aggregate fair market value of all of the corporation's assets over the aggregate basis of the corporation's assets at the time of conversion from C to S status. §§ 1374(c)(2), 1374(d)(3) and 1374(d)(4). For example, if a corporation has unrealized built-in gains of $100 and unrealized built-in losses of $60 on the conversion date, only the net unrealized built-in gain of $40 is subject to tax under § 1374. Thus, the appreciation in assets purchased after the conversion date and subsequent appreciation in existing assets is generally not subject to the § 1374 tax.

Generally, the net recognized built-in gain is taxed under § 1374 in the year in which the corporation recognizes such gain, subject to a taxable-income limitation (as modified by the 1988 Act for corporations making S elections on or after March 31, 1988). Under this taxable-income limitation, the net recognized built-in gain for any taxable year may not exceed the corporation's taxable income (as determined under § 1375(b)(1)(B)), and any excess is carried forward to a subsequent year. § 1374(d)(2). For example, if an S corporation has a recognized built-in gain of $100 and a current operating loss of $100 in the same year, the recognized built-in gain is not taxed under § 1374 for the current year because the corporation's recognized built-in gain ($100) exceeds its taxable income ($0). The untaxed portion of the recognized built-in gain ($100) is carried forward and taxed under § 1374 in the succeeding year (during the recognition period), subject to the taxable-income limitation for such succeeding year.

Under the 1988 Act, recognized built-in gain includes any income which accrued before the corporation's first taxable year as an S corporation but which is recognized for tax purposes during the recognition period. § 1374(d)(5)(A). Thus, a "disposition" includes not only income from sales or exchanges but also other income-recognition events that effectively dispose of the corporation's right to receive income (such as collection of accounts receivable). Recognized built-in losses include amounts which are allowable as a deduction during the recognition period but which accrued before the corporation's first taxable year as an S corporation. § 1374(d)(5)(B). The 1988 Act also clarified that the built-in gain tax applies to assets acquired from C corporations (or from another S corporation subject to § 1374) in certain nonrecognition transactions. § 1374(d)(8). Finally, the Service has announced that built-in loss property contributed to a corporation shortly before an S election for the purpose of reducing the net built-in gain will be subject to "anti-stuffing" rules similar to the rules of § 336(d)(2). IRS Ann. 86–128.

Section 1374 is both underinclusive and overinclusive. On the one hand, if the corporation is sufficiently patient, it can avoid the § 1374 tax by waiting out the 10–year period before liquidating or otherwise disposing of its assets. On the other hand, the burden is on the taxpayer to establish the amount of the net recognized built-in gain. If the taxpayer is unable to meet this burden, not only pre-election but also post-election gain may be swept under the § 1374 tax, even though appreciation in assets while in S solution is normally subject to only a single level of tax.

(d) *Coordination With § 1375.* The special taxes on passive investment income and built-in gain are coordinated to prevent double taxation if income would otherwise be subject to both provisions. The 1988 Act provided that the amount of passive investment income is determined by excluding any recognized built-in gain or loss for any taxable year during the 10–year recognition period. § 1375(b) (4). Thus, net recognized built-in gain is subject only to the § 1374 tax.

(e) *Reduction in Pass-Through for Taxes Imposed.* The special taxes on passive investment income and built-in gains are also coordinated with the pass-through rules of § 1366. Under § 1366(f) (2) and (3), the amount of recognized built-in gain or passive investment income passing through to shareholders is reduced by a proportionate share of the tax imposed under §§ 1374 and 1375. The combined corporate and shareholder-level tax rate under these special taxes is as high as in the case of a C corporation; moreover, both levels of tax are imposed at once, regardless of when the income is distributed.

(f) *LIFO Recapture.* The 1987 Act added a new provision requiring a C corporation electing S status to include in income its LIFO "recapture amount." § 1363(d). The LIFO recapture amount is the excess of the FIFO value of the corporation's inventory over its LIFO value at the close of the corporation's last taxable year as a C corporation. § 1363(d)(3). The basis of the inventory is increased to reflect the amount subject to the recapture tax, which is payable in four equal installments. §§ 1363(d)(1) and 1363(d)(2).

(g) *Installment Treatment.* The 1988 Act added new § 453B(h) to permit nonrecognition of gain at the corporate level if an S corporation distributes certain installment obligations in complete liquidation. Distribution of such obligations is tax free to the corporation, however, only to the extent that receipt of the obligations by the S shareholders does not constitute payment for their stock under the rules of § 453(h)(1) applicable to C corporations. *See* Chapter 6. The shareholders report gain or loss upon receipt of payments under the obligation, and the character of such gain or loss is determined under the pass-through rules of § 1366(b). In addition, the corporation recognizes gain on distribution of an installment obligation to the extent that gain from sale of the underlying property is subject to the built-in gain tax.

§ 8. Distributions of Appreciated Property

Liquidating and nonliquidating distributions of appreciated property (other than the corporation's own obligation) are treated as recognition events at the corporate level. This rule (formerly codified in § 1363(d)) prevents S shareholders from receiving a stepped-up basis in appreciated property without corporate-level recognition of the unrealized appreciation in the property. Accordingly, the corporation is treated as if it had sold the appreciated property to the distributee at its fair market value. The deemed sale may trigger the built-in gain tax and may also affect the character of the gain (*e.g.,* ordinary income treatment under § 1239 if property is depreciable in the hands of a related shareholder). The 1988 Act repealed former § 1363(d) and clarified that, pursuant to § 1371(a), the provisions of Subchapter C apply to distributions of property by an S corporation in determining recognition of gain or loss.

To determine the tax treatment of a distribution of appreciated property, the amount of the corporate-level gain and any corporate-level tax must first be determined. Second, the shareholder's basis must be increased for his pro-rata share of corporation's gain on the distribution (net of any corporate-level taxes). Third, the taxability of the distribution to the shareholder must be determined under the normal distribution rules of § 1368.

Example. The sole shareholder of an S corporation has a basis of $10 in his stock at the beginning of the year, and the corporation distributes appreciated property with a basis of $10 and a fair market value of $100 on December 31. If the § 1374 built-in gain tax does not apply, the corporation's entire recognized gain of $90 will pass through to the shareholder, increasing the shareholder's basis in his stock to $100 ($10 plus $90 of

pass-through income). § 1367(a)(1). The shareholder's basis will be reduced by $100, the fair
market value of the distributed property, and the
shareholder will take a $100 basis in the distribut-
ed property. §§ 1368(b)(1) and § 301(d). The shareholder will recognize no gain on the distribution,
but his stock basis will now be zero. If the § 1374
built-in gain tax applied, however, the increase in
the shareholder's stock basis would be limited to
the excess of the corporate-level gain over the
corporate-level tax; the amount of the tax-free
distribution under § 1368 would be correspondingly reduced, and the amount of taxable gain under
§ 1368(b)(2) would be greater.

In the case of liquidating or nonliquidating distributions by an S corporation, gains (but not
losses) are recognized. Thus, an S corporation may
have an incentive to sell any loss property in order
to recognize the loss. Of course, any loss recognized by the S corporation will reduce the shareholder's basis in his stock under the pass-through
rules, thereby increasing any gain or decreasing
any loss to the shareholder upon the liquidation.

§ 9. Family Income-Splitting

An S corporation may be a useful device for
channelling profits from a business into the hands
of lower-bracket family members. Under
§ 1366(e), however, the Service may reallocate income among members of the family group if a
family member furnishes services or capital to the
corporation without "reasonable compensation."

In addition, a transfer of shares in an S corporation to children must not be a mere "paper" transaction, *i.e.,* the children must enjoy beneficial ownership of the stock as well as possess legal title. The 1986 Act, however, curtails the benefits of family income-splitting by taxing certain minor children's unearned income at the highest marginal rates of their parents. § 1(i).

§ 10. Worthless Stock or Debt

If the stock or debt of an S corporation becomes worthless, the shareholder may be entitled to a deduction under § 165(g) or § 166(d). Under § 1367(b)(3), the adjustments to stock and debt basis for the S corporation's separately and non-separately stated items of income or loss are made before the deduction for worthlessness of stock or debt is determined. The effect of this rule may be to convert some or all of the loss from a capital loss (under § 165(g) or § 166(d)) to an ordinary loss. Shareholders of an S corporation that meets the requirements of § 1244 may also be entitled to an ordinary loss on sale or worthlessness of their stock within the limits of § 1244, just as in the case of a C corporation.

§ 11. Post-Termination Transition Period

Under § 1371(e), S shareholders are entitled to tax-free treatment of cash distributions from an S corporation which has previously taxed but undistributed income at the time its S election terminates, to the extent that the distribution does not exceed the AAA as defined in § 1368(e). The distributions must occur within the so-called "post-termination transition period," generally the one-year period after termination. § 1377(b). Distributions of cash (but not other property) are treated as tax-free during the post-termination transition period, and reduce stock basis.

Example: A calendar-year S corporation's election terminates on July 1, 1990, when its AAA is $25,000, and it has $15,000 of taxable income during its C short year. On December 31, 1990, the corporation distributes $30,000 to its shareholders. The shareholders will treat $25,000 of the distribution as tax-free recovery of their stock basis and the remaining $5,000 as an ordinary dividend from the corporation's current e & p.

If S shareholders have previously disallowed losses in excess of stock basis at the end of the last taxable year for which the corporation is an S corporation, such suspended losses are treated as if they were incurred on the last day of the post-termination transition period. § 1366(d)(3)(A). Thus, to the extent that the shareholders' stock basis increases during the post-transition termination period (*e.g.*, through additional capital contributions), the loss will be allowed currently and reduce stock basis. §§ 1366(d)(3)(B) and 1366(d)(3)(C). Only stock basis (not debt basis) is considered in determining whether suspended losses may be used during the post-termination period.

§ 12. Other Advantages of S Election

The principal advantages of an S election are that income from business operations or liquidation will generally be subject to only a single shareholder-level tax. In addition, an S election offers other substantial tax advantages over operation as a C corporation: (i) the corporate alternative minimum tax does not apply; (ii) the corporate penalty taxes (the accumulated earnings tax and personal holding company tax) do not apply; (iii) the cash method of accounting may generally be used; (iv) compensation paid to officers and key employees is less likely to be challenged as unreasonable by the Service; and (v) passive losses from an S corporation may offset passive income from other sources. Although an S corporation is less flexible than a partnership with respect to allocations of income or loss, the limited liability offered by the corporate form may be an important consideration. Because of its hybrid corporate-partnership characteristics, an S election is likely to be increasingly attractive for eligible corporations.

*

INDEX

299

308 *INDEX*

S CORPORATIONS—Cont'd
Family income splitting, 294–295
LIFO recapture, 291–292
Pass-through treatment,
        Generally, 268, 275–282, 291–294
    Limitations on losses, 277–282, 296
Passive investment income, 273, 286–288, 291
Taxable year and accounting method, 17, 274–275, 297
Worthless stock or debt, 295

SALE OF A CORPORATE BUSINESS
        See also Collapsible Corporations; Complete Liquida-
                tions
    Generally, 149–158
Mirror transactions, 159–160
Section 338 election,
    Basis, allocation of, 156–158
    Consistency requirements, 154–155
    Mechanics, 150–154
    Protective carryover election, 155–156
Subsidiary stock sale treated as asset sale, 156

SECTION 306 STOCK
    Generally, 185–194
Defined, 186–188
Exceptions to ordinary income treatment, 191–193
Preferred stock bailout, 185–186
Redemptions of, 188–190
Sale of, 188–190
Uses of, 193–194

SECTION 338 ELECTION
See Sale of a Corporate Business

STOCK DIVIDENDS
        See also Section 306 Stock
        Generally, 170–194
Basis, allocation of, 171–172, 182–183
Convertible preferred stock, 179
Deemed distributions, 179–182
Disproportionate, 174–177

†